D0205660

Kishwaukee College Library
21193 Malta Road
Malta, IL 60150-9699

The Praeger Handbook of Transsexuality

Kishwaukee College Library
21193 Malta Road
Malta, IL 60150-9699

THE PRAEGER HANDBOOK OF TRANSSEXUALITY

Changing Gender to Match Mindset

Rachel Ann Heath

Sex, Love, and Psychology
Judy Kuriansky, Series Editor

Westport, Connecticut
London

Library of Congress Cataloging-in-Publication Data

Heath, Rachel Ann.
The Praeger handbook of transsexuality : changing gender to match
mindset / Rachel Ann Heath.
      p.   cm. — (Sex, love, and psychology, ISSN 1554–222X)
   Includes bibliographical references and index.
   ISBN 0–275–99176–8 (alk. paper)
1. Transsexualism.   2. Gender identity.   I. Title.   II. Title: Handbook
of transsexuality.   III. Series.
   HQ77.9.H43   2006
   306.76'8—dc22   2006011953

British Library Cataloguing in Publication Data is available.

Copyright © 2006 by Rachel Ann Heath

All rights reserved. No portion of this book may be
reproduced, by any process or technique, without the
express written consent of the publisher.

Library of Congress Catalog Card Number: 2006011953
ISBN: 0–275–99176–8
ISSN: 1554–222X

First published in 2006

Praeger Publishers, 88 Post Road West, Westport, CT 06881
An imprint of Greenwood Publishing Group, Inc.
www.praeger.com

Printed in the United States of America

The paper used in this book complies with the
Permanent Paper Standard issued by the National
Information Standards Organization (Z39.48–1984).

10 9 8 7 6 5 4 3 2 1

I wish to dedicate this book to my family in recognition of their loving support over many years.

CONTENTS

FOREWORD

What does it mean to be a man or a woman? People increasingly debate this question in these modern times, when gender roles are being redefined. Yet gender identity is also being called into question, as natal males and females become more confident about finding out just who they are "really, at their core." Psychology Professor Rachel Ann Heath addresses these issues in an exceptionally impressive academic—and humanistic—way in this book, *The Praeger Handbook on Transsexuality: Changing Gender to Match Mindset.*

I encountered this subject over a quarter of a century ago when, in the early days of more widespread recognition of transsexuality in this country, I served on a medical team evaluating whether applicants were eligible for the "sex-change operation." Some, seeking to escape depression or repressive masculine roles, were denied. As such, I admire Heath's brilliant consideration of all the latest knowledge about the topic, and about factors affecting people who want their bodies to conform to their inner self. The depth and breadth of knowledge in this book gives the professional as well as the lay reader a complete picture of the biological, psychological, and cultural factors that influence the decisions about whether one feels truly male or female. The historical context—ranging from stories of other cultures to a New York governor dressed as a female—is captivating. I've been in American Samoa where *fa'afāfines,* transgendered males, are honored for their place in the family.

Through Heath's tutelage, we learn how voice and facial structure affect gender presentation and learn details about how the medical procedures are completed. Most importantly, we are presented with a sex-positive view of persons with transsexuality and transsexed people (postoperative), considering them not as candidates for "gender reassignment surgery," which implies pathology, but for "sex-affirmation surgery," which affirms self-realization.

Heath's presentation does honor to people like club performer Jayne (nee Wayne) County from the punk rock Andy Warhol days, who as a guest on my LovePhones radio advice show talked about her autobiography, *It Takes a Man to Be a Woman*, and chronicled her transformation. It also honors the character of Bree Osbourne (nee Stanley), portrayed by actress Felicity Huffman in the award-winning film "Transamerica," which follows a transsexual father's cross-country trip with her newly reunited son, on her way to sex-affirmation surgery—and to finding self-respect for herself and from others.

Judy Kuriansky, PhD
Series Editor, Sex, Love, and Psychology

PREFACE

Upon realizing she is pregnant, a woman's thoughts lead inevitably to the question, "Will my baby be a boy or a girl?" Then often the excited couple shares this question, deciding whether to keep it unanswered until the baby is born or to harness modern technology to resolve the uncertainty before birth, usually the sooner the better.

That is not an unusual request. The first question 80 percent of people ask a new parent is whether the newborn is a boy or a girl. Once the new baby's sex is known, in Western societies 75 percent of girls are given pink clothes, and similarly 79 percent of boys have some blue in their outfits.[1]

Although the baby's sex is usually confirmed before or shortly after birth, occasionally the medical team is unsure whether the baby is a boy or a girl. Then follows uncertainty and distress as medical experts wonder how to tell the parents that they are unsure about the baby's sex. Malformed or ambiguous sexual organs contribute mostly to the confusion, leading to difficult medical and ethical decisions for both the doctors and the parents of the child with such a condition.

Even when a child's biological sex is accurately determined, a few years later an even more disturbing situation for parents may occur when their young child insists on behaving like a child of the opposite sex. The little boy may insist, persistently over a period of years, that he be dressed like his sister and play with dolls. A girl may with equal determination and persistence detest frilly frocks, heading straight for the comfort of baggy trousers and short hairstyles and preferring rough-and-tumble play with boys and trucks and trains over dolls, dishes, and utensil. Such behavior—which, as we will see in a later chapter, can be a common part of universal child development—may demonstrate in extreme cases a dissociation between born-sex, as defined by the genitals, and gender identity, as evidenced by behavior preferences. Eventually, such people may escape society's gender encapsulation and assume both the body and behavior of their affirmed gender identity, one that is different from that corresponding to their sex at birth. They become "people with a transsexed condition," and in some societies may qualify for medical intervention to relieve their suffering.

How often, when required to specify your sex as male or female, have you hesitated before ticking the "appropriate" box? For people of transsexual background, who identify with the alternative response, it always feels wrong to tick the male or female box. For most, this bureaucratic requirement never coincides with their individual balance between masculinity and femininity, even if they do not exhibit cross-gendered behavior. They wonder why telling someone about their sex is necessary, especially if they are never likely to be a sexual partner of the questioning person. So one can imagine how difficult it is for people of both sexes who have a deep, possibly lifelong, commitment to being treated as, and living the role of, the sex opposite to that of their birth. Many transsexed people suffer enormously from their distress and require appropriate treatment to live happy, productive lives.

Transitioning from one sex to the other, either permanently or temporarily, has occurred in most human societies throughout recorded history. From Native American two-spirit people, to the hijras of India, and to the more familiar drag queens and drag kings seen in clubs worldwide, people have been enthralled by, and generally respectful of, gender-variant people. Reports of people transitioning from one sex to the other incite public interest, especially in autobiographies that offer fascinating insights into their authors' lives. Many may question their own gender feelings after reading about the anguish of another's search for happiness and a better life, especially when the hostile environments of family upheaval, employment prejudice, and other barriers accompany the transition.

This book provides an up-to-date account of current knowledge about gender and sex and their relationships when people transition from one gender role to another, and ultimately into their affirmed sex following surgery. Recent research provides readers, especially those in the transgender and transsexed communities and their expert advisors, with a valuable resource to inform their own decisions and to assist others in understanding the complex issues involved. The book considers aspects of gender identity and sexual development and relates this basic knowledge to transsexuality, emphasizing the hoops transsexed people must jump through in order to attain happiness and an identity they can call their own.

The book begins with a history of transsexuality and its prevalence, and considers people's attitudes towards those of transsexual background.

Next a summary of the biological bases of sex determination and gender identity formation is presented, followed by information on the psychological aspects of gender differences. After discussing correlates of gender identity and sexual orientation, attention is focused on the assessment and diagnosis of the medical condition known as transsexualism, highlighting the needs of both adults and young people. Next follows an account of hormone therapy for transsexed men and women, as well as surgical and supplementary treatment options. After discussing social and legal aspects of transsexuality, the book concludes with consideration of future prospects for people of transsexual background, improvements in their own management of their situation, services, and tolerance, as well as some speculation on the biological and psychological causes of the condition. A small but representative number of Internet resources are contained in the appendix.

Although I have been flexible with terminology so far, many people of transsexual background are sensitive to the labels used to describe them. In particular, they detest being called "transgendered," a term that includes part-time cross-dressers and drag performers with whom those of transsexual background do not identify. I apologize in advance if my choice of terminology causes offense.

Bockting[2] recommended *transexual* with only one *s* to remove the connotation that gender has only two values, masculine and feminine. The "trans" idea disrupts the binary gender divide and leads to a gender continuum from male to female, just like the colors of a rainbow.[3] Indeed, as we will discover in chapter 6, personality tests reveal such a gradated form of gendered experience.

In the title of this book I have preferred the term *transsexuality* to the more common term *transsexualism,* simply because the latter refers to a purported medical condition (now superseded by the even more prejudicial term *gender identity disorder*) to describe the pathologization of gender variance by psychiatrists and clinical psychologists. *Transsexuality* is a more neutral collective term. The subtitle of the book *Changing Gender to Match Mindset* suggests that persons of transsexual background change their gender-role representation (but NOT the sex with which they identify, that is, their affirmed sex) from one corresponding to their birth-sex to one more closely matching their experienced gender identity. Later in the book I describe recent research that suggests a biological basis for this affirmation. However, the findings are suggestive, correlative, and not causal, so the jury is still out with respect to the precise biological basis for transsexuality.

Throughout the book I use the term *transsexed,* rather than *transsexual* or *transexual,* when referring to people transitioning from their natal sex to their affirmed sex, that is, the sex they know they always have been. For example, *transsexed people* is a shorthand version of *people of transsexual background.* For clarity I use *transsexed woman* to refer to someone who is transitioning to the female sex—a woman of transsexual background—and *transsexed man* for someone transitioning to the male sex—a man of transsexual background. These terms only refer to the transition process, since most transsexed women consider themselves to be women following surgery, and similarly, transsexed men are men after surgery, even though for the latter genital surgery is difficult. I use *gender* to refer to the social role and its behavioral and subjective attributes adopted by people of both sexes.

Transsexed people wish to change their genital sex to more closely approximate their affirmed gender mindset, even when medical, financial, and social problems as well as surgical inadequacies prevent them from achieving their goals. Transgendered people of both sexes are satisfied to live a cross-gendered life, either part-time or full-time, without necessarily indulging in surgery or other medical interventions. Transvestites, who are most commonly heterosexual males, enjoy the experience of cross-dressing either in private or with others who share their predilection. They have no intention of affirming their sex as a female by medical means.

Most writers use the term *sex reassignment surgery,* or *genital reconstruction surgery,* to refer to what is commonly called a "sex-change operation." However, some contemporary writers prefer *sex affirmation surgery* to signify that such surgery affirms the person's brain-sex from birth by altering the genitals appropriately. For example, Rachael Wallbank states that "[t]he aspect of sex affirmation treatment involving surgical intervention is referred to as **sex affirmation surgery**" (italics and bold in original).[4]

Using two terminologies can be confusing, so I have concentrated on the mechanics of the surgery by using *genital reconstruction surgery* (GRS) throughout. This is more appropriate, since the surgeon's goal is to reconstruct the genitals to more closely approximate those of the client's affirmed sex. When GRS is mentioned in the text it always refers to the surgery itself rather than to any more generalized outcome.

The terms *homosexual* and *heterosexual* are awkward, especially when the former is used with, or instead of, *gay* and *lesbian.* Alternatively, I use *gynephilic* and *androphilic* to refer to a sexual preference for women and men, respectively. Gynephilic[5] and androphilic derive from the Greek meaning love of a woman and love of a man, respectively. So a gynephilic man is a man who likes women, that is, a heterosexual man, whereas an androphilic man is one who likes men, that is, a gay man. For completeness, a lesbian is a gynephilic woman, a woman who likes other women. Gynephilic transsexed woman refers to a woman of transsexual background whose sexual preference is for women. Unless *homosexual* and *heterosexual* are the more readily understood terms in a given context, this more precise terminology will be used throughout the book. Since homosexual, gay, and lesbian are often associated with bigotry and exclusion in many societies, the emphasis on sexual affiliation is both appropriate and socially just. *Natal woman* refers to someone whose birth-sex is female, *natal man* referring to a person born as a male. Natal men and women have no intention to transition.

Details of statistical analyses are not included here. The terms *statistically significant* and *not statistically significant* can be assumed whenever a finding is expressed in either the affirmative or negative, respectively. The minimum odds that a difference is wrongly claimed are 1 in 20, in accordance with scientific convention. Rather than report the average ages of research participants, the terminology *25-year-old* is used to imply that the average age is *25* for all participants in that group.

Research methodology is an important consideration when the literature employs small populations that cannot be sampled randomly. Just because a finding has been published in a peer-reviewed journal does not mean that it will be accepted unqualified. Rather, each outcome is evaluated using the scientific and ethical criteria demanded by contemporary medical, social, and psychological research. When research findings conflict with the impressions of transsexed people, the practical utility of such findings are correspondingly downgraded. The community of transsexed people, the homosexual and bisexual communities, and those with intersexed conditions have suffered too long at the hands of uninformed "experts" for this book to serve as a platitudinous reiteration of distorted truths.

How people become aware of their transsexuality is little understood and somewhat mysterious. Although many transsexed people claim to have been aware of their transsexuality from a very early age, others report a sudden revelation that their body-sex is inconsistent with how they feel, that is, with their brain-sex. This situation can follow a major life stressor, such as the death of a spouse. In many situations, people experience abrupt change in their feelings, leading to a state of "spiritual awakening."[6] This change can be permanent, leading to a feeling of ultimate freedom and happiness. Perhaps such a revelation characterizes some cases of transsexuality in which the person suddenly becomes aware of their mind-body disharmony.

ACKNOWLEDGMENTS

I thank Judith Gatland and Dr. Grant Keene for their expert help in reading and offering comments on an earlier version of the book. I thank Emeritus Professor William Walters for his encouragement in completing this project and his expert advice on transsexuality. I thank Rachael Wallbank for her expert advice on terminology and legal aspects of transsexuality. I would also like to thank all those people within the transcommunity who encouraged me to bring this project to fruition.

I am indebted to Associate Professor Andrew Heathcote from the University of Newcastle, Australia, for assisting me in many ways to complete the research and production of this book. Finally, I appreciate the dedicated assistance from my editor at Greenwood Press, Ms. Debbie Carvalko, who offered me encouragement and who was always prompt in advising me on editorial aspects of the project.

It was impossible to research this book without referring to the extensive Internet resources on gender, sex, and transsexuality. Many hours spent communicating with transsexed people and others, both in real life and on the Internet, have informed much of the book's contents. It is impossible to write a credible account of these complex issues without considering the collective experience and wisdom of the transsexed community.

Figures 10.1 to 10.5 have been reproduced by kind permission from the copyright holder, Blackwell Publishing, Oxford, United Kingdom.

ABBREVIATIONS

5α-RA	5α-reductase activity
16PF	16 personality factors
17β-HSD3	17β-hydroxysteroid dehydrogenase 3 deficiency
ACL	Adjective checklist
ACTH	Adrenocorticotropic hormone
ADHD	Attention-deficit/hyperactivity disorder
AIDS	Auto-immune deficiency syndrome
AIS	Androgen insensitivity syndrome
BSRI	Bem Sex Roles Inventory
BST	Bed nucleus of the stria terminalis
BSTc	Central region of the bed nucleus of the stria terminalis
CAH	Congenital adrenal hyperplasia
CAIS	Complete androgen insensitivity syndrome
CAT	Computerized axial tomography
CGI	Childhood gender identity
CGN	Childhood gender nonconformity
CPA	Cyproterone acetate
DHT	Dihydrotestosterone
DSM	Diagnostic and Statistical Manual
FFS	Facial feminization surgery
FSH	Follicle-stimulating hormone
GD	Gender diagnosticity
GEDAD	Gender expression deprivation anxiety disorder
GIA	Gender identity atypicality
GID	Gender identity disorder

GIDAANT	Gender identity disorder of adolescence and adulthood, nontranssexual type
GRS	Genital reconstruction surgery
HBIGDA	Harry Benjamin International Gender Dysphoria Association
hCG	Human chorionic gonadotropin
HDL	High-density lipid
HIV	Human immunosuppressive virus
hK2	Human glandular kallikrein
HRT	Hormone-replacement therapy
INAH-3	The third interstitial nucleus of the anterior hypothalamus
LDL	Low-density lipid
LH	Luteinizing hormone
LHRH	Luteinizing hormone-releasing hormone
MePD	Posterodorsal component of the amygdala
MIS	Mullerian-inhibiting substance
MMPI	Minnesota Multiphasic Personality Inventory
MRI	Magnetic resonance interferometry
PA	Plasminogen activation
PAI-1	Plasminogen activation inhibitor 1
PSA	Prostate specific antigen
RLE	Real-life experience
SCN	Suprachiasmic nucleus
SDN-POA	Sexually dimorphic nucleus of the preoptic area
SHBG	Sex-hormone-binding globulin
SOC	Standards of care
SOM	Somatostatin expressing
SPA	Spironolactone
tHcy	Total homocysteine
tPA	Tissue-type plasminogen activation
UK	United Kingdom
U.S.	United States
VIP	Vasoactive intestinal polypeptide

Chapter One

TRANSSEXUALITY: HISTORY, VIEWPOINTS, AND PREVALENCE

Transsexuality is associated with the behavior of changing one's sex from either male to female or female to male and living thereafter in the opposite gender role. Not only does such behavior attract the attention of significant others, but it threatens the foundations of modern society, particularly institutions such as marriage and the family. The burden endured by transsexed people challenges the medical and legal professions to devise an easier path so transsexed people can attain both happiness and fulfillment.

When writing about a sensitive issue such as transsexuality, the temptation to right the wrongs is always present. However, it is equally important to offer readers a critical evaluation of what is known. By so doing, transsexed people will not be deluded by half-truths, and professionals and researchers will not be deterred by uninformed claims from disenchanted clients. This book treads a fine line between upholding the human rights of a downtrodden minority and ensuring that what is known about transsexuality and related conditions is presented accurately and understandably.

Before embarking on a detailed survey of gender, sex, and transsexuality, a brief history of transsexuality and its associated medical conditions is provided. Then follows an account of people's attitudes towards transsexuality based on surveys conducted in Sweden and more widely over the Internet. This material is tempered somewhat by disturbing incidents of prejudice against transsexed people. The chapter concludes with information on the prevalence of transsexuality, a contentious issue.

A BRIEF HISTORY OF TRANSSEXUALITY

Transsexuality has accompanied human existence since antiquity. According to Green,[1] the Greek goddess Venus Castina reacted sympathetically to feminine souls locked up in male bodies. The earliest mention of transsexuality, in terms of current definitions of the term, was in reference to the Assyrian king Sardanapalus, who dressed in women's clothing and spun thread with his wives. Later instances of transsexuality were reported by Philo of Judaea, who lived during the Roman Empire.[2] In Ovid's Metamorphoses the male Teresias is transformed into the woman Teresa upon striking two copulating snakes with a stave. When Teresa strikes the snakes again she is transformed back into a male, so gender identity is temporary and a person can be transformed from one sex to another.[3]

Transsexuality during the Middle Ages is illustrated by the sixth-century story by Gregory of Tours. A man dressed in a nun's habit who lived secretly in a nunnery was forgiven for his indiscretion provided he agreed to be castrated. Since childhood he had worn female clothes, as he suffered from "an incurable disorder of the groin."[2]

In the 1200s, Pelagia originally lived as a woman dressed in a monk's outfit so that her previous life as a prostitute would not be discovered. She then lived as a man, Pelegius, whose female sex was only discovered when she died. Around the same time another woman assumed a male role to escape an unhappy marriage. Although women can often get away with dressing as men, even today male transvestism, men dressing as women, is shunned by society as it represents a status loss for that person as well as for all other men.[2] This is especially the case in societies that devalue women and their impersonators.

Later on, Chevalier d'Eon (1728–1810), a French diplomat who spent the second half of his life living full-time as a woman, was a mistress to King Louis XV of France. D'Eon was so convincing in appearance that he rivaled Madame Pompadour for Louis XV's attention. Eonism, a term first mentioned by the famous sexologist, Havelock Ellis, has been used ever since as a synonym for cross-gendered behavior in nonhomosexual males.[4] The first colonial governor of New York, Lord Cornbury, came from England fully attired as a woman and remained so during his time in office.[2]

The loss of social status for men who cross-dress as women, relative to their female counterparts, is not new. Von Krafft-Ebing, a nineteenth-century German psychiatrist, considered transsexed women to be "failed men," whereas transsexed men were accomplished, intelligent, and independent women (sic). In the 1860s, Ulrichs regarded the homosexual, a term proposed by Kertbeny in 1869, as a third sex. During the nineteenth century, homosexuality was also considered a gender inversion by which the "soul of a woman [is] confined to the body of a man."[5] The sissy, who represents undesirable male qualities such as weakness, dependency, and helplessness, is a considerable threat to maleness. The confusion of male transvestism with homosexuality still remains.

Hirschfeld coined the term transvestism in 1910. Later, in 1923, he used the term transsexualism for the first time, more than a quarter of a century before Cauldwell used the same term in 1949. In 1918, Hirschfeld revealed that the first genital reconstruction surgery (GRS) occurred in Berlin as early as 1912. This pioneering surgery resulted in an incomplete female-to-male genital conversion, to be followed in 1920 by crude genital surgery performed on a male-to-female client.[6] So Hirschfeld identified the clinical category of transsexualism that was later developed and popularized by Benjamin.[1] Hirschfeld also stated rather pessimistically that "to attempt to medically treat transvestism would be as foolish as to try to treat some star to make it behave differently in its relation to the solar system."[7]

Hirschfeld maintained that "transvestism" is an innate affliction that becomes more intense with age, with any sudden stressor leading to its full expression. Hirschfeld distinguished ten types of transvestites: the extreme, the partial, a transvestite in name alone, a constant transvestite, a periodic transvestite, a narcissistic transvestite, a metatropic transvestite, defined as being attracted to mannish females in the case of males, as well as bisexual and homosexual transvestites.[8] This detailed categorization of transsexed people was elaborated further by Benjamin and, more recently, by others.

The sudden appearance of full-blown transsexuality in middle age and beyond is a common phenomenon that is seldom recognized by current pathologization of the condition. So Hirschfeld was way ahead of his time. For example, "Inez," Benjamin's ninth client, first made contact when she was 52. She subsequently underwent a three-stage GRS procedure involving castration, removal of the penis, and vaginoplasty, the construction of a vagina using most commonly the inverted skin of the penis. This is basically the same technique currently used in male-to-female GRS.

Lili Elbe, born as a male in Germany in 1886, was one of the first recorded GRS cases. Unfortunately she died a year after an attempt was made to surgically remove rejected ovaries that were placed in her abdomen during the original GRS. Since her blood contained more estrogen than testosterone, her feminization probably resulted from Klinefelter syndrome. This would imply that she had a 47, XXY sex-chromosome karyotype containing an extra X chromosome. So one of the first transsexed people publicized widely in the media was probably intersexed.[9]

Abrahom performed the first GRS in the United States in 1931.[10] However, such surgical solutions for the medical condition of transsexualism only became widely known after Christine Jorgensen's publicity in 1953 following successful GRS in Denmark. In the 1960s, it was realized that hormonal chemical castration without risky surgery might provide relief for some transsexed people. Traditionally, psychotherapy that is beneficial for some transsexed people does not provide a complete resolution of their problems. More often than not, hormone therapy and genital modification are also needed. During the sixties and seventies, many transsexed people suffered at the hands of ignorant psychiatrists who tried to "cure" them using electric shock therapy.

DR. HARRY BENJAMIN'S LEGACY

In her historical review of transsexuality in the United States, Ettner[11] highlighted Harry Benjamin's outstanding accomplishments. Benjamin started his long career as both an endocrinologist and a gerontologist. Benjamin's colleague, Professor Steinach from Vienna, introduced him to "gerontotherapy" techniques for hormone replacement in older people and offered him experience in sex-organ transfer between animals.

In 1948 Kinsey, perhaps the most famous U.S. sexologist, introduced Benjamin to a youth named Van who had desperately requested GRS. Due to the lack of surgical expertise in the United States, Van eventually had surgery in Europe in the mid 1950s, thanks to Benjamin's sympathetic concern. Among Benjamin's more interesting clients was a cross-sexed couple, the husband wanting to become a woman and the wife wanting to become a man. Christine Jorgensen, who was treated by Benjamin before heading off to Denmark for GRS, and who enjoyed considerable fame upon her return to the United States, initiated a lifelong correspondence and friendship with Benjamin.

Benjamin first used the medical term "transsexualism" in a December 1953 symposium held by the Association for Advancement of Psychotherapy.[12] Benjamin's Sex Orientation Scale, one of the first quantitative measures of sexual behavior, was used to discriminate the so-called "true transsexed" from others. The "true transsexed," who score V and VI on a six-point scale using Benjamin's test, are also more likely to score at the "homosexual" end of the Kinsey Scale. This suggests they be classified as nonheterosexual, a contentious situation given recent transsexual politics decrying any necessary association between sexual orientation and transsexuality. Benjamin believed that "true transsexuals" would need to have GRS in order to live happy and fulfilling lives.[13] The distinction between "true" or primary transsexed people, who usually transition at a relatively young age, and secondary transsexed people, who live an apparently normal masculine life prior to transition in mid-life or beyond, persists as a diagnostic typology today.

A review of Benjamin's first 10 transsexual cases between 1938 and 1953 reported that Benjamin helped more than 1,500 gender-atypical clients during his long career. Many of these early clients came to Benjamin self-diagnosed based on early cross-gendered behavior, secret cross-dressing, purges, isolation, and lots of guilt. The first 10 clients included 1 transvestite as well as 6 category V and VI transsexed people. One of the three category IV transsexed people—who may not necessarily request GRS—was Otto Spengler, who was his mother's dress model and the inspiration for Hirschfeld's early writings on transvestism. Benjamin used the term *transgender* to refer to cross-dressing behavior before eventually using both terms *transsexual* and *transvestite* to describe his clients' behavior. Evidently, problems with terminology existed even in Benjamin's time.[13]

Meanwhile, the Americans were working hard to assist transsexed people live successful and happy lives. The Gay and Lesbian Historical Society of Northern California[14] reviewed transgender activism in the Tenderloin district of San Francisco between 1966 and 1975. Tenderloin, located within San Francisco's red-light district, had been a refuge for transsexed people who had no other means of support.

The U.S. radical transgender movement started after a riot in Compton's Cafeteria in the Tenderloin district in August 1966. Many of the bars and clubs in this part of San Francisco were frequented by "queens," transsexed women who lived full time as women, and who were sexually active with men. Some of the "queens" underwent hormonal and surgical procedures to pass more successfully as women.

The Methodist Church was the first religious organization to care for homosexual and transsexed people in the Tenderloin district, successfully reducing police brutality and providing a safe meeting place for transsexed people. Transsexed prostitutes engaged in sex work to survive economically, as they had no other employment opportunities. Sadly, a similar situation occurs today due to the high cost of GRS and associated feminization procedures, especially for otherwise unemployable and destitute transsexed people.

Benjamin advised his first transsexual client in the Tenderloin area during a summer visit in the late 1940s. His clinic, which operated during the 1950s and 1960s, attracted many transsexed people who sought information and access to hormones and surgery. Benjamin disseminated the innovative ideas developed by Hirschfeld in Germany. This allowed GRS to be conducted in the United States even when there was no physical deformity, a requirement that was accepted surgical practice for physically intersexed people at that time.

The Erickson Educational Foundation, funded in 1964 by Reed Erickson, furthered the education and treatment of transsexed people in the San Francisco and Los Angeles areas. Prior to 1966, GRS, breast enhancement, and hormone therapy for transsexed people were not generally available in the United States. Exceptionally, the urologist Belt performed GRS in Los Angeles in the 1950s and 1960s, and three GRS procedures were performed on transsexed women in San Francisco between 1954 and 1964.

The first gender counseling service in the Tenderloin was set up in 1971 by Laura Cummings. Her technique discriminated drag queens and transvestites from transsexed people, since the latter would benefit from female hormones whereas the others could not tolerate the disruption to their sexual activity from erection problems resulting from hormone treatment. Only the truly transsexed can celebrate the loss of their libido following doses of estrogen.

In 1972, the Salmacis Society organized meetings of lesbian natal and transsexed women for femme-femme relationships. This enlightened period for transsexed people did not reappear until the 1990s, when a new generation of transsexed people became actively involved in reevaluating their social situation.

THE PATHOLOGIZATION OF GENDER DIVERSITY

Cohen-Kettenis and Gooren[15] reviewed modern aspects of the presumed medical condition of transsexualism, including its etiology, diagnosis, and treatment.

Transsexualism first appeared as a psychiatric diagnosis in the third edition of the American Psychiatric Association's *Diagnostic and Statistical Manual,* DSM-III, in 1980. Transsexualism was subsequently replaced in the fourth edition, DSM-IV by the term *gender identity disorder*. Fisk[16] proposed the term *gender dysphoria syndrome* to represent the distress experienced by those whose gender identity does not correspond to their biological sex.

Beginning in the late 1960s and early 1970s, "gender dysphoria" clinics were opened in the United States, Australia, the UK, Canada, the Netherlands, and elsewhere. Most of these clinics, often associated with university medical schools, employed similar diagnostic and treatment protocols for clients who were observed to express dysphoria, that is, discomfort, with their gender diversity. John Money opened the first U.S. clinic in 1965 located in the Johns Hopkins Medical School in Baltimore. Following a controversial and reportedly unscientific adverse report on its operation, the clinic closed in 1975.[17]

At about the same time, the Monash Gender Dysphoria Clinic in Melbourne, Australia, was opened. Its staff consisted of two psychiatrists, a gynecologist, a plastic surgeon, an endocrinologist, a psychologist, a speech therapist, and a social worker. Referrals to the clinic came from general practitioners, specialists, and other health professionals. A number of clients also self-referred. All new clients were screened by a psychiatrist for accompanying psychiatric conditions such as delusions, psychosis, and mood disorders, and a life history was taken. After evaluation by an endocrinologist, and possibly a clinical psychologist, the assessment team met to determine a candidate's suitability for entry into the program. Successful clients partook in a real-life experience, which required them to live in their preferred gender role full-time for at least 18 months. During this time, hormone therapy commenced, as did ancillary requirements such as speech therapy and facial hair removal for transsexed women. Further counseling was offered, including possible consultations with families.[18]

In the UK transsexed people could use both public and private avenues for the diagnosis and treatment of their presumed condition. The operation of the UK public system is both interesting and alarming in its inconsistency, delays for initial treatment and surgery, and the poor facilities that exist in the more remote parts of this densely populated country.

Murjan, Shepherd, and Ferguson[19] sent questionnaires to directors of UK health authorities seeking information on services for transsexed people, obtaining an 82 percent response rate. Twenty percent of authorities reported a local "transgender" service, although not all of these had surgical facilities. Sixty percent of the remainder had no services for transsexed people but referred cases to other health boards for assessment and treatment, especially the "gender dysphoria" clinic at Charing Cross Hospital in London. Three local health boards reported no facilities for treating transsexed people due to a reported lack of demand.

The absence of a comprehensive system of care in the UK meant that some clients were obtaining hormone therapy without sufficient medical resources for surgery, an unsatisfactory state of affairs. Some transsexed people traveled long distances for treatment. It was claimed that some of these people began hormone therapy with insufficient counseling, and without a psychiatrist and/or psychologist confirming that they were "sick." Only six gender clinics in the UK offered comprehensive services, there being no standardized protocols for assisting transsexed people. In their desperation, some UK transsexed people sought a private and more expensive route to obtain hormone therapy and GRS. This attractive alternative includes surgery in overseas locations, such as the United States, Canada, and, commonly, Thailand. If proper care for transsexed people is so difficult to obtain in a modern medical system such as that in the UK, how much more difficult must it be in poorer, less-organized countries?

The availability of proper medical treatment for transsexed people differs between countries depending on the diversity of cultural, social, and legal environments. For example, during the first 10 years of operation of the German Transsexuals' Act, transsexed women, whose average age was 34, tended to present for treatment at a later age than did transsexed men, whose average age was 30. The average delay between a legal name change in a German law court and change of sex status following GRS was two years, about the same as in most Western countries.[20]

Cultural, political, and religious considerations determine the relative frequency of surgery for transsexed people. For example, the first GRS case in China, a 20-year-old male, occurred in the 1980s. She had been reared as a girl from a young age and had avoided masculine pursuits, such as rough-and-tumble play.[21] Although GRS has been available in other Asian countries such as Thailand for some time, the first GRS in Japan occurred as recently as 1998.

TRANSGENDER POLITICS

Transgenderism might be usefully defined as "changing the social perception of one's everyday gender through the manipulation of non-genital signs."[22] This criterion distinguishes transgenderism from transsexuality, the latter almost always implying that the person has undergone, or intends to undergo, GRS.

Since transsexed and transgendered people have received such a rough deal from people in power for some time, those brave enough to out themselves as either transsexed or transgendered have campaigned unceasingly for improved rights, especially since the 1990s. Transgender activists, such as Leslie Feinberg and Riki Wilchins, proclaim that transgendered and transsexed people should take responsibility for their own histories and political initiatives, including ownership of a unique shared identity. Whereas transgender politics seeks to challenge and destabilize the binary gender system, gender identifiers still exist in such terminology as *transsexed men and women*. According to this political stance, the prefix "trans" does not denote transcendence of gender when the labels "man" and "woman" remain as a suffix.[23]

Examples of binary gender transgression include those transsexed men and women who claim not to be real men or women, respectively. Transgenderists who live as part man and part woman might assume an "intersexed identity" that is more social than biological in origin. Such gender deviations challenge biological, sociological, and legal experts to devise a more appropriate gender classification.

Transsexuality in its various forms has a colorful past, harking back to our earliest recorded history. The modern recognition of the condition was realized when relatively safe GRS procedures became available in a small number of locations in the 1950s. Since then, there have been considerable advances in assistance to transsexed people, as well as in the recognition of transsexed people as productive members of society. The situation continues to improve in the new century with an increase in social tolerance accompanied by improvements in surgical and other medical procedures. Even so, news about "sex-change" gets immediate media attention, especially in cases of regret. Like many newsworthy phenomena, overexposure in the media of regretful cases might lead the general public to believe that regret following GRS is a routine event.[24] However, this is not the case. Skilled treatment leads to a marked improvement in the transsexed person's quality of life and their ability to make beneficial contributions to society. A good indicator of a society's maturity is how well it treats a stigmatized group such as the transsexed community. The next section discusses the sociocultural basis of transgenderism and transsexuality by comparing the approaches of both traditional and Western societies.

SOCIOCULTURAL ASPECTS OF TRANSGENDERISM AND TRANSSEXUALITY

Cross-gendered behavior was recorded in early human records. Laqueur[25] suggested that some premodern European tribes consisted of one sex and two genders, the basic sex being male. These people considered the vagina, a defining characteristic of the female, to be an inverted internal penis. This idea contrasts with the modern concept of sex based on external, rather than internal, genitals.

Considered in its broader cultural context, gender is "a complex, temporally extended system in which issues such as renown, age, and rank are all at work."[26] Gender is something people do—a way they behave—rather than a quality they possess. Every society has people who display gender differently from their society's norm. For example, the Burmese Dayaks consider universal humanity to be feminine, a gender role assumed by shamans and other religious people who are considered to be women with a penis. In Kenya's Turkana society, a child is initially neuter or androgynous until the appropriate sex is determined at puberty during initiation rites. According to ancient belief, Turkana women undergo removal of inappropriate "male" parts in order to attain sexual purity.

Since gender expression is a performance or imitation, transgenderism represents an "imitation of an imitation."[27] So, drag shows and temporary transvestism survive provided the performance adheres to accepted male or female behavior. Medical treatment of transsexualism in Western societies adheres to this same gender divide, especially when successful passing in one's preferred gender role is encouraged. Whereas ambiguous gender behavior is scorned in Western societies, this is not the case in other societies within which "third-gender" people play important cultural roles.

The third-gender concept was originally introduced by Martin and Voorhies, who suggested that in some cultures gender is not partitioned into two categories. In general, the third gender represents any gender embodiment that does not lie within the binary gender scheme of man and woman, rather than implying the more restrictive idea of only three different genders. Because such third genders are common in non-Western cultures, perhaps a transsexed person's claim that they were born into the wrong body is equivalent to having been born into the wrong culture. Although third-gender people are generally revered, they often suffer similar levels of prejudice to that endured by transsexed and transgendered people in Western societies.[28] This is certainly the case for the so-called "sistergirls," transgendered indigenous Australians. Whereas "sistergirls" are revered within Aboriginal society and perform important feminine tasks within their families, they suffer discrimination, child abuse, and many other forms of discrimination in the wider community that can adversely affect their mental health.[29]

Chevalier d'Eon, the famous French cross-dresser, experienced an increase in religious experiences following a change in gender presentation. Such spiritual conversions occur in traditional societies such as the two-spirited people in North America, who mediated between physical and spiritual aspects of their people's lives. Other spiritually esteemed transgendered people include the *acault* (transgendered women) in Myanmar, and the *maa khii* (transgendered men) in northern Thailand.[30]

In Thailand masculine women and feminine men are called *tom* and *kathoey*, respectively. Such people are socially homosexual, being sexually attracted to people of their same natal sex. Perhaps Thai culture does not distinguish between homosexuals and transgendered people.[31]

The "sworn virgins" are transgendered women who assume a male role in rural Albania and Kosovo. These women become honorary males and do not marry but assume the role of household head. They exhibit a masculine speech style as well as masculine activities and body language. They also change their name to reflect their new masculine social role. Few, if any, of these women participate in lesbian activities, suggesting a dissociation between gender identity and sexual orientation in their community.[32]

Transgendered behavior in Japan, including that shown on the relatively uncensored Japanese Internet sites, is diverse. Both male female-role and female male-role actors partake in stage-shows, suggesting that the Japanese entertainment industry is tolerant of homosexuality and transgenderism with sexual license being common, particularly for men. Transgendered and transsexed women who work in the Japanese sex and entertainment industry are called "new-half" people. Although they communicate using female speech patterns, some "new-half" transsexed people adopt an intermediate sexual identity that is not entirely female. So in Japan there is a sanctioned departure from the binary gender norm that is mainly limited to entertainment and discrete communication.[33]

Most Aravanis, a transgendered hijra community in Tamil Nadu, India, accept the Hindu belief that the feminine gender is primordial whereas transformation into a masculine gender is only needed to maintain patriarchal roles in society. Aravanis are asked to bless newborn babies because their "third-gender" status offers its own special spiritual significance.[34]

Aravanis are men who dress as women and work in nontraditional occupations such as cooking and dance. Although they occasionally provide sexual services to men, they dress differently from men, avoid sexual relationships with women, and do not indulge in sexual relationships within their own community. The Aravanis assume a female sexual identity and refer to each other in female terms. Since they are often shunned by male family members, they offer both material and emotional support to each other. Many Aravanis take hormones and have "sex-change" surgery to more adequately fulfill their female role. They occasionally assume a monogamous liaison with a man they call their husband.[34]

The gender beliefs of Aravanis were investigated by asking them to judge the appropriateness of gender transgressions in one of two stories, one involving a boy who behaves like a girl, the other telling of a girl who behaves like a boy.[34] Aravanis tolerate all types of gender transgression. Aravanis believe that a girl is more likely to become a boy in the next life than a boy will become a girl because of their good Karma. However in their current life, they believe that a girl could not become a boy whereas a boy could easily become a girl. Gender presentation is important since if a boy dresses and behaves like a girl then he would become a girl. But even if a girl dressed and acted like a boy, a gender transformation was considered impossible. For the Aravanis a male gender identity is more fluid than a female one. In most Western societies the opposite applies, there being greater tolerance of girls dressing and behaving like boys than vice versa. Whereas male gender transgression results in status loss in many Western countries, it is a male prerogative in some parts of India. So cultural factors are important determinants of gender expression and tolerance.

Many transsexed and transgendered people respond to society's stigma by maintaining the traditional male-female gender divide, especially for those who value passing. Feminist authors might be expected to be tolerant of individual differences and to eliminate pathological labeling of transsexed women. However, Raymond[35] restricts "womanhood" to natal women, a proscription that explicitly excludes transsexed women.

HOW DO PEOPLE VIEW TRANSSEXUALITY?

Transgendered behavior has been considered abnormal, anomalous, and scandalous in Western societies. This negative attitude towards transgendered people's behavior reflects long-term sanctions based on religious and legal impositions. However, recently such negative attitudes have softened, especially in the entertainment industry, where drag queens and drag kings have provided comic relief for the masses. Perhaps the best-known exponent of this art is *Dame Edna Everage*, the mature-aged female persona developed by the Australian actor Barry Humphries. However, such lampooning of cross-gendered behavior incites incredibility in transsexed people who must live permanently in their affirmed sex without parody.

The attractiveness and seductiveness presented by some transsexed women threatens masculine values. Movies with a transgendered theme such as *Some Like It Hot* and *The Silence of the Lambs* invoke both amusement and horrified repulsion in viewers, leading to an inevitable ambivalence in people's attitudes towards transsexed and transgendered people.

Television has brought transgendered and transsexed people into the public gaze. These shows range from the outlandish representation of transsexed people on the *Jerry Springer Show* to the more refined interviews that occasionally occur on the *Oprah Winfrey Show*. Recently, documentaries with a transsexed theme have appeared on television, as have a number of notable feature-length movies involving transsexed or transgendered themes. The popular films *Priscilla Queen of the Desert, Mrs. Doubtfire,* and the rather disturbing *Boys Don't Cry* are noteworthy. Felicity Huffman's winning of a Golden Globe award in 2006 for her starring role of Bree, a transsexed woman, in *Transamerica* is a notable achievement. People were either amused or outraged by the TV show *There's Something about Miriam,* in which a group of unsuspecting young men unknowingly become infatuated with an attractive preoperational transsexed woman. The participants' subsequent outrage indicated the disservice such a show does to the transsexed community.

The public can now read autobiographies by transsexed people.[36] More than any other medium, the written word, accompanied frequently by life-history photographs, has described the agonies and joys experienced by transsexed people brave enough to share their experiences. Of special significance is the way partners, family, and work colleagues have accommodated themselves to the changes transition imposes upon their loved ones. Inevitably, such stories provide a glimpse of humanity that is scarcely experienced by most people in a lifetime.

The Internet has provided more information on transgenderism, transsexualism, and the intersexed than was previously available. Nowadays, people can explore their transgender feelings by reading informative web pages on the Internet. They can also communicate directly with transgendered and transsexed people in chat-rooms and by email.

SURVEYS ON ATTITUDES TOWARDS TRANSSEXUALITY AND THE INTERSEXED

As in many other matters of social interest, Sweden is an ideal place to conduct a survey on transsexuality. Since 1972, GRS has been covered by that country's national health scheme, and postoperative people are able to live as their affirmed sex and enjoy the same rights as other citizens, including marriage and adopting and raising children. In 1998, Mikael Landén and Sune Innala[37] sent a questionnaire designed to explore people's views on transsexuality to almost 1,000 Swedish people aged between 18 and 70, obtaining a good response rate of 67 percent. For the purposes of this survey, the medical condition of *transsexualism* was defined as follows:

> **Transsexualism** occurs in both men and women, and is characterized by a gender identity of the opposite sex. A transsexual person is often said to be trapped in the body of the wrong sex, and have a strong desire to live and be accepted as a member of the opposite sex and to "change sex." A sex change implies a new name, treatment with the hormones of the opposite sex, and surgery of the genitals to make his or her body as congruent as possible with the preferred sex. Transsexualism is **not the same as transvestism,** which refers to men who occasionally dress in women's clothes. A transvestite does not wish to change sex.[38]

The survey produced a number of interesting findings. More women than men returned the questionnaire. Interestingly, 65 percent of respondents believed that transsexuality has a biological cause (the *Biological* group), whereas the remainder considered that a socially determined cause (the *Social* group) was more likely.

In terms of medical and social implications, only 22 percent considered transsexualism to be a treatable disease, 64 percent supported a transsexed person's desire for a name change, 52 percent approved a change in identity, and 53 percent approved access to hormone treatment. Fifty-six percent supported transsexed people's desire for GRS. Sixty-three percent of respondents believed that the individual should pay for their medical treatment; 56 percent approved of marriage following GRS; and 52 percent opposed the idea that single sex-affirmed persons should adopt and raise children, whereas 43 percent approved the transsexed person's right to raise children provided they were married. Sixty-one percent of respondents considered that a sex-affirmed person, no matter what their new gender, could work with children. Seventy-one percent would be pleased to work with a sex-affirmed person, and 60 percent would be prepared to have such a person as their friend. However, 84 percent of respondents would not want a transsexed person as their partner. People agreed that the media provides adequate, but not excessive, attention to transsexed people. Only 8 percent of respondents knew a transsexed person, and 38 percent of people believed that the incidence of transsexuality had increased in Sweden over the last 20 years. Interestingly, 53 percent of people considered the transsexed to be born that way, reinforcing slight majority support for a biological basis for the condition.

Searching for a biological basis for transsexuality, rather than assuming that the lifestyle is socially determined, is worthwhile as fewer of the people who consider transsexuality to be biologically determined believe it is a disease. More women than men considered transsexuality to not be a disease. Similarly, a greater number of younger people, when compared with older people, considered transsexuality to not be a disease. These results suggest community support for the removal of gatekeeping from the medical assistance provided to transsexed people. Gatekeeping occurs when a transsexed person's transition is controlled, sometimes excessively, by medical and other requirements.

Biological respondents of all ages, including more women and younger people, supported a change in name and identity for a transsexed person. They also thought that transsexed people should be treated with hormones followed by GRS, if they so desire. *Biological* respondents favored the transsexed using their own financial resources to pay for GRS, as also did the younger respondents. More *Biological* respondents thought transsexed people should be able to marry in their new sex, as also did more women and younger respondents. Nevertheless, *Biological* respondents were not so keen for single transsexed people to adopt and raise children by themselves. However, this situation changes dramatically if the couple is married, the *Biological* respondents supporting the idea that transsexed people should be able to look after children, an attitude they shared with female respondents in general. *Biological* respondents favored postoperative transsexed people being allowed to work with children, a liberal view they shared with women. More *Biological* respondents, as well as most women, would be prepared to work with a transsexed person and to have a transsexed person as their friend.

The Swedish survey demonstrated that country's liberal attitudes towards transsexed people and their desire for a normal life. Overall, women and those who believed that transsexuality has a biological basis were the most supportive of transsexed people. Such findings, if replicated in other Western societies, would provide considerable encouragement for those transsexed people who proceed to GRS.[39]

A biological correlate for transsexuality has been discovered based on a discrepancy between brain sexual differentiation and born-sex. The central region of the bed nucleus of the stria terminalis (BSTc) in the hypothalamus is female in appearance for transsexed women, using as evidence postmortem brain micrographs. This difference cannot result from estrogen exposure, as men treated with estrogen for medical conditions other than transsexualism had a male BSTc size. Other studies have demonstrated both genetic and finger-length ratio differences between the transsexed and others. Such discoveries bolster the hopes of those transsexed people who believe that their condition has a firm biological basis, especially when tolerance is enhanced once people realize that transsexuality is a biological condition. Evidence for the biological basis of transsexuality is contained in chapter 2.

Much research into sex differences, as well as homosexuality and transsexuality, maintains the superiority society attaches to heterosexuality. Rogers[40] criticized the unconfirmed, biased viewpoints of both evolutionary psychologists and sociobiologists who have made unsubstantiated claims about the ancestral differences between men and women. Such claims demean women and lower their social prestige. Such an injustice can be doubly devastating to transsexed people, who deserve absolute indifference to any preordained gender differences.

The most devastating outcome for transsexed people is transphobia, defined as "skepticism about the existence of the transsexed or a dislike or hatred of, and occasionally hostility toward, them."[41] Transphobia is not limited to the general public but is occasionally exhibited by members of the psychological and medical professions, even those treating transsexed people. Raj[41] outlined various forms of clinical transphobia, the irrational attitudes of clinicians directed towards their transsexed clients. These include unethical treatment strategies applied to those without accompanying psychological disability, such as:

(a) pathologizing clients by suggesting that transsexuality is a symptom of serious psychiatric illness;
(b) insisting upon client compliance towards therapy based on outdated ideas;
(c) employing unethical and unproven diagnostic methods such as physiological responses to erotic stimuli;
(d) using unproven techniques such as psychoanalysis to effect a "cure";
(e) using behavior modification techniques with young people who exhibit gender atypical behavior to deter them from an anticipated homosexual lifestyle;
(f) discriminating against gynephilic transsexed women, i.e., those who are sexually attracted to women, but not applying this restriction to androphilic transsexed men, i.e. those who are sexually attracted to men;
(g) excluding those from the real-life experience, i.e. living full-time in their preferred gender, who are unemployed or not studying full-time, and who cannot "pass" in their affirmed gender role;
(h) showing prejudice towards those transsexed people, mainly women, who engage in sex-work;
(i) only providing hormone therapy for those who intend pursuing GRS when some transsexed people cannot undergo GRS for personal, health, or financial reasons; and
(j) frustrating transsexed people by imposing excessive "gatekeeping."[41]

A shift in focus to transsexuality being considered a normal variant of gendered behavior rather than a pathological condition is required. The therapist's role should change from clinical provider to client-facilitator. Improvements in support for transgendered and transsexed people include a more diverse client population, more therapists with transsexual backgrounds, improved access to GRS and other medical procedures by government and insurance companies, and better training of professionals who assist transsexed clients.[41]

Fearing an incorrect and unexpected "misdiagnosis," transsexed clients are often antagonistic towards their medical advisors, simultaneously challenging the need for expensive clinical assessment. Some advisors serve as gatekeepers by setting up eligibility criteria and clinical thresholds, while the client *demands* hormones and surgery. Such antithetical positions can be moderated by offering greater decision-making responsibility to the client. Such cooperative strategies emphasize client-directed, collaborative, self-determined medical management based on a de-medicalized, social diversity approach.[41]

Whatever the treatment strategy, it should be person-centered and solution-focused using the most appropriate procedure for each client. Few psychologists have certified training in transsexual counseling to serve as informed and innovative counselors. More often than not, transsexed clients know more about their lifestyle needs than do their therapists.[41]

People who believe that transsexuality has a biological basis are more understanding and sympathetic to the needs of transsexed people. On the other hand, when professionals treating transsexed people are as antagonistic to their needs as is the general public, transsexed people can be justifiably aggrieved. Education is needed to achieve a change in people's attitudes towards transsexed people.

THE PREVALENCE OF TRANSSEXUALITY

Controversy exists regarding the prevalence of transsexuality, due to the condition's relative rarity, and the tendency for some transsexed people to transition "in stealth" without medical supervision. A large latent population of transgendered people who have not attended gender clinics further complicates the task of assessing prevalence. Most of the prevalence estimates have been obtained from clients of gender clinics who have been pathologized with the medical condition of transsexualism. So it is nearly impossible to determine the incidence of the normal gender variant known as transsexuality.

A retrospective study of 1,285 transsexed people who attended a Dutch gender clinic between 1975 and 1992 included 949 men and 336 women. The annual number of applicants increased over the time period, with numbers stabilizing in the late 1980s. The ratio of transsexed women to men of about 3:1 remained relatively constant over the 17-year period. Seventy-seven percent of the men and 80 percent of the women progressed to hormonal and/or surgical treatment. Sixty-seven percent of transsexed women and 78 percent of transsexed men were young, having presented for treatment in their late teens or early twenties. A smaller proportion of older transsexed women, those transitioning in middle age and beyond, underwent GRS than did the younger transsexed women. Of those who progressed to GRS, only five transsexed women regretted their decision. This small number, representing 0.7 percent of the applicants, contained only older transsexed women. Overall, the prevalence of transsexualism as a medical condition was estimated to be 1:11,900 for natal men and 1:39,400 for natal women, values a third less than those published in DSM-IV, the *Diagnostic and Statistical Manual* used by psychiatrists and clinical psychologists worldwide.[42]

Prevalence rates can vary widely over time and between societies. In 2000 in the Czech Republic, the incidence of transsexualism for both males and females was 1:10,000, the average age for GRS being 29.[43] The prevalence of gender dysphoria, the distress resulting from gender atypicality, in Scotland is about 1:12,225, a relatively high ratio.[18] Since many people suffering from gender dysphoria are not diagnosed with transsexualism, this prevalence figure is probably an overestimation.

In West Germany between 1981 and 1990 there were 1,422 cases of diagnosed transsexualism. Most transsexed people were in the 25–34 age bracket, the next most common age range being the following decade, 35–44. The estimated prevalence of transsexualism was 1:36,000 for transsexed women and 1:131,000 for transsexed men, a sex ratio favoring transsexed women by about 3:1.[20]

Other observations, not yet firmly supported by systematic study, suggest an even higher prevalence of transsexuality. Gender problems are occasionally masked by other conditions such as anxiety, depression, bipolar disorder, conduct disorder, substance abuse, dissociative identity disorders, borderline personality disorder, other sexual disorders, and intersexed conditions, so people presenting with these other conditions will not be counted in medical estimates of the prevalence of transsexualism. Some transvestites, female impersonators, and homosexuals may also exhibit gender atypicality but not be counted. Since the intensity of gender problems tends to fluctuate, some people may not present with any problems at all in prevalence studies. Finally, gender variance among females is relatively invisible in Western societies, so many transsexed men are not counted.[44]

Since an unknown number of transsexed people are not counted in studies of transsexuality prevalence, the true prevalence must be much higher than any of the published figures suggest. For example, Lynn Conway[45] argued that the prevalence of transsexuality is up to 100 times greater than figures quoted in the literature. Such a high prevalence is reasonable since many people never undergo GRS and so never appear in the diaries of psychiatrists and surgeons. Many people never seek medical help because they can obtain black-market hormones, or else have family and job commitments that deter them from approaching a gender specialist. When those who do not undergo GRS, or are otherwise unaccountable, are excluded the prevalence of transsexuality in natal males is more than three times the figure proposed by Green and others.[42]

Although precise estimates are difficult to obtain and tend to vary from one country to another, the current best published estimate of the prevalence of the medical condition of transsexualism is about 1:10,000 for natal men and 1:30,000 for natal women, based on data collected mainly in the Netherlands. These figures are about three times larger than those quoted in DSM-IV. Clearly, a more carefully conducted epidemiological study is required, not only to inform transsexed people how very special they are, but to allow health and support agencies to estimate current and future demands on their services. If Conway is correct and the prevalence of transsexuality expressed in all of its forms as gender variance among natal men alone is 1 in 250, we have a major public health issue on our hands, certainly one that is far more widespread than diseases such as multiple sclerosis, which has a prevalence of about 1 in 1000.

SUMMARY

Following a brief review of the historical origins of transsexuality, the rapid advances in recognition, assessment, and help provided for the condition were summarized. This review highlighted the important contributions of pioneers such as Harry Benjamin and transsexed pioneers such as Lili Elbe and Christine Jorgenson. These people encouraged medical professionals to expand their skills into a challenging and potentially stigmatized field while simultaneously paving the way for the many transsexed people who would follow in their footsteps. A few examples of pioneering gender clinics were provided.

Although many transsexed people comply with socially proscribed gender roles and pass if they can, others live their lives either in an androgynous way or in a more radical form akin to the "third-gender" role that is tolerated in many non-Western societies. A Swedish survey investigating people's attitudes towards transsexed people and their desire for proper treatment indicated a high level of tolerance, especially among those who believed that, rather than being merely some social whim, there is a biological basis for transsexuality. This positive approach was dampened somewhat by those professionals who exhibit similar prejudice towards transsexed people as does the general public. Prevalence studies indicated that, despite the large variability between estimates, the latest figures suggest that transsexualism as a medical condition may be about three times more prevalent than is recognized in the most recent version of the DSM-IV. Sampling difficulties and the tendency for many transsexed people to live in "stealth" ensure that such estimates are highly unreliable in the absence of properly conducted epidemiological studies. However, common sense suggests that the prevalence of transsexuality may be rather high, more so than for many recognized medical conditions that attract generous research funding and medical facilities from governments and other agencies.

Chapter Two

THE BIOLOGICAL BASIS OF GENDER IDENTITY FORMATION

Of the gender differences occurring in humans, perhaps the most basic are those occurring in the brain, resulting possibly from prenatal hormonal and genetic effects. These differences between males and females are likely causes of human variability in both sexual orientation and gender identity. This chapter examines the biological basis of gender identity and sexual orientation, showing some interesting differences in brain structures between men and women, as well as between transsexed people and others of their natal sex.

PRENATAL DEVELOPMENT OF SEX DIFFERENCES

Sex differences originate in the differentiation process that determines whether the human embryo will become male or female. The outcomes of such biochemical changes are brain regions with quantifiable sex differences.

During the first six weeks of fetal development, male and female genitals are indistinguishable. Differentiation begins around week seven in the male fetus in response to testosterone stimulation. The major sexual differentiation event is the transformation of a rudimentary gonad into either a testis or an ovary, a process initiated by the SRY gene, which is located on the Y chromosome. This gene is responsible for the proper development of the testes. In the male fetus, Sertoli cells start secreting Mullerian-inhibiting substance (MIS) at seven weeks. MIS remains at high concentrations in male blood for several years postnatally. However, by puberty, the MIS concentration decreases to a low level that is maintained throughout adulthood. MIS can be detected in females between puberty and the onset of menopause at a level similar to that occurring in a newborn male.[1]

Differentiation of the external male genitals requires the transformation of testosterone to dihydrotestosterone (DHT) by the enzyme 5-α-reductase. Two pairs of genital ducts develop within the urogenital ridge. The Wolffian duct is located in the central rear section of the urogenital ridge, draining the embryonic kidney and entering the urogenital sinus from the rear. In the absence of MIS in females, these ducts eventually form the fallopian tubes, the uterus, and the upper portion of the vagina. Without MIS, the Mullerian duct starts regressing by day 51 and disappears by day 64. MIS affects both sex cells and body cells during gonad formation.

In males, the first stage of testicle formation occurs when a urogenital ridge forms in the rear wall of the abdominal cavity around day 28. During the seventh or eighth week, Leydig cells appear in testicular tissue. These cells produce androgens, such as testosterone, that increase in concentration within testicular tissue, fetal blood, and amniotic fluid, attaining a peak concentration around week 16. The initial and terminal gonad configurations for males and females are depicted in Figure 2.1.[2]

At two critical periods during early development, males are exposed to greater levels of testosterone than are females. The first critical period occurs during weeks 8 to 10 as well as in the five weeks after the testes start secreting testosterone. The second period occurs during the first six months of neonatal life, when another testosterone surge occurs. Evidence from non-human species indicates an optimal testosterone level, with sexual behavior being reduced when the testosterone concentration is either too small or too large.[3]

A sexually dimorphic brain region is one that shows clear differences between men and women. Sexually dimorphic neural structures are not necessarily determined solely by sex differences in gonadal hormone levels, but could be determined by genetic differences.[4] In mice, for example, over 50 different genes express their biological effects differently in male and female brains even before hormonal sexual differentiation occurs. Research using animals in which the Y chromosome had no testis-determining SRY gene shows that sex chromosomes are responsible for sex differences in the number of dopamine receptors that control nerve message transmission in the developing brain, even when there are no associated hormonal influences.[5]

Although genetics may serve as a precursor of brain sexual differentiation, the genetic basis for transsexuality, when compared with other intersex conditions, is especially scant. Using genetic material from 30 transsexed women and 31 transsexed men, no association between the presumed medical condition of transsexualism and any chromosomal abnormalities has been found.[6]

Figure 2.1
**The Sexual Differentiation of Embryonic Undifferentiated Gonads into
Their Male (Bottom Left) and Female (Bottom Right) Configuration**

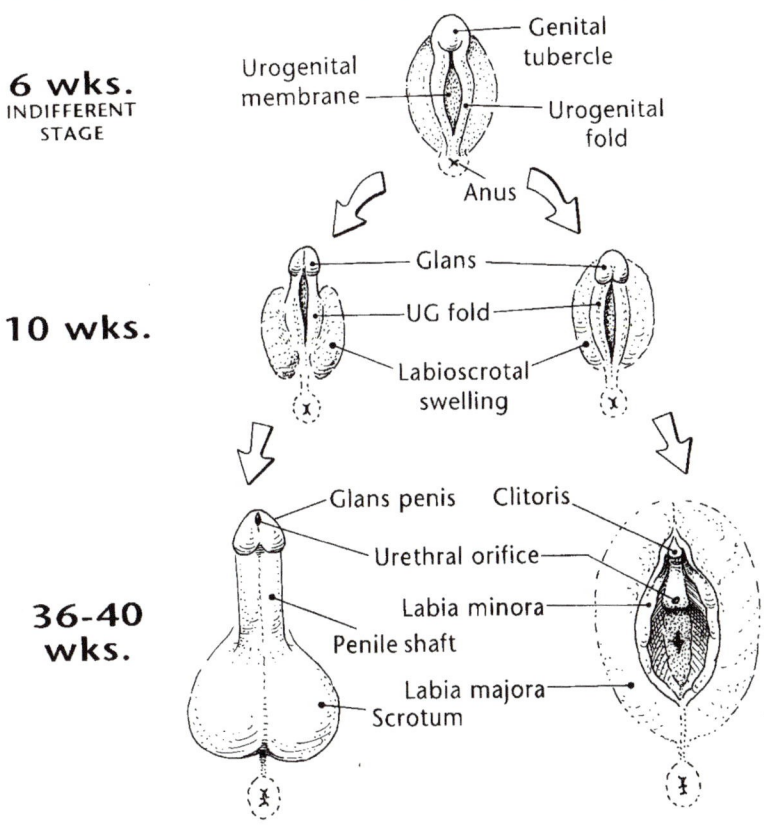

Source: Reprinted with permission from the Annual Review of Medicine, Vol. 45 © 1994
by Annual Reviews, www.annualreviews.org.

However, genetic effects may be rather subtle. When the genetic structures of 29 transsexed women were compared with those of 229 natal women, there were differences in the genetic sequences that govern the function of the sex hormones, estrogen, and testosterone (a type of androgen), as well as in genetic sequences for aromatase, the chemical that converts testosterone to estrogen.[7]

SEX DIFFERENCES IN BRAIN FUNCTION

Recent research has revealed some interesting differences in the brains of men and woman. These differences occur throughout the brain and are responsible for associated behavioral differences. The hypothalamus, a small lower brain region that controls vegetative functions such as hunger, thirst, reproduction, and sleep and regulates hormone release by stimulating the pituitary gland, is sensitive to sex differences. Imaging techniques such as magnetic resonance interferometry (MRI) reveal interesting sex differences in the living brain.

Previous research had suggested that brain-sex differences in males, arising around the time of birth, result from the effects of testosterone secreted by the developing testes. Such sex differences were thought to persist throughout adulthood, since the brain was assumed to remain relatively fixed through-out the lifespan. However, sex differences in the posterodorsal nucleus of the medial amygdala, an emotional center that is larger in males than in females, are not only determined prenatally but persist postnatally. Within four weeks after adult male rats are castrated, the posterodorsal nucleus volume decreases to female levels. A corresponding increase in posterodorsal nucleus volume occurs when female rats are given testosterone injections. Therefore, the adult brain changes in response to hormonal influences that occur after birth.[8]

Hormone effects in adults are revealed by changes in brain structure. For example, testosterone acts on the spinal nucleus of the bulbocavernosus, which enervates the penis, to change both the size and connectivity of neurons that control penis function. In females, estrogen causes the ventromedial nucleus of the hypothalamus to produce new synapses. Therefore, hormones pro-duce reversible changes in the brain. Estrogen-controlled synapse formation also occurs in the hippocampus, a lower-brain region involved in memory and learning, in tune with the estrous cycle of the female rat. Environmental influences such as enriched learning and stress produce neural change in the hippocampus. Therefore, life experiences affect behavior by interacting with hormonal influences.

Sex differences exist in brain regions outside of the amygdala, hypothalamus, and hippocampus regions and may include the corpus callosum, the nerve tis-sue connecting the two brain hemispheres. The corpus callosum is more richly connected in females than in males,[8] suggesting that the brain hemispheres might have less specialized functions in women than in men.[9]

Although the female brain weighs about 100g less than that of males, the metabolic activity per unit volume is about the same. The corpus callosum has a larger area in males than in females, but this anatomical difference, which is rather small, does not produce sex differences in behavior.[10]

Figure 2.2[11] provides a more detailed view of the locations of specific nuclei within a frontal slice through the hypothalamus.

Sex differences are widespread in the human hypothalamus. The volume of the sexually dimorphic nucleus of the preoptic area (SDN-POA) in men is more than twice as large as that for women, this sex difference fluctuating

Figure 2.2
Schematic Frontal Section through Two Subdivisions of the Bed Nucleus of the Stria Terminalis (BST) That are Hatched

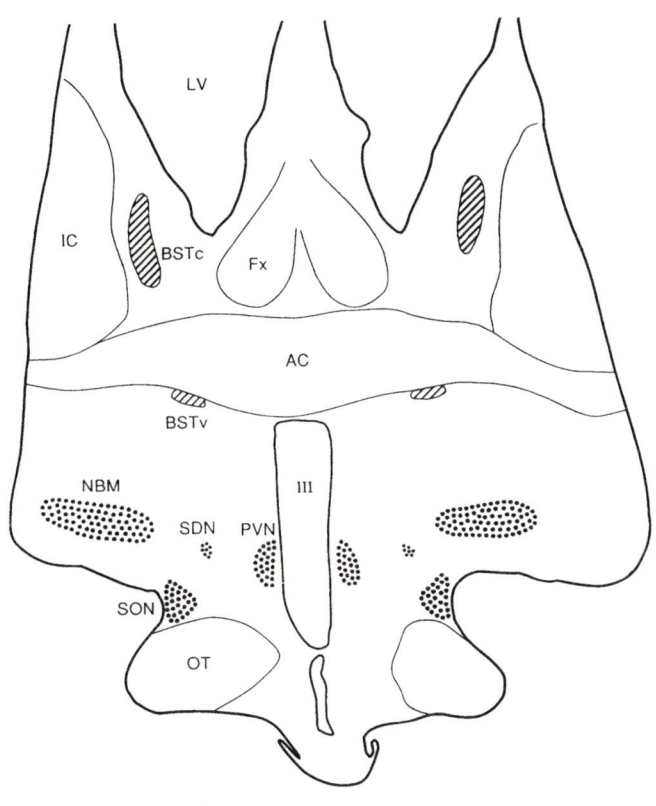

Note: III: third ventricle; AC: anterior commissure; BSTc and BSTv: central and ventral subdivisions of the BST; FX: fornix; IC: internal capsule; LV: lateral ventricle; NBM: nucleus basalis of Mynert; OT: optic tract; PVN: paraventricular nucleus; SDN: sexually dimorphic nucleus; SON: supraoptic nucleus.

Source: Reprinted by permission from Macmillan Publishers Ltd: Nature, Vol. 378, 6552, p. 68–70, 1995.

with age. There is a correspondingly larger number of androgen and estrogen receptors in this site for men than for women. The central section of the bed nucleus of the stria terminalis (BSTc) is a small region of the hypothalamus defined by its dense vasoactive intestinal polypeptide (VIP) innervation, probably originating in the amygdala. The BSTc is also characterized by its somatostatin nerve fiber network and associated neurons that exhibit clear sex differences. The BSTc is 40 percent larger in men than in women and has almost twice as many somatostatin neurons in men.[12]

Somatostatin is a peptide chemical involved in nerve message transmission. For example, deficits in somatostatin accompany both epilepsy and Alzheimer's disease.[13] Data obtained from 10 47-year-old men and 14 41-year-old women indicated that males have a higher somatostatin density in both the temporal and frontal cortical regions of the brain than do females, suggesting that somatostatin-receptor density in the cerebral cortex is related to gender identity.[14]

Sex differences in the SDN-POA first become evident around four years of age, when the number of cells decreases for girls but stays relatively constant for boys. There is a rapid decrease in cell numbers for men over 50 and a corresponding decrease in cell numbers for women over 70. In men, the reduction in SDA-POA cell count occurring between 50 and 60 years leads to a small sex difference. Thereafter, a decrease in cell count occurs for women over 70 but not for men, resulting in older men having a larger SDA-POA cell count than do older women.[12]

The VIP-containing subnucleus of the human suprachiasmic nucleus (SCN), a region of the hypothalamus controlling hormone cycles, is twice as large in young men as in women of comparable age. This sex difference reverses beyond 40 years of age when the subnucleus size for women becomes larger than that for men. Therefore, age can be an important factor affecting the direction of brain-sex differences.

Vasopressin is responsible for body fluid retention and may cause an increase in blood pressure. Young males exhibit greater vasopressin neuron activity in the supraoptic nucleus than do women. This sex difference disappears after age 50, suggesting that a region with no structural sex differences can nevertheless reveal a sex difference in how it functions.

The volume of the darkly staining posteromedial component of the bed nucleus of the striata terminalis, another sexually dimorphic part of the hypothalamus, is 2.5 times larger in men than in women. Women have higher percentages of slow-wave sleep and lower percentages of stage one sleep than men do. In addition, women have twice as many sleep bundles in their brain's electrical activity and tend to spend more time sleeping than do men.[12]

The volume of the suprachiasmic nucleus (SCN) of the hypothalamus may be related to sexual orientation, as it is 1.7 times larger and contains about twice as many mainly vasodepressin-expressing neurons in homosexual men than in heterosexual men. Interestingly, there is a lower cell death rate with increasing age in the SCN for homosexual men. The number of VIP-expressing neurons in the SCN is larger in men aged from 10 to 40, and larger in women between the ages of 41 and 65. The increased number of VIP-expressing neurons in homosexual men suggests a difference from heterosexual males in early brain development.

However, there is no difference in the size of the BSTc between homosexual and heterosexual men, unlike the situation for natal and transsexed women, where similarities have been observed in postmortem specimens. Except for this case, homosexual men have some brain structures that differ from those of both heterosexual men and women.[12] Nevertheless, such brain structure differences may not result in differences in brain function, since the homosexual lifestyle is also affected by psychological and social factors.[15]

The search for biological correlates of homosexuality has been reasonably successful. As noted, the suprachiasmic nucleus that controls both circadian rhythm and sexual behavior is larger and more elongated in both homosexual men and heterosexual women when compared with non-homosexual men. The third interstitial nucleus of the anterior hypothalamus (INAH-3) is smaller in homosexual men than in heterosexual men, its size being similar to that of women. By contrast, the midsagittal plane of the anterior-commissure is larger in homosexual men than in heterosexual men and women, this brain region being larger in women than in men. The isthmus of the corpus callosum, which is larger in women, is larger by 13 percent in right-handed homosexual men when compared with nonhomosexual men. Its size is also related to left-handedness in men. Homosexuals tend to sleep less than heterosexuals, possibly resulting from differences in circadian regulation.[16] Lifestyle such as late-night partying might also influence sleep patterns in some young people.

It is unlikely that a small brain area such as INAH-3 causes behavior as complex as homosexuality. Since the brains studied were from deceased AIDS victims, the observed differences in brain structure might be due to the illness. It is impossible to verify the assumption that the presumed heterosexual clients were not homosexual. In any case, small sample sizes make it difficult to discern reliable differences in INAH-3 size between homosexuals and nonhomosexuals.[15]

A BIOLOGICAL BASIS FOR TRANSSEXUALITY

The bed nucleus of the stria terminalis (BSTc) exhibits a female form in transsexed women, whereas a more male-like BSTc was observed in one transsexed man. These differences did not depend on hormone treatment. During its development in animals, the BSTc is sensitive to the effects of testosterone, suggesting that a reduction in prenatal androgens may be responsible for transsexuality in natal men.[17]

Using postmortem brain samples from six transsexed women collected over an 11-year period, the volume of the BSTc (see Figure 2.2), a brain area essential for sexual behavior, was found to be similar in size and shape for natal women and transsexed women (compare Figures 2.3B and 2.3D). BSTc size was not affected by sex hormones in adulthood nor was it related to sexual orientation. A small BSTc volume was found in the transsexed women (see Figure 2.3D)—52 percent of that for heterosexual males (see Figure 2.3A) and 46 percent of that for homosexual males (see Figure 2.3C).[17]

When considered together with animal data, these results suggest that gender identity atypicality in transsexed people results from abnormal interactions between brain development and sex-hormone concentrations. However, such a claim is impossible to evaluate empirically, since causal influences cannot be inferred when there is no experimental manipulation.

Sex differences in BSTc size might result from differences in its neural connectivity with the amygdala, which forms part of the limbic, or emotional, system of the brain. The number of somatostatin-expressing (SOM) neurons in the BSTc was determined using postmortem brain samples from 42 men and women with disparate sexual orientation, intersexed conditions, and gender identities. The number of SOM neurons for heterosexual men was 71 percent higher than that for heterosexual women. The numbers of neurons for homosexual and heterosexual men were similar, whereas the number of SOM neurons was 81 percent higher in homosexual men than for heterosexual women.[18]

The number of neurons was similar for transsexed women and heterosexual women, the data for one transsexed man being located within the natal male range. The number of neurons for transsexed women was 40 percent less than that found for heterosexual men. There was no difference in the number of BSTc neurons for young compared with middle-aged transsexed women, suggesting that BSTc size depends on gender identity rather than age at transition. Young transsexed women usually start transitioning from male to female in their late teens or early twenties, whereas other transsexed women start their transition when they are middle aged or beyond.[18]

The number of SOM neurons in the BSTc was not affected by hormone levels, suggesting that hormone therapy may not affect neuron numbers, especially in transsexed women. An old man with a strong untreated cross-gender identification whose BSTc neuron count lay in the female range further evidenced absence of an effect of hormone therapy on BSTc neuron count. A 31-year-old man with a feminizing adrenal tumor had a BSTc neuron count that was within the male range. So estrogen treatment, orchidectomy (testicle removal), antiandrogen treatment that minimizes the effect of testosterone, and hormonal changes in adulthood do not influence BSTc neuron numbers. Perhaps BSTc neuron numbers are determined by testosterone exposure during brain development, leading to sex-dimorphic brain regions that determine one's gender identity. This inference is complicated by the observation that unexpectedly a greater concentration of α-estrogen receptors occurs in the BSTc for males than for females.[18]

Figure 2.3
Representative Sections of the BSTc Innervated by Vasoactive Intestinal Polypeptide (VIP)

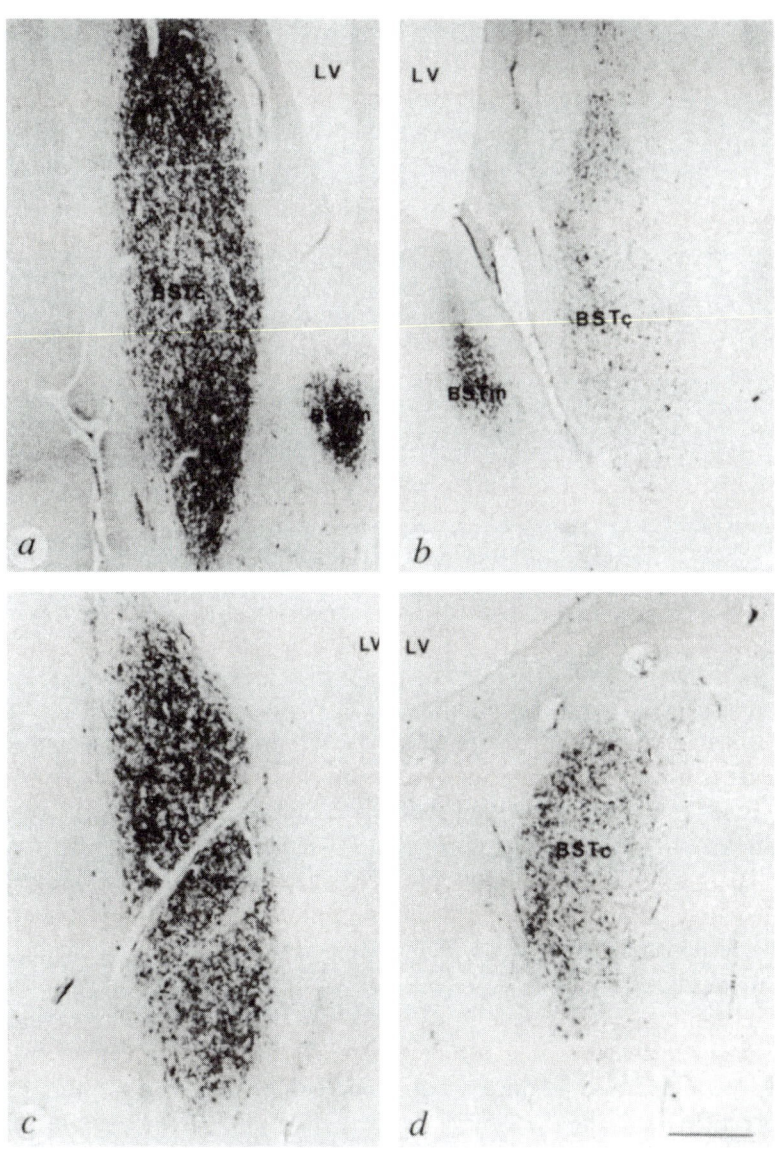

Notes: A: heterosexual man; B: heterosexual woman; C: homosexual man; D: transsexed woman. Bar=0.5 mm. LV: lateral ventrical. There are two parts of the BST in A and B: small-sized medial subdivision (BSTm) and large oval-sized central subdivision (BSTc).

Source: Reprinted by permission from Macmillan Publishers Ltd: Nature, Vol. 378, 6552, p. 68–70, 1995.

Figure 2.4
Changes in Relative BSTc SOM Volume with Age for Males and Females

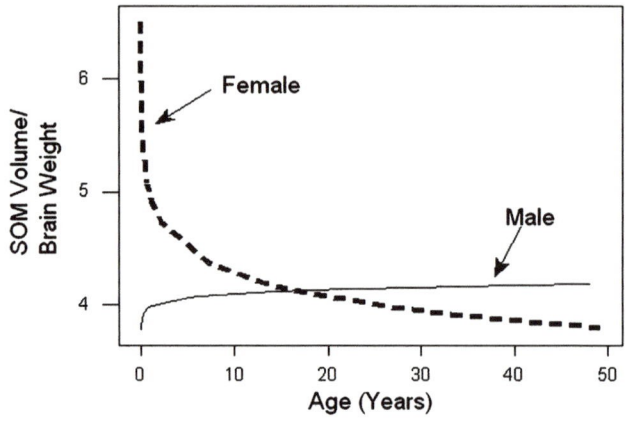

BSTc Volume vs. Age for Males and Females

Calculated From Data in Table 1 of Chung et al. (2002)

Note: The curves are smoothed versions produced by a statistical analysis of data.

Source: The original data are contained in Table 1 in Chung et al. (2002).[19]

Anatomical properties of the BSTc were examined using postmortem evidence from 25 males and 25 females whose ages ranged from about 27 weeks after conception to 49 years. Data from the 50 brain samples showed that BSTc volume increased with age for both males and females, so that at its maximum, the adult BSTc volume was 39 percent larger for males than females. BSTc volume was only larger for males from about puberty onwards, suggesting that differences in sex-hormone concentrations around puberty might be responsible for final BSTc size. This sex difference might depend on activity produced by the SRY gene located on the sex-determining region of the Y chromosome. This gene is transcribed in the hypothalamus of adult males, but not in females. The later development of nerve connections from the amygdala might also produce sex differences in BSTc size in adults.[19]

To investigate this effect in more detail, I divided the BSTc somostatin innervation measure, labeled "SOM Volume," by brain weight to control for changes in brain weight with age. Statistical analysis showed that this ratio could be predicted accurately both by the sex of the brain sample donor and by the separate effects of age for both males and females. Figure 2.4, which shows the predicted relationships between relative BSTc SOM volume and age for both males and females, indicates that the greater relative volume for males only occurs in late adolescence. Interestingly, this is a time when many young transsexed women first seek help for their gender identity atypicality. However, most transsexed people report feelings of "gender difference" much earlier than this, suggesting that other brain structures might influence transsexuality. Although a developmental change in gender identity might be responsible for later changes in BSTc structure, further brain-sex differentiation and possibly the persistence of hormonal effects occur well into adulthood.

The findings of Chung et al. raise interesting questions about the proper role of BSTc in sexual functioning, especially among those transsexed people who experience gender identity atypicality before puberty. Doubt exists regarding the significance of BSTc as a causal influence on transsexuality given the clear sex-reversal effect that occurs around 16 years.[20]

Men have higher androgen-receptor immune responsiveness than do women, the highest effect occurring in the mamillary body complex, a region of the hypothalamus involved in both sexual behavior and cognition. Androgens regulate aromatase activity, which is responsible for converting testosterone into estrogen, in several brain regions and so indirectly affect estrogen concentrations. The clearest difference in androgen-receptor concentrations occurs in the medial nucleus of the mamillary body, a brain region involved in sexual arousal. Here the density of such receptors is much greater in males than in females. The relatively weak androgen-receptor density compared with estrogen-receptor density, especially in the BST region of the hypothalamus, suggests that the process that converts a form of testosterone into estrogen more likely controls sexual behavior. Therefore, any difference in BST size for transsexed people is probably not the result of androgen activity in this part of the brain as has been claimed.[18]

Nonreproductive organs, including the brain and especially the hypothalamus, are sensitive to the effects of sex hormones. The greater prevalence of estrogen receptors in blood vessel walls may explain why women are more protected against cardiovascular disease than are men. On the other hand, women have a greater concentration of α-estrogen receptors in the ventromedial hypothalamic nucleus of the lower-brain region than do men. Perhaps transsexed women have a lower density of α-estrogen receptors in the ventral perimamillary part of the histaminergic tuberomammilary nucleus of the hypothalamus than do natal men, another interesting brain difference.[21]

SEX DIFFERENCES IN BRAIN STRUCTURE

Interesting sex differences have been observed in intact living brains using MRI, which can display brain structure in living organisms. Although the brain is 10 percent smaller in women than in men, relative to overall brain size women have a greater cortical grey matter volume as well as larger volumes in brain regions associated with language, such as Broca's area and the superior temporal cortex. When compared with men, women have larger hippocampus volumes, larger caudate and thalamic nuclei, a larger anterior cingulated gyrus, dorsolateral prefrontal cortex, and right inferior parietal lobe, and a greater volume of white matter in the corpus callosum. Men, on the other hand, have larger brain volumes in the limbic and paralimbic regions, the hypothalamus, and in the paracingulate gyrus.[22] So, many brain regions are sensitive to a person's natal sex.

When men and women are matched on age, handedness, education, and IQ, MRI data reveal larger sex differences in regions having a greater number of sex-hormone receptors. Women have larger brain volumes than do men in the frontal and medial paralimbic regions, the precentral gyrus, and the fronto-orbital cortex, as well as in the superior frontal and lingual gyri.[22]

The limbic system consists of the anterior cingulate, the amygdala, the hippo-campus, and the insular cortex. When selectively stimulated, the limbic system's activity can be measured using positron tomography. Men have a greater response on the left insula than do women, whereas women have a greater response on the left amygdala than do men.[23] These sex differences might be related to the generally greater emotional responsiveness in women.

Viewed using similar MRI technology, the caudate and, possibly, the globus pallidus and hippocampus are larger in female than in male brains, whereas the amygdala is smaller in female brains. This finding is possibly due to there being mostly androgen receptors in the amygdala and mostly estrogen receptors in the hippocampus. The smaller amygdala in women might explain their greater proneness to emotional disorders whereas the larger caudate nucleus in women might protect them from typically male problems such as attention-deficit/ hyperactivity disorder (ADHD) and Tourette's syndrome.[24] However, behav-ioral correlates of sex differences in brain regions are difficult to determine.

The volume of the posterodorsal component of the amygdala (MePD) is 65 percent greater in male than female rats. Administration of testosterone to female rats produces an increase in MePD volume to match more closely that of males. After 30 days, MePD volume of castrated male rats decreases to the female size. Sex differences in MePD volume result from changes in circulating androgens. Therefore, hormones in adulthood might affect brain structures associated with sexual behavior. Perhaps some sex differences are caused solely by circulating steroids in adulthood, moderating the effects of prenatal hormone exposure.[25]

Although androgens are important for masculine behavior development, in nonhuman animals the hormone progesterone counteracts the effects of androgens and protects the female fetus brain from excessive masculinization.

However, androgen effects are more subtle in humans. When mothers are treated with medroxyprogesterone acetate (Provera) during pregnancy, there is minimal effect on their male offspring's behavior. However, their females indulge in more exaggerated feminine behavior and rarely exhibit that typical of a tomboy.[26]

Sex differences in brain function may be responsible for sex differences in the prevalence of physical and mental disorders. For example, predominantly female disorders include anorexia nervosa, bulimia, senile dementia, multiple sclerosis, anxiety disorder, post-traumatic stress disorders, and unipolar depression. Predominantly male disorders include Kallmann's syndrome, sleep

Table 2.1
Documented Sex and Gender Identity Differences in Brain Structures

Brain Region Difference	Sex Difference	Gender Identity
Posterodorsal nucleus of medial amygdala	M > F	
Corpus callosum connectivity	F > M	
Corpus callosum volume	M > F	
Sexually dimorphic nucleus	M > F	
BSTc	M > F, age > 15	TF = F, TM = M ?
VIP subnucleus	M > F	
BNST-dspm	M > F	
Suprachiasmic nucleus	M > F	
Left insula of limbic system	M > F	
Left amygdala	F > M	
Androgen receptor immune response	M > F	
Cortical gray matter volume	F > M	
Broca's area and superior temporal cortex	F > M	
Hippocampus volume	F > M	
Caudate and thalamic nuclei	F > M	
Anterior cingulated gyrus	F > M	
Dorsolateral prefrontal cortex	F > M	
Right inferior parietal lobe	F > M	
Limbic and paralimbic volume	M > F	
Hypothalamus	M > F	
Paracingulate gyrus	M > F	
Fronto-orbital cortex	F > M	

M = male; F = female; TF = transsexed female; TM = transsexed male apnea, autism, ADHD, dyslexia, schizophrenia, stuttering, substance abuse, and learning disability.[9]

Table 2.1 shows brain regions, especially in the hypothalamus, that exhibit clear sex differences. Many of these differences result from prenatal hormone influences. However, the available evidence is circumstantial, since some sex-linked biological processes also influence adult brain development. The similarity between brain structures for natal women and transsexed women in the BSTc region of the hypothalamus is interesting. Whether this result is moderated by age is difficult to evaluate, since only postmortem samples were analyzed. In the next chapter, we examine psychological influences on gender identity development. Eventually, we may be able to link psychological effects with their associated brain structures.

SUMMARY

Several brain regions, particularly the hypothalamus, provide evidence for reliable sex differences in brain structures that appear to be related to gender identity. These brain regions are different from those responsible for human variation in sexual orientation. The discovery of a small region of the hypothalamus that may be related to transsexuality was quite an achievement, even though more research is needed to assess any causal relationship.

Chapter Three

THE PSYCHOLOGICAL BASIS OF GENDER IDENTITY FORMATION

This chapter discusses the psychological development of gender identity in children and adults and considers how this process is disrupted for children and adolescents with gender identity atypicality.

PSYCHOLOGICAL ASPECTS OF GENDER IDENTITY FORMATION

The difference between sex and gender is difficult to define. *Sex* is primarily limited to biological differences between males and females, such as the sex chromosomes, gonads, genitals, hormonal balance, and differences in brain structures. *Gender* commonly refers to our feeling masculine or feminine, depending on our own identity and society's expectations of our role.

Chromosomal sex usually involves XY chromosomes for the male sex and XX chromosomes for the female sex. However, the situation is not that simple. Variations of the more common sex-chromosome combinations result in various intersex conditions. For example, some XX individuals have a male genotype, or behavioral expression, and similarly a few XY people have a female genotype, due to anomalous arrangements of sex-determining genes.

Gonadal sex involves organs producing germ cells—ovaries in women producing eggs, and testicles in men producing sperm. Hormonal sex represents the different combinations of hormones that characterize the two sexes. Generally, men have mostly testosterone and women estrogen. However, for good reproductive and homeostatic reasons, both sexes have a little of the other sex's hormone. For example, testosterone in females is important for libido. Although brain-sex, sex differences that occur in the brain, is important for all aspects of human behavior, it is little recognized as a major contributor to our sexual behavior and, in particular, our gender identity.

Gender, the psychological and social correlate of our sexual existence, includes the concepts of *gender identity* and *gender role. Gender identity* refers to a person's feeling of being either a man or a woman, or some combination of both. *Gender role* refers to characteristic gendered behavior sanctioned by society, such as the antiquated idea that women should be responsible for child rearing and other domestic duties while men should work to support their family. These aspects of gender can be compared and contrasted with aspects of sexual behavior such as *sexual orientation,* which represents sexual preference involving the same sex, a different sex, or a combination of both; and *sexual identity,* which refers to the most common role assumed by a person in their sexual encounters. For example, a fluid bisexual identity occurs when homosexual roles are assumed occasionally by those who are mostly heterosexual.[1]

Gender identity is considered as "the structured set of gendered personal identities that results when the individual takes the social construction of gender and the biological "facts" of sex and incorporates them into an overall self-concept."[2] Gender identity also refers to a person's awareness of, and feelings about, their own gender category, whether that be man, woman, or some combination of the two.

Forming a gender identity is different from being male or female based on one's genital appearance at birth. Like our identity of self, gender identification takes time. It is influenced by our physiological and sexual endowments as well as by what we learn from parents and significant others. Ordinarily, gender identity corresponds with sexual identity. Females are expected to develop a feminine gender identity whereas males will develop a masculine gender identity. However, occasionally there is a mismatch between sexual and gender identities leading to distress and a need to reconcile the two.

During the gender identity phase of development, the child learns to label herself and others appropriately. Next, the child learns about gender stability, understanding that once you are a boy or a girl, you will grow up to be a man or a woman, respectively. In the gender constancy stage, the child realizes that gender attribution is permanent and cannot be affected by cultural and personal whims, such as temporary changes in hairstyles and clothing.[3]

A child's first acceptance of a consistent gender descriptor, such as "I am a boy no matter how I present myself," requires the attainment of concrete operational thought, a cognitive process that occurs when the child is between four and six. Children have attained concrete operational thought when they understand that a quantity of fluid remains the same irrespective of the dimensions of containers into which it is poured.[3]

So a simultaneous process of cognitive and gender identity development occurs. Children first discover their own gender identity, followed by the realization that their gender identity does not change over time, leading to the concept of gender stability. Finally, the child recognizes that gender identity is unaffected by changes in circumstances such as wearing gender-inappropriate clothing, a process known as gender consistency.[4] Attainment of gender consistency depends on mental age rather than chronological age, confirming a nexus between gender identity development and cognitive development.

Gender identity development can be explained by Kohlberg's fundamental principles of active and constructive processes. The child acquires a gender identity by actively interacting with environmental cues arising from parental and peer-group influences. Children can also create their own gender-consistent environment by selecting appropriate same-sex playmates and sharing experiences during play activities. In this way, the child becomes aware of appropriate gender stereotypes that guide subsequent behavior, even before the child exhibits a clear gender identity of his own.

Acquiring a consistent gender identity requires the eventual attainment of gender constancy by means of a number of developmental stages starting in infancy. By six months, babies can discriminate male voices from female voices, indicating both rudimentary categorization ability and better hearing than vision. The baby can distinguish male and female faces by nine months, when they are more sensitive to visual cues. Interestingly, gender categorization occurs before the learning of language. Finally, by the time they are one, toddlers can associate male/female faces with male/female voices, thus generalizing further their concept of gender.

A two-year-old child displays gender-consistent toy preferences as well as an ability to recognize her own gender from photographs, an ability that first appears when the child is about 18 months old.[5] Accurate verbal labeling of males and females occurs when the child is between two and two and a half years old.

Three-year-old children can sort photographs into their appropriate gender categories without assistance. A year earlier, when they are two, children prefer socializing with other children of their own gender. Spontaneous gender-based toy choice, girls playing with dolls and boys playing with cars, for example, also occurs around this time. Six-year-old children play with children of their own gender 11 times more often than they do with children of the opposite gender.[6]

Sixty-seven percent of 27-month-old children can correctly identify their own sex. Fifty-six percent successfully completed a gender-labeling task, with girls out-performing boys, and 23 percent labeled toys correctly in terms of gender stereotype, for example, dolls for girls and trucks for boys. However, only 13 percent correctly categorized gender-identified activities, such as boys playing rough-and-tumble sports and girls wearing pretty dresses. When children choose their toys, girls spent more time playing with dolls than did boys.[6]

Developing a stable gender identity depends on acquiring an understanding of one's own gender identity. By the time they are three, most children begin understanding gender stereotypes such as "big," "fast," and "strong" to describe boys and "small," "scared," and "slow" to describe girls. A child's initially rigid conception of gender becomes more flexible as they get older.[7]

The expression of gender-specific behavior depends on socioeconomic status, upper-class children exhibiting behavior that is more flexible. Working-class children, on the other hand, are more likely to behave traditionally in terms of expressiveness for girls and goal achievement for boys.[8]

Once children can correctly tell whether someone is a boy or a girl, they spend much more time playing in same-sex groups. This preference for same-sex play increases with age and becomes firmly established during the first few years at school. Such in-group affiliation reinforces both their own gender identity and the expected behavior of children in same-sex groups.[5]

Girls become less aggressive once they can label another's gender properly. Although groups of boys tend to play in larger groups and have more physical contact than do groups of girls, girls are generally less domineering than boys are and more readily form within-group friendships. Boys tend to dominate their own-group conversations, whereas girls form good relations with their peers by communicating equitably. Whereas boys maintain a circle of friends, girls tend to have a single best friend to whom they show considerable support and devotion.[8]

The Pre-School Activities Inventory assesses gender-role development, gender-role preference, and acquiescence in preschool children. The average gender-role score for boys is higher than that for girls. The difference between boys' and girls' scores almost doubles between two and a half and five years of age, indicating a progressive increase in gender-role discrimination ability during this period.[9]

Gender-role attitudes have been measured for children between four and six years of age, a period of gender development that progresses from a generally well-established own-gender identity to acquiring gender constancy. When children's gender-role attitudes are assessed using structured doll-play and story telling, they select a doll that is the same gender as the subject of a story. Male gender typing is evident in boys by four years of age, this ability improving with age. However, four-year-old girls take longer to achieve the same degree of male gender-role knowledge as boys. Complementary results for female gender stereotyping indicate that girls achieve superior attainment to that of boys by four years of age. Between four and six, children attend more to members of their own sex, but this preference declines with age.[10]

Attaining a stable gender identity relies on forming gender schemas defined as "dynamic knowledge representations that show age-related development as a function of interactions between the individual and his or her environment as well as changes in response to situational variations."[11] A gender schema refers to one's own gender identity, the role expected of someone of that gender, and how gender determines appropriate behavior, both individually and in response to social influences. When children rely primarily on same-sex interactions, their gender schemas are less flexible than when children are also free to explore cross-sex relationships.

The most important factor in gender schema development is physical appearance. Young children readily categorize tall, short-haired people as males and short, long-haired people as females, irrespective of other discriminating characteristics. Once gender identification has occurred, children consider a newly learned fact about one of their girlfriends as pertaining to all girls, a typical stereotypical response. For example, once a child discovers that a girl has "estro" (a fictitious reference to "estrogen") in her blood, she will think that all girls have this quality, possibly including herself. Children also pay greater attention to, and have better memories for, gender-appropriate tasks than gender-inappropriate ones.[5]

The formation of gender schemas has been studied in 11-year-old children as well as in adults. The most gender-typical scenarios reported by children are childcare (female), mechanical (male), and cooking (female), with boys showing more gender-stereotypical behavior than do girls. For adults, a scenario involving male and female executives can elicit gender stereotypes. The proportion of imagined female leaders is higher for those who saw a videotape showing women in management than it is for participants who did not view the video.[12] So, stereotypes can be modified, highlighting how environmental influences affect both gender roles and the formation of gender schemas. Parent's and their children's gender schemas are similar, the relationship being greater for mothers than for fathers. Gender stereotypes are less prevalent in single-parent families and in those families in which both parents work.[13]

After discriminating sex and gender, we can consider developmental aspects of acquiring a stable gender identity. Gender recognition occurs as early as six months of age, well before the acquisition of language and the start of gender identity formation when the child is about two. Gender identity development progresses in parallel with cognitive development, through several stages of increasing abstraction, until gender constancy is attained when the child is six. At this stage the child's gender identity is unaffected by peripheral changes such as clothing and the choice of toys. Further development of gender identity occurs when the child understands gender schema that incorporate not only the child's own identity but also her understanding of appropriate gender-role behavior in response to environmental demands. In the next section, atypical gender identity development is considered, leading possibly to adjustment problems in children and adolescents.

DEVELOPMENTAL ASPECTS OF GENDER IDENTITY ATYPICALITY

The most common cross-gendered behavior exhibited by girls, such as dressing in boys' clothes, playing boys' games, and playing with boys' toys, increases in frequency from when the girl is between two and three years of age to when she is four or five. Thereafter, cross-gendered behavior declines, only to increase again when the child is six or seven. The decline in cross-gendered behavior once the child is five may result from peer pressure at school.[14]

Appropriately gendered behavior requires children to develop and understand social norms for acceptable behavior as exhibited by parents and significant others. Related aspects of gender constancy include gender-stereotypic norms for appearance and conduct as well as norm-flexibility, so violation of social expectations does not affect gender identity. For example, even though boys play football, it is acceptable for girls to play football too. This behavior by girls does not mean that they have suddenly switched genders unless there is a consistent preference for behaving more typically like boys. So normal fluctuations in behavior do not imply that gender constancy has been violated. Gender constancy implies that sex might also remain the same except in rare cases of genital surgery to correct an intersex condition.

Gender identity atypicality (GIA) occurs when the child identifies with the opposite sex, the first signs of which occur just before the child starts preschool. Parents of children with this normal but rare variation in gender identity do not usually seek specialist assistance until the child is about seven. Boys with GIA internalize their feelings more and exhibit less social competence than do other boys. A comparative analysis of children with GIA in Canada and Holland showed that boys had significantly poorer peer relations than did girls.[15]

Atypical gender behavior in young people is indicated by a preference for friends of the opposite sex, a characteristic that decreases by the time they are 12. Cross-gendered behavior by children younger than 12 is characterized by their preference for opposite-sex toys and the opposite-sex role in spontaneous play. Cross-dressing is more prevalent in boys younger than 12 who are more interested in clothes and jewelry than it is in older children. Some children with GIA who are older than 12 do not attend school regularly. There is a greater incidence of depression for girls with GIA than in boys with atypical gender behavior. Children with GIA who are older than 12 have relationship difficulties with parents and siblings, more boys than girls suffering from harassment. All gender-atypical children, but girls in particular, dislike their appearance. To complicate matters further, children older than 12 are more likely to indulge in self-harm and drug-taking than are their younger peers. Twelve years may be a critical age for confirming an atypical gender identity.[15]

In a study of sex-typed behavior and sexual orientation in children, approximately equal numbers of feminine and nonfeminine boys started attending a gender clinic for gender identity issues when they were seven years old. When interviewed again in late adolescence, 75 to 80 percent of the feminine boys were homosexual or bisexual, compared with about 4 percent of the nonfeminine boys. Relatively few of the feminine boys exhibited GIA as adolescents.[16]

Masculine behavior in girls is more common than feminine behavior in boys. Categories used to classify early cross-gendered behavior include rough-and-tumble play, toy and activity preference, imagined roles, cross-dressing, preference for male or female friends, social reputation as a sissy, tomboy, or loner, and gender identity. Homosexual male adolescents are more likely to recall gender-typed behavior than are heterosexual male adolescents, the scores for both groups being higher than those for females. Early cross-gendered behavior predicts 51 percent of male homosexuality compared with only 6 percent of female homosexuality. Childhood cross-gendered behavior in males is associated with lower self-esteem, higher levels of anxiety and depression, and a greater suicide risk when they become adults.[16]

Based on reports from their parents, feminine seven-year-old boys are distinguished from their nonfeminine peers by being more likely to wear feminine clothing, to wish to be a girl, to play with dolls, and to be interested in women's clothing. They are less likely to partake in rough-and-tumble play and to desire to grow up to be like their father. However, except for the feminine boys being more attractive, there are no socially important influences, such as father absence, that discriminate between the two groups.[17]

The hypothesis that children with GIA have a delayed onset of gender constancy can be evaluated by comparing the performance of children with gender identity issues with a comparison group containing siblings of those with GIA, children being assessed for clinical conditions, and children with no documented problems. In a study of this issue, the two groups only differed in social class, for which the GIA group scored slightly higher. Apparently, children from more disadvantaged families receive a less-sympathetic response from parents who maintain conventional gender roles in their family, so they are much less likely to seek voluntary referral to a gender specialist.[18]

Children referred for gender assessment were delayed in their attainment of both gender stability and gender constancy. Children with GIA were more likely than other children to draw an opposite-gendered person in their first attempt at the Draw-a-Person Test. They also participated less often in same-sex play with typically male and female toys. Children with GIA exhibited more confused emotional responses when asked questions related to gender than did other children, suggesting a lower level of emotional maturity.

Overall, children with GIA demonstrated developmental lags in gender identity development.[18]

Physical characteristics contribute to gender identity confusion. The traits *pretty, beautiful, tomboyish, cute, attractive, all-boy, rugged,* and *handsome* reflect a progression from the most feminine to the most masculine traits exhibited by children. *Attractive, beautiful, handsome,* and *pretty* are traits ascribed more often to photographs of boys with GIA than to other boys. In contrast, *attractive, beautiful, cute,* and *pretty* are traits attributed less often to photographs of girls with GIA than to photographs of girls who show no evidence for GIA.

Physical attractiveness is commonly associated with feminine behavior in boys with GIA, who are rated as more *attractive, beautiful, handsome,* and *pretty* than other boys. Whereas boys without GIA are rated less *cute* as they get older, the ratings change very little with age for boys with GIA. In a study of six-year-olds, girls with GIA were rated less *attractive, beautiful,* and *pretty* than girls without GIA, including a group of sexually abused and emotionally disturbed girls. The older the girl with GIA was, the less *attractive* she was rated.[19] Eight-year-old boys with GIA are rated more *handsome* but less *all-boy, masculine,* and *rugged* than a sample of other boys equated on age, IQ , and the parents' social class and marital status. On the other hand, six-year-old girls with GIA are judged more *masculine* and *rugged* than a matched group of other girls.[20]

Psychological problems attributed to gender identity atypicality, especially in children and adolescents, derive from a disruption of the normal developmental progression through the stages of gender identity formation. Confusion sometimes occurs when the assumption is made that feminine boys exhibit the early manifestations of a homosexual sexual orientation. Although such an outcome is reasonably common, it cannot explain the high level of distress experienced by children with atypical gender identity.

SUMMARY

Several investigators have found evidence to support the basic assumptions of Kohlberg's stages of gender identity formation. The normal progression through the various developmental stages leading to gender constancy, a feeling of gender that is unaffected by outward appearances, occurs at similar ages to that of cognitive development, at least until the attainment of concrete operational thought. Ultimately, cognitive representations of gender lead to a conceptualization in terms of a schema that reflects environmental constraints on gendered behavior. When things go wrong during gender identity development, the attention of parents and caregivers is directed towards finding professional help for children with atypical gender identity development.

Chapter Four

GENDER DIFFERENCES IN COGNITION, PERSONALITY, AND SOCIAL BEHAVIOR

Since the brains of men and women differ, men and women should also differ in their behavior. This chapter considers gender differences in cognition and personality as well as in social and emotional behavior. Interpreting gender differences is complicated, especially when masculinity and femininity do not lie on opposite ends of a single dimension but are multidimensional concepts.

SEX AND GENDER

Sex refers to biological aspects whereas *gender* is affected by social and cultural influences and may not be biologically determined. Transsexed people might be considered as "intersexed" to the extent that they have the body and genitals of one sex and the brain-sex of the other. Any reconciliation of the two can only be achieved by changing one's body rather than one's mind, since brain-sex is more deeply rooted than are the bodily manifestations of sex.[1] Even when we suspect that transsexuality is dependent on brain-sex, based on biological evidence, the official diagnostic category for the medical condition of transsexualism is gender identity disorder (GID), a psychological condition with no necessary reference to brain structure or function.[2]

Sex has been defined as "the biologically based categories of male and female," whereas gender involves "the psychological features frequently associated with these biological states, assigned either by the observer or by the individual subject."[3] In the following discussion I use "gender" instead of "sex" since many gender differences cannot be biologically verified. "Sex" is used when referring to biological entities such as the brain, hormones, and nonhuman species.

Most gender differences in psychological characteristics and behavior are small, with a large overlap between the score distributions for males and females. Although people often consider boys to excel at mathematics when compared with girls, even this small gender difference is probably culturally determined. Stereotypes suggest that male behavior represents authority, status, competence, and social influence, whereas female behavior is characterized by low status, incompetence, and a relative lack of influence. Nevertheless, female behavior is often nurturant and adaptive whereas male behavior is often associated with negative consequences such as violence. Although gender stereotypes might have a firm basis in our psychological or biological makeup, they mask the similarities in behavior between men and women, leading to social injustice and prejudice for those who violate society's gender norms. A comprehensive review of gender differences could only find substantial differences in childhood play and in aggressive tendencies, such is the extent of overlap between the behaviors of males and females.[4]

PERCEPTUAL AND COGNITIVE DIFFERENCES

Rather than observing their respective genitals, King Solomon determined the sex of two twins using gender-discriminating behavioral measures, such as how they would catch an apple and how they would throw the apple back. Throwing differs between men and women, as any comparison of male and female softball players will reveal.[5] This example illustrates how reliable the behavioral expression of gender can be. In this section, some illustrative differences between men and women in both their abilities and temperament are considered.

Men do better than women on mathematical reasoning, mental rotation, perception of the horizontal, and targeting accuracy, whereas women perform better at verbal memory and finger dexterity and have larger color vocabularies. Women also obtain higher scores than men do on tests of object-location memory. In this task, people are shown randomly relocated objects and are required to recall which objects have been moved.[6]

Gender differences in cognitive performance depend on hormonal influences. For example, the optimal level of testosterone required for men's spatial performance is in the low male range. Women's relative performance on spatial and verbal fluency tasks depends on the menstrual cycle phase, their performance improving on spatial tasks and declining on verbal fluency tasks during the postovulation stage when estrogen levels are low. Men perform better on spatial tasks in the spring when their testosterone is low and worse early in the morning when their testosterone levels are high. Homosexual men perform less well than heterosexual men on spatial reasoning and horizontal perception tasks. They perform worse than heterosexual men on targeting tasks, their performance being similar to that of women.

Gender differences are mainly evident for verbal ability, mathematical ability, visual-spatial ability, and aggression. Gender differences in mathematical ability appear from adolescence onwards, yet only 1 percent of test-score differences in mathematics can be attributed to gender. Men and boys with high mathematical ability perform better than women and girls on difficult algebra problems, but both groups perform similarly on less difficult mathematical problems.[7]

Only about 5 percent of the individual differences in spatial ability are gender dependent, better performance by men being restricted to mental rotation and horizontal-vertical discriminations. Gender differences in cognitive abilities have decreased over time, suggesting that environment and learning play important roles in moderating such differences. Women score higher than men in work motivation, but men score higher in both job mastery and competitiveness.[3]

The cognitive ability of young people with GIA measured prior to their being exposed to hormone therapy indicates that males perform better than females in rotation and visualization tasks but there is no difference between people with GIA and others, suggesting that cognitive ability is unrelated to atypical gender identity.[8] A study of transsexed men before and after three months of testosterone therapy showed an increase in spatial ability, as indicated by performance on the rotated-figures test and a decline in verbal skills as measured by word and sentence production.[9] Transsexed women's performance declined on spatial-ability tasks whereas that of transsexed men improved over a 12-month period. Therefore, larger cognitive changes can be detected over a longer testing period.[10]

Girls use a greater variety of colors than do boys when drawing. Girls prefer warmer colors such as pink and red. Boys concentrate their attention on object movement and location, whereas girls concentrate on form and color. Female vision is biased towards using the parvocellular visual system, which is specialized for identifying objects (*what is it?*) whereas male vision makes greater use of the magnocellular visual system, which is specialized for locating objects (*where is it?*). Women are also generally better at recognizing faces than are men.[11]

Human attractiveness is associated with a biologically determined preference for healthy and fertile mates. People rate the composite face generated by averaging a sample of arbitrarily selected faces as the most attractive. Women rate men with slightly feminized faces as more caring, cooperative, and honest. They also consider such men as making better parents. On the other hand, women prefer more masculinized faces during the fertile period of their menstrual cycle. Large eyes and small noses are more attractive in women, as also are larger lips and more fatty deposits in the upper cheek area. Generally, men judge a smaller lower facial region in women as more attractive.[12]

Figure 4.1
Horizontal and Vertical Facial Features Required for Recognition of the Gender of the Human Face

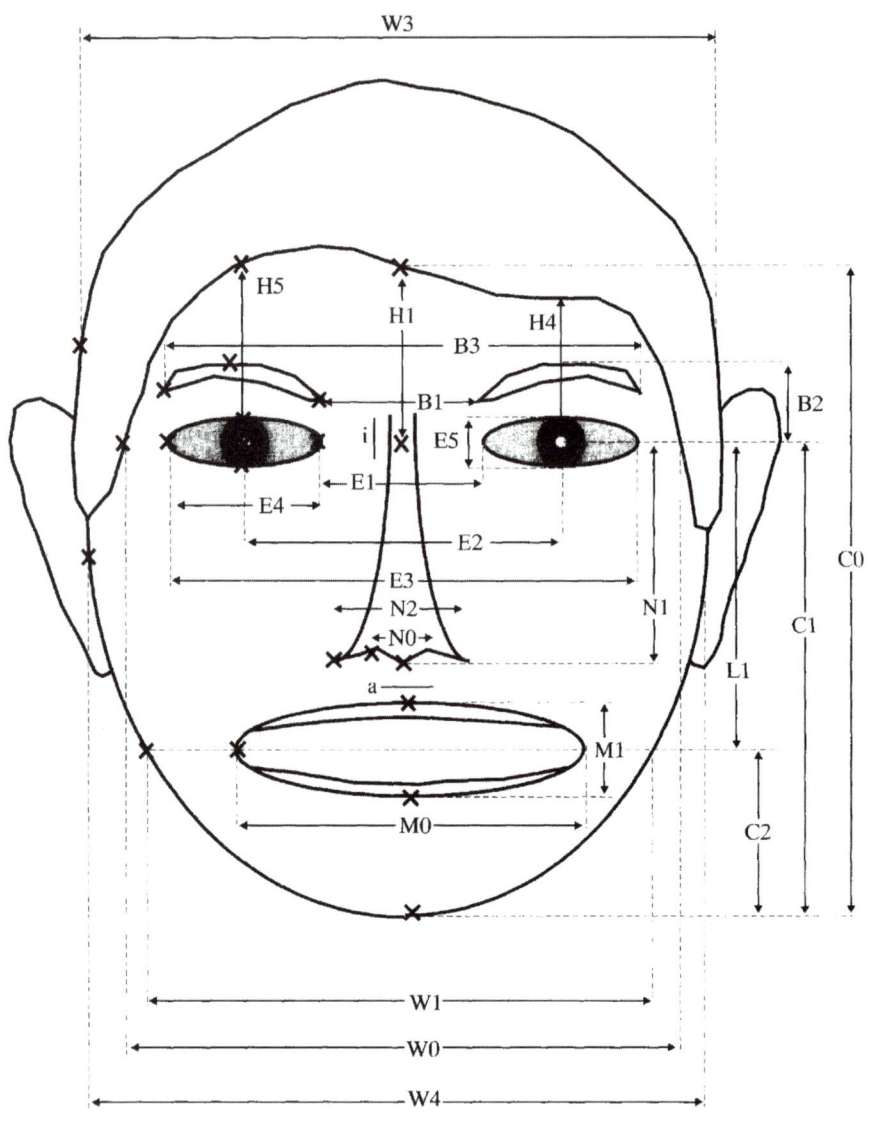

Source: J.-M. Fellous, Gender discrimination and prediction on the basis of facial metric information, 1997 Vision Research, 37, 1961–1973. Figure 1, page 1964. Reprinted by permission from Elsevier.

People assess gender using face shape, mouth size, cheek position, and eye size. Judgments of male faces rely on eye spacing, nose size, and eyebrow shape, whereas judgments of female faces use nose size and a combination of eye spacing and eyebrow shape. Removing the eye region makes it difficult to detect female faces, whereas removing the nose makes it hard to recognize male faces. So different facial features discriminate gender in males and females.[13]

Male faces are wider and longer than female faces. Important correlates of gender are eyebrow thickness, nose width, mouth width, eye-to-eyebrow distance, forehead height, and the distance between the inner corners of the eyebrows. Measures of 24 facial features shown in Figure 4.1 can be reduced to five basic facial dimensions that distinguish between male and female faces. These dimensions are the distance between the outermost corners of the eyes (E3), which is larger in women; the distance between the two cheek bones (W4), which is larger in men; the width of the nose (N2), which is larger in men; the distance between the eyes and eyebrows (B2), which is larger in women; and the distance between the eyes and mouth (L1), which is larger in men. When these five dimensions are substituted into the following masculinity index equation, male faces are correctly classified 87 percent of the time, and female faces 92 percent of the time.

$$\text{masculinity index} = -0.9\text{E3} + 0.2\text{W4} + 0.5\text{N2} - 0.4\text{B2} + 0.2\text{L1}$$

A positive masculinity index indicates a masculine face whereas a negative value indicates a feminine face. Femininity is indicated by large distances between external eye corners and between the eyes and eyebrows, as well as by a small nose and a narrow, rounded face. Masculinity is characterized by a large nostril-to-nostril width, wide cheekbones, a lengthy face, a small distance between the eyes, and a short distance between eyes and eyebrows. Most gender-discriminating distances in the human face involve horizontal and vertical directions rather than diagonals. The distances estimated from Figure 4.1 are E3 = 6.4 cm, W4 = 8.5 cm, N2 = 1.5 cm, B2 = 1.1 cm, and L1 = 4.2 cm. Substituting these values into the masculinity index produced a value of -2.9, suggesting that the face in Figure 4.1 has feminine characteristics.[13]

The masculinity index might be used to determine whether transsexed women should consider facial feminization surgery (FFS). Too masculine a face might be problematic for passing in their new gender. The effect of FFS should be to transform the masculinity index from a positive value to one in the female range. FFS for transsexed women is described in chapter 11.

Gender differences in speech processing may depend on differences in brain hemisphere asymmetry. For example, the left side of the brain is responsible for gender differences in speech-recognition ability. Since brain lateralization is greater in men than in women, the extent to which one brain hemisphere processes speech more effectively than the other would be greater for men than for women.[14]

Prenatal exposure to high levels of testosterone causes retarded development of the left hemisphere and enhanced development of the right hemisphere, resulting in a greater prevalence of left-handedness in males, as well as such debilitating conditions as stuttering and dyslexia.[15] So there is a close relationship between hormonal influences on brain development and cognitive performance in later life.

Gender differences in how people use language have biological as well as developmental and social causes. There is a sufficient difference in the average voice pitch range for men and women to be distinguished on that basis alone, even though the voice pitch ranges for men and women overlap to some extent. Gender differences in intonation pattern are a far more important cue for gender identification than are most other linguistic forms. These gender differences in speech assist transsexed women to feminize their voice and speech patterns. Such speech differences complement other cross-culturally universal gender identifiers such as hair style and dress, body posture, facial expression, and gesture patterns, especially those involving hand and finger movements.[16] Voice training for transsexed women is described in chapter 11.

A number of commonly used linguistic conventions differentiate between male and female speech. Women tend to use words that men rarely use, such as the color *mauve*, ancillary adjectives such as *divine, cute,* and *sweet,* and tag questions, such as "We're staying, *aren't we?*" Women tend to be more polite in their choice of words and use more uncertainty in phrases such as *I guess, I hope,* etc. Women are more likely than men to use intensifiers, such as *so, very,* and *really,* as well as excessively correct grammatical forms. Women's speech is characterized by a rising intonation at the end of phrases. Some of these linguistic features suggest that women are more interested in maintaining good social relationships than are men. In terms of social language use, men interrupt women's speech more often then women interrupt men in mixed-sex groups.[16]

An important distinguishing feature of text written by female, when compared with male, authors is their more frequent use of pronouns. Female authors tend to involve their reader more in their discourse, whereas male authors use the text primarily for presenting facts. The pronouns *I, she,* and *you* are used more often by women than men whereas men tend to use determiners, such as *a, the,* and *that* more frequently. Fiction is normally written in a feminine style, whereas nonfiction is more consistent with a masculine writing style, irrespective of the author's sex.[17]

Electronic communication, especially using email and Internet chat lines, reveals gender differences in language use. Fifty-two percent of females, compared with 41 percent of males, use computers for communication, whereas

76 percent of males, compared with 62 percent of females, use computers to play games. Just as in speech, women are more likely than men to use emotional references and intensive adverbs ("the game was *really* good") and to make compliments and use minimal responses such as "mmmm." They are also more likely to ask questions and employ polite language. In same-sex email messages, women express more emotions, personal information, hedges ("it was sort of OK"), and intensive adverbs than do men.[18]

Most female and almost all male Internet users can be identified using a composite score derived from how they phrase email messages.[19] Such fundamental differences in how men and women use language in conversation make it difficult for transsexed people to mimic the speech patterns appropriate for their new gender even when they have mastered changes in average pitch and frequency modulation.

EMOTIONAL AND PERSONALITY DIFFERENCES

Gender accounts for about 5 percent of the individual differences in aggression scores, but mainly when such aggression is provoked. About 1 percent of the individual differences in conformity can be accounted for by gender, women being more easily influenced than men. Although women are generally better than men in their use of nonverbal cues, this gender difference is small.[3]

Hormone levels generate differences between men and women in their emotional responses to environmental events. Estrogen depletion in women often produces depression and anxiety that can be alleviated by hormone-replacement therapy. Following menopause, there is a greater prevalence of serious anxiety and depressive disorders in women. Such gender differences in emotional response may result from sex differences in the brain's neurotransmitter systems that control the flow of nerve messages.[20]

Instrumental behavior, as indicated by competitiveness and aggression, is usually associated with masculinity, whereas expressive behavior, such as gentleness and nurturance, is more often associated with femininity. A positively androgynous person, someone who scores highly on both femininity and masculinity, exhibits independence, compassion, ambition, and tolerance. On the other hand, a negatively androgynous person, someone who has low scores on both masculinity and femininity, is submissive and selfish but can also be both temperamental and aggressive. An undifferentiated androgynous person is above average on both positive and negative masculinity and femininity. Positively androgynous people exhibit better mental health and adjustment than those with either positive masculinity or positive femininity but not both.[21]

Gender differences in personality are indicated by women scoring higher on neuroticism and agreeableness than men, and women scoring lower than men on self-esteem. Women score higher than men on warmth, gregariousness, and positive emotions but lower on assertiveness and excitement seeking. Gender differences in personality are greater in healthy and prosperous cultures in which women enjoy a greater variety of educational opportunities. However, such differences are not especially large, larger differences occurring within, rather than between, genders due to the overlap of scores for both males and females.[22]

The three most characteristic aspects of femininity reported by young people are being critical of one's own appearance, being concerned with outward appearance, and emotionality, whereas the two most characteristic aspects of masculinity are being career oriented and independent. Masculinity is less diversified, less unstable, and less subject to change than is femininity. "Sex seen as power/empowering" is a masculine rather than feminine trait, whereas "reading for pleasure" is a typically feminine pursuit. Being family oriented is especially feminine whereas being career oriented is a masculine trait. Perhaps gender unites men but divides women due to the relatively greater instability of feminine prototypical attributes. These days, over a five-year period, women become less dependent on a partner for maintaining social status than was the case in previous generations.[23]

People can be categorized on gender using the relative likelihood that they would exhibit masculine compared with feminine interests by using a gender diagnosticity (GD) score. GD, a people-things measure in vocational-interest tests, distinguishes transsexed people from others better than do measures of masculinity and femininity. The inheritance of GD is greater than it is for both masculinity and femininity, suggesting that GD has a possible genetic basis.[24]

Crying is a uniquely human characteristic that has its origins early in life when it is a baby's only way to signal distress. Gender differences in emotionality are revealed when women cry more easily and for longer periods than do men. A lot of crying occurs when people are alone and when they lack both social and emotional support.[25]

There are two types of crying, an emotional outpouring that is intense, long-lasting, and persistent, and a more transient form that is easily controlled, for example, when watching a sad movie. Crying results from a complex interaction between biological, social, and cognitive processes. From the biological view-point, crying is associated with both parasympathetic and sympathetic arousal. The sympathetic nervous system prepares us for action whereas the parasympathetic nervous system prepares us for feeding and rest. Crying proneness seems to be more biologically based, whereas crying frequency is mainly determined by environmental needs.[25]

When people are emotionally affected by helplessness, for example, the parasympathetic nervous system activates the lachrymal nucleus in the brain stem, the nerve center that initiates the flow of tears. Tears contain high concentrations of prolactin, adrenocorticotrophic hormone, leucine-enkephalin, and manganese. Gender differences in crying propensity depend on fluctuating prolactin levels that are higher in women, especially following childbirth, a time of depressed mood for some new mothers.[25]

Crying occurs more frequently in situations involving the death of a loved one, a broken romantic relationship, and during sad movies. Crying is also invoked by interpersonal conflicts such as being rejected and experiencing low self-esteem. Men report crying more often in response to positive events whereas women cry more easily when they are powerless. There is a gradual increase in crying likelihood between 4 A.M. and 11 P.M. as the day progresses. Both men and women cry more easily when women are present, women often consoling a man when he is crying. Gender differences in crying do not arise until a person is at least 13. People who are emotionally disconnected from themselves and others are less likely to cry.[25]

SUMMARY

Gender differences occur in many aspects of human life. These include cognitive processes, such as spatial and verbal memory, vision, learning, and facial recognition. There are also differences between men and women in personality, language, and emotionality. Some of these differences, for example, in memory, learning, and perhaps personality, have a firm biological basis in terms of differences in brain function. Other differences, such as in language and social behavior, require adherence to gender norms imposed by cultural and social influences, as well as biological processes in the case of crying. Such gender differences should be considered by transsexed people. Successful living in their new gender role requires adapting their behavior and values to those typical of their affirmed sex, a difficult task for many transsexed people.

Chapter Five

INTERESTING CORRELATES OF GENDER IDENTITY AND SEXUAL ORIENTATION

Because the distinction between gender identity and sexual orientation is often confused and misunderstood by the general public, it is important to define these two terms clearly. Most people assume that men prefer women as their sexual partner, and women prefer men. However, some men prefer men, and some women prefer women. Although some men present as women, this transgendered preference provides no information about their sexual preferences, and a similar situation applies to women who present as men. A person's sexual orientation is considered with respect to their born-sex.[1] If a transsexed woman prefers men as her sexual partners, she is considered homosexual. If she prefers women, as is often the case when a married partner transitions, then she is nonhomosexual, or perhaps heterosexual. A similar situation applies to transsexed men.

This chapter discusses both gender identity and sexual orientation. Relationships between sexual orientation and gender identity are discussed, as are individual differences in sexual orientation. Health issues for gay, lesbian, bisexual, and transsexed/transgendered people are considered, as are also the personal characteristics of gender-variant people.

GENDER IDENTITY, SEXUAL IDENTITY, AND SEXUAL ORIENTATION

Various interpretations of the differences between gender identity and sexual identity have been proposed. A novel representation considers the range of sexual identities as "spokes in a wheel that has the heterosexual norm in the center."[2]

So every sexual identity, including gay and lesbian, is connected in some way to the heterosexual norm. Gender and sexuality have been defined as follows:

> [G]ender [encompasses] both an institutionalized interpretation of what it means to live as a woman or a man (including rules of belonging) and individual interpretations of what it means to live as a woman or a man. Sexuality [is] the way we represent and enact bodily pleasures and desires, a term that engages concepts of the body (both real and symbolic) and concepts of gender, if only to negate them, and which is not reducible to them. Sex [is] the mostly anatomical features by which social designations of female, male, and intersexed bodies are made.[3]

Many people believe that homosexual men are necessarily effeminate and, conversely, that feminine men must be homosexual. Although transsexed women consider themselves to be feminine, they are not generally homosexual. Moreover, homosexual men do not usually have a feminine identity, suggesting that sexual orientation and gender identity are relatively unrelated lifestyle characteristics. Some early studies considered transvestism to be an exclusively heterosexual characteristic, whereas transsexuality was more closely associated with homosexuality. These days, gender identity and sexual orientation are recognized as mutually exclusive characteristics, even though the effeminate homosexual person is no exception, nor is a transsexed woman who is homosexual.

In a study comparing the psychological adjustment of transsexed women and homosexual men, transsexed women had a stronger feminine gender identity, as exhibited by their earlier preference for girls' games, cross-dressing, and imagining themselves as female. All participants were well adjusted psychologically.[4]

INDIVIDUAL DIFFERENCES IN SEXUAL ORIENTATION

Between 2 and 5 percent of men and between 1 and 2 percent of women are homosexual. Generally, homosexual men recall being feminine boys whereas lesbian women recall being masculine girls, and this cross-gender identification continues to some extent into adulthood. Since identical, or monozygotic, twins are more likely to both be homosexual than is the case for fraternal, or dizygotic, twins, there is probably a genetic basis for homosexuality, the heritability ranging from 30 percent to 60 percent. Gay men have more homosexual uncles and cousins through the maternal, rather than paternal, line than do heterosexual males. Finally, there is controversial evidence of a genetic marker for exclusively male homosexuality on the sex chromosome Xq28.[5]

Homosexual people differ from heterosexual people in some aspects of their cognitive behavior. For example, during spatial navigation through a maze, the left side of the hippocampus is activated to a greater extent in men while the right parietal and prefrontal regions of the brain are activated to a greater extent in women. Homosexual men perform more poorly on mental rotation tasks but better on verbal fluency tasks when compared to heterosexual men. Homosexual men are also less accurate on visuomotor targeting tasks when compared with heterosexual men. Homosexual men perform in a feminine fashion on object-location memory, a spatial task in which women usually perform better than men. Like women, homosexual men demonstrate relatively lower spatial ability than do heterosexual men.

Since the brains of homosexual men are more bilaterally organized for language, similarly to heterosexual women, they behave like heterosexual women in many cognitive tasks. Developmental instability, such as facial asymmetry resulting from the effects of stress hormones during fetal development, affects heterosexual transsexed women more than it does homosexual males.[5]

In a controversial exposé of homosexuality and transsexuality, J. Michael Bailey[6] proposed that a typical gay man displays more feminine behavior than 90 percent of straight men. Although gay men tend to speak in a more feminine way than other men, no one knows exactly how gay men's speech differs from that of women. Homosexual men also tend to exhibit body movements that are considered stereotypical and, in some cases, closer to feminine movements. However, this generalization does not apply to all homosexual men. In all the studies mentioned by Bailey, homosexual men displayed a greater variety of distinctive behaviors than those exhibited by heterosexual men. Evidence for a genetic basis for homosexuality is provided by the observation that 52 percent of identical twins and 24 percent of fraternal twins, but only 11 percent of adoptive brothers, are gay if their brother is also gay. This result suggests primarily a moderate genetic basis for homosexuality, with environmental factors playing an important role.

There are two major categories of lesbians, women with a sexual preference for other women. Stereotypically, butch lesbians present with short hair, little or no makeup, and clothing that is atypical of women. Femme lesbians, on the other hand, differ very little in presentation from most other women. The differentiation between butch and femme lesbians started in the United States in the late 1940s, and by the 1950s, assuming one or the other of these identities was virtually obligatory for all lesbians. Among lesbian partners, those considered more femme tend to have less testosterone. They recall gender blending, being a tomboy as a child and then emerging with a more feminine teenage persona accompanied by either homosexual feelings or a desire to date men. Often femme lesbians view their butch partners as transgendered women who display a masculine persona while dating and initiating sexual relationships.[7]

HEALTH ISSUES FOR TRANSSEXED PEOPLE

Transsexed people, especially those who work in the sex industry either as their only source of income or to obtain social acceptance and support, are frequently exposed to health risks. The incidence of HIV-positive respondents in one survey of transsexed sex workers was as high as 22 percent, highlighting their risky lifestyle.[8]

Transsexed women are at a greater risk of drug abuse and prostitution than are transsexed men. Of 292 transsexed women interviewed in San Francisco, 32 percent were sex workers, 62 percent were depressed, 33 percent had attempted suicide, 20 percent had serious mental health problems, and 35 percent were HIV-positive. In terms of social disadvantage, 60 percent of the transsexed women had experienced harassment or violence and 37 percent had experienced economic discrimination.[9] In another study conducted in San Francisco in 1998, 34 percent of transsexed women and 18 percent of transsexed men reported intravenous drug use at some time in their lives.[10]

The suicide ideation rate in transsexed and transgendered people is as high as 33 percent. Often ignored is the mental health of transsexed people's partners, many of whom suffer significant emotional distress similar to post-traumatic stress disorder.[11] Of concern, occasionally transgendered and transsexed students are not well treated in educational institutions such as medical schools.[12]

The incidence of HIV in transsexed sex workers is as high as 74 percent in Italy and 68 percent in the United States. Although wishing to maintain their passability as women to ensure both their safety and self-esteem, the experiences of HIV-positive transsexed women in healthcare delivery include alienation, leading to a reduction in their perceived quality of care. Depression and suicidal ideation are also quite common. They are concerned about whether their HIV status would disqualify them from obtaining electrolysis and other forms of feminization, including genital reconstruction surgery (GRS).[13] Transsexed men who tend to have unprotected sex more often than transsexed women are also at risk from HIV infection.[14]

PERSONAL CHARACTERISTICS OF GENDER-VARIANT PEOPLE

Some homosexual people have personality types akin to those of the opposite sex. So there may be interesting relationships between sexual orientation and gender identity, even though in principle the two characteristics are logically unrelated and probably rely on the activation of different brain regions. Such relationships are relevant for the understanding of gender identity atypicality as it relates to sexual preferences.

Family issues are important, since a child's cross-gendered behavior, for example an aversion to gender-typical activities such as rough-and-tumble play in boys, is often associated with emotional distance from the same-sex parent. This lack of interest in typically masculine activities in transsexed women might produce a self-concept characterized by inadequate masculinity, a feeling reinforced by peers and significant others.[15]

Gender-variant people differ both in their physical characteristics and in their behavior from those who are gender-congruent. Homosexual transsexed women tend to be lighter and shorter than men of the same age.[16] They also tend to be shorter and lighter in build than nonhomosexual transsexed women.[17] These findings might explain why on average homosexual transsexed women pass more easily than their heterosexual counterparts.

A study of sexual preferences in groups of transvestites, transsexed women, and gay men showed that whereas over 80 percent of transvestites were attracted to women, and a similar proportion of gay men were attracted to men, about half of the transsexed women were attracted to men and a quarter attracted to women, the remainder reporting no sexual preference. Perhaps transsexed women change their sexual preference from women to men during the transition period. Most transvestites identified either as a man with a feminine side or simply as a person who enjoys wearing opposite-sex clothing. Most of the transsexed women reported feeling like a women trapped in a male body, or else they just felt like a woman without reference to their physical embodiment. About a quarter of the transvestites were taking feminizing hormones, whereas over 80 percent of the transsexed women were either undergoing hormone therapy or had already completed GRS.[18]

The terms sex and gender are somewhat difficult to dissociate even when we stipulate that sex is biological and gender is sociocultural. Perhaps this problem arises from the complex intertwining of gender identity and sexual orientation that pervades both the literature and popular convention. The association of homosexuality with cross-gendered behavior has been observed in many cultures, with those exhibiting such traits being frequently revered. Health issues are important for homosexual as well as for transgendered/ transsexed people. Some find access to medical care limited and prejudice rife even though, in this more enlightened era, we might expect professionals to be sensitive to gender-identity and sexual-orientation variance. The scourge of HIV/AIDS highlights the need for special treatment of such people within the healthcare system.

THE GENETIC BASIS OF HOMOSEXUALITY AND GENDER NONCONFORMITY

Discovering a biological cause for both homosexuality and gender nonconformity would be useful both for understanding the origins of such conditions and for ameliorating the social stigma associated with minorities. The Australian National Health and Medical Research Council Twin Register was used to study genetic and environmental influences on sexual orientation, as indicated by responses to Kinsey test items that measured sexual fantasy and attraction. Childhood Gender Nonconformity (CGN) and Childhood

Gender Identity (CGI) scores successfully predicted the degree of nonhetero-sexuality, suggesting that CGN is a possible precursor of homosexuality. Male twins recalled their nonheterosexual co-twin as being more gender noncon-forming as a child than they were. Both CGN and CGI were greater for male identical twins than for male fraternal twins, whereas such differences were only found for CGN in women.[19]

A genetic analysis indicated that CGN is an inherited trait for both men and women. For women, sexual orientation, CGN, and especially CGI are good predictors of a person's current gender identity. For men, on the other hand, both sexual orientation and CGN, but not CGI, reflect their current gender identity. However, environmental variables are also important, espe-cially for men.[19]

HANDEDNESS AND DEVELOPMENTAL INSTABILITY AS CORRELATES OF SEXUAL ORIENTATION AND GENDER IDENTITY

Handedness is an interesting psychological correlate of both sexual orienta-tion and gender identity. Since handedness does not change with age and is unaffected by environmental and social influences, it may be associated with transsexuality. Handedness is determined by week 15 of the gestation period. Larger than usual testosterone levels might affect development in the right hemisphere of the brain, leading to the non-right-handedness that occurs, for example, in women with congenital adrenal hyperplasia, an intersex condition resulting from excess exposure to testosterone during gestation.

The incidence of right-handed thumb-sucking in human fetuses corre-sponds almost exactly with the 92 percent incidence of right-handedness in human populations. Historically, right-handedness is the ideal, whereas left-handedness is maladaptive. Indeed, the Latin word for left, *sinistra*, is the origin of the English word *sinister*. Left-handedness is associated with various neurodevelopmental problems including dyslexia, mental retarda-tion, autism, schizophrenia, cerebral palsy, and epilepsy. All of these prob-lems occur more frequently in men than in women, as men are more likely to be left-handed.[20]

Left-handedness is associated with *fluctuating asymmetry*, a developmental anomaly producing anatomical differences between the left and right sides of the body. Consistent with the cultural stereotype, left-handedness is associated with a smaller number of offspring, more stillbirths, a lower birth weight, more serious accidents, and a shorter lifespan. The incidence of left-handedness in men is greater the larger the number of their older brothers.[21]

In women, non-right-handedness is associated with masculinity, suggesting a tendency towards dominance and independence. Left-handed people of both genders tend to show more dominance and less nurturance than right-handers. Non-right-handedness in men is associated with female-oriented occupational interests and self-rated femininity. By contrast, non-right-handedness in women is associated with male-oriented occupational interests.[22]

Richard Green and Robert Young studied handedness and sexual preference in 443 transsexed women and 93 transsexed men. The comparison group contained 144 natal men and 140 natal women. Transsexed women and transsexed men, no matter what their sexual orientation, were less often right-handed when compared with natal men and natal women respectively. Jacob Orlebeke and colleagues also reported a greater prevalence of left-handedness in transsexed people. Hand preference was assessed in 93 transsexed women and in 44 transsexed men. The survey showed that 19 percent of the transsexed women and 18 percent of the transsexed men were left-handed. This represents a greater incidence of left-handedness in transsexed people than the 11 percent that occurs in the general population.[23]

There is also a higher prevalence of left-handedness in women with congenital adrenal hyperplasia, a birth disorder that has a masculinizing effect. Left-handedness is more common in boys with gender identity atypicality (GIA) (20 percent) than in a comparison group (8 percent).[24] Also, right-handed transsexed men exhibit a more extreme version of right-handedness than do natal men.[21]

Other hand features also show gender differences probably resulting from prenatal causes. Dermatoglyphics, which measures the number of finger ridges on each hand, can be obtained using ink-pad recordings. A leftward asymmetry in the number of finger-tip ridges is determined during week 13 of gestation and is fully developed between weeks 16 and 19. Women exhibit this asymmetry more often than men do, whereas men have a higher total ridge count on both hands than do women. Ridge development is also affected by environmental influences, such as alcohol and anticonvulsant drugs consumed during pregnancy.

Fingerprint asymmetry was measured in 270 transsexed women and 54 transsexed men, as well as in a comparison group containing 123 natal men and 99 natal women. Of the transsexed women, 31 percent were heterosexual, 22 percent were homosexual, 38 percent were bisexual, and 9 percent were asexual. Almost all of the transsexed men were homosexual. Fingerprints were taken from the thumb and little finger of each hand, as these fingers are least likely to produce a zero ridge count. There was no difference in ridge count for the male and female comparison groups, nor was there any difference in ridge count for the left and right hands. However, transsexed women had a higher average ridge count.[25]

Adextrality is the extent to which fingerprint ridges tend to be more prominent on the left hand than on the right. For those with a rightward fingerprint ridge shift, comparison-group participants had a greater frequency of adextrality than did the heterosexual transsexed group. By contrast, for those with a left-ward fingerprint ridge shift, heterosexual transsexed participants had a greater frequency of adextrality than did heterosexual members of the comparison groups. Heterosexual transsexed participants also showed a greater frequency of adextrality than did homosexual transsexed participants, suggesting an interesting criterion for distinguishing young and often homosexual transsexed people from older transsexed people who frequently report nonhomosexuality.

When data were averaged across sex, homosexual transsexed people differed in dermatoglyphic asymmetry from both heterosexual transsexed people and members of the comparison groups. After removing extreme measurements, nonhomosexual transsexed women exhibited greater fluctuating asymmetry, an indicator of body asymmetry, than did the other groups. Overall, dermatoglyphic characteristics depend on sexual orientation rather than gender identity.[25]

DIGIT-RATIO AS AN INDICATOR OF SEXUAL ORIENTATION AND GENDER IDENTITY

Digit-ratio is obtained by dividing the length of the index, or second, finger by the length of the ring, or fourth, finger. With the palm upwards, finger-length is usually measured as the distance from the basal crease, where the finger joins the palm, to the tip of the finger. Digit-ratio is a stable sexually dimorphic characteristic resulting perhaps from the effect of prenatal testosterone exposure around week 14 of gestation. The greater the exposure the longer will be the ring finger and the lower the digit-ratio. An individual's digit-ratio is determined by the Homeobox genes that regulate both sexual differentiation and skeletal development around the same time of embryonic development.[26]

Since digit-ratio is a marker for prenatal testosterone, low values of digit-ratio, less than 1.0, are typical of men, whereas values of 1.0 or greater are more characteristic of women. However, the overlap in digit-ratio for both men and women is large. Interestingly, digit-ratio tends to be lower in homosexual women and more similar to the values for heterosexual men. Also, digit-ratio tends to be lower still in "butch" lesbians, these effects of sexual orientation applying to the right hand only. However, no differences in digit-ratio are found between transsexed men and heterosexual nontranssexed women.[26] Although the physiological basis of these differences in digit-ratio is not known, estrogen might feminize a male homosexual brain, whereas masculinization of other body features might result from the effect of dihydrotestosterone (DHT), a derivative of testosterone.

If the intersex condition congenital adrenal hyperplasia (CAH) results from excess masculinization during fetal development, then we might expect people with CAH to exhibit masculine digit-ratios. When the lengths of the left-hand fingers were measured using X-ray photographs, non-CAH boys had a lower digit-ratio than non-CAH girls (0.918 vs. 0.927). There was no difference in digit-ratio between the non-CAH and CAH girls, suggesting that left-hand digit-ratios are unaffected by fetal masculinization. Since masculinization effects are detected for the right-hand digit-ratio, maybe the left and right hands differ in their fetal development.[27]

When digit-ratio was measured for both right and left hands, the digit-ratio was less for men than women, with no differences in digit-ratio being observed between the hands. The average ratios were similar: 0.97 for men and 0.99 for women. When the data were combined for men and women, the left-hand digit-ratio was larger for those scoring high on neuroticism, a typically feminine trait, and smaller for those having high scores on psychoticism, a typically masculine trait related to aggression. However, the relationships between digit-ratio and personal characteristics were rather slight.[28]

Despite measurement and methodological difficulties, digit-ratio is an interesting, and readily available, indicator of fetal-developmental processes that may also be associated with sexual differentiation. The tendency for men's digit-ratios to be less than those of women is reflected further in suggestions that homosexual men have larger digit-ratios than do heterosexual men. Likewise, there is a tendency for lesbian women to exhibit slightly larger digit-ratios than heterosexual women do. The suggestion that masculinizing hormonal effects influence digit-ratio only on the right hand is interesting. Perhaps digit-ratio differences observed for the left hand reflect personality and gender identity differences, a topic for further research.

The digit-ratios of transsexed men and women have been compared with those of natal men and women. For right-handed participants, the right-hand digit-ratio for transsexed women is no different from that of natal women but larger than the right-hand digit ratio for natal men, whereas the left-hand digit-ratio is similar for natal men and transsexed women. Since digit-ratio may be influenced by prenatal hormone activity, perhaps this is further evidence for a biological basis for transsexuality. The greater prevalence of left-handedness among transsexed women together with the discovery of no differences in digit-ratio between left-handed transsexed women and others is a puzzling finding.[29]

BIRTH ORDER, SEXUAL ORIENTATION, AND GENDER IDENTITY

Homosexual men tend to have more male siblings than do nonhomosexual men. A study of birth order and sibling sex-ratio in two samples of Dutch gender-atypical men indicated that for the homosexual group, 57 percent of their siblings were male, compared with 53 percent male siblings for the non-homosexual group, a value that did not differ from the general population value of 52 percent. Compared to their own age, homosexuals had a larger number of older siblings than younger ones, the opposite being found for the nonhomosexuals.

Gender identity atypicality in nonhomosexual men may be associated with an earlier birth order than occurs for homosexual men with gender identity atypicality. Hence gender-atypical nonhomosexual people are more likely to be firstborns or only children than are their homosexual counterparts.[30]

Homosexual transsexed women have a later than usual birth order and a larger number of older brothers than do other transsexed women. The odds that a transsexed woman is homosexual increases by 40 percent with each older brother.[31] The finding that homosexual males are more likely to be late-born is fairly universal; it is also observed among transgendered males in Polynesia.[32]

In a study of the families of transsexed women and transsexed men, categorized as asexual, homosexual, heterosexual, or bisexual, the transsexed women had slightly more maternal aunts than maternal uncles. The heterosexual group also had an excess of aunts. Asexual transsexed women had a predominance of uncles on their father's side, with an average of 1 aunt compared with 1.5 uncles.[33]

RELATIONS BETWEEN GENDER IDENTITY AND SEXUAL ORIENTATION

Young transsexed women are more likely to be nonheterosexual than are older transsexed women. Transsexed men tend to be nonheterosexual irrespective of their age at transition. This generalization suggests that the independence of gender identity and sexual orientation is difficult to discern, especially for transsexed men.

A contentious idea is to associate heterosexual transsexed people with autogynephilia, the tendency to be sexually aroused by one's own image as a woman. Hirschfeld, a pioneer sexologist, first referred to a similar idea when he recounted that some transvestites were attracted to the "woman inside them."

The term *autogynephilia* was introduced by Ray Blanchard,[34] a clinical psychologist and head of the Clinical Sexology Programme of the Clarke Institute of Psychiatry in Toronto, Canada. Blanchard defined autogynephilia as "a male's paraphilic tendency to be sexually aroused by the thought or image of himself as a female."[35] According to Blanchard, there are only two fundamentally different types of transsexuality in males: homosexual and nonhomosexual. In his view, nonhomosexual transsexed women, that is, those with a sexual preference for women, are characterized by their propensity towards autogynephilia.

Autogynephilia in nonhomosexual transgendered men and transsexed women may compete with heterosexual relationships. There are both behavioral and anatomical versions of autogynephilia in which the fantasies may involve masturbation while contemplating working as a typical woman or while imagining that one has female sex organs and/or secondary sex characteristics.

Blanchard's study involved 238 cases from a large database of clients at a gender identity clinic. Only those clients presumed to be nonhomosexual were included in the investigation. The sample was further reduced by including only those who answered "Yes" to one of the following questions (with the percentage answering "Yes" and their presumed classification shown in brackets):

> Which of the following pictures of yourself has been most strongly associated with sexual arousal?
> a. as a nude female (40 percent, the "nude" group)
> b. as a female dressed in only underwear, sleepwear, or foundation garments (for example, a corset) (28 percent, the "underwear" group)
> c. as a fully clothed female (32 percent, the "clothed" group)

Those in the "clothed" group were older than those in the other two groups. The degree of reported gender "distress" was greatest, and cross-gender fetishism least, for the "nude" group. It was assumed that those who are more sexually aroused by themselves as "nude" would desire female anatomies, and hence GRS, whereas the "clothed" group might be content as fetishistic nonoperational transgendered men.

Autogynephilia is characterized by fetishistic cross-dressing. Masturbation fantasies undertaken by some people with purported autogynephilia involve pretending that they are pregnant, menstruating, lactating, and even breast-feeding. Such activities might also include the fantasy that the rectum is a vagina. This behavior might be accompanied by the practice of potentially fatal autoerotic asphyxia in extreme cases of sadomasochism. More commonly, people with purported autogynephilia imagine themselves in a female role whenever they indulge in sexual intercourse.[36]

A test of Hirschfeld's hypothesis that autogynephilia would compete with heterosexual interest was based on the idea that the extent of autogynephilia and the degree of heterosexual interest would be greatest for those people lying intermediate between homosexuality and heterosexuality. A similar result was also expected for transvestism, fetishism, masochism, and sadism. Questionnaires were distributed to men who had been regular cross-dressers since they were thirteen, and to people who had experienced autogynephilic feelings, at least sporadically. Over 90 percent of the respondents reported distress due to their gender identity atypicality.[36]

The predicted relationship between autogynephilia and heterosexuality was obtained. There was a steady decrease in androphilia and gender discomfort associated with an increase in heterosexual interest. Interest in fetishistic cross-dressing was greatest for those who rated themselves highest on heterosexuality.

So autogynephilia might involve competition from those developmental processes that are responsible for individual differences in heterosexual interest.[36]

Nonhomosexual transsexed women report some erotic arousal when cross-dressing, whereas only a minority of homosexual transsexed women, those whose sexual preference is for men, report such arousal.[37] However, this is difficult to understand, especially when drag queens and other cross-dressed homosexual people might indulge occasionally in erotic acts.

Blanchard obtained responses from 256 diagnosed transsexed women, from whom he selected 64 participants on the basis of their pattern of scores on his Modified Androphilia-Gynephilia index. This index measures a person's sexual attraction towards women, gynephilia, and towards men, androphilia. There was a decline in gynephilia with an increase in androphilia for those scoring above average on androphilia; that is, homosexual transsexed women preferred sexual relationships with men rather than women.

Those with low androphilia scores, presumably the heterosexual candidates, exhibited widely distributed scores on gynephilia. This result led to a rather arbitrary categorization of the candidates into four equal-sized groups: high gynephilia–high androphilia (bisexual); high gynephilia–low androphilia (heterosexual); low gynephilia–high androphilia (homosexual); and low gynephilia–low androphilia (asexual). Homosexual participants were younger, at 24, than the other three groups, whose average age was 36. Questionnaire responses indicated that the homosexual transsexed women exhibited greater femininity than did members of the other three groups.

Homosexual transsexed women (transsexed woman whose sexual preference is for men) experience less fetishistic arousal when cross-dressed than do nonhomosexual transsexed women and are more likely to recall participating in feminine games during childhood. Homosexual transsexed women present themselves for help at a gender clinic at a much younger age of 23 on average than do heterosexual transsexed women, who are on average 38 when first seen at a clinic.[38]

Fewer homosexual men answered "Yes" to the rather inappropriate question: *Have you ever been sexually aroused by the thought of being a woman?* than did heterosexual men. However, homosexual men might prefer to be associated with a male image than a female one. Hence this critical question for the assessment of autogynephilia may not be particularly relevant for people in all of the four sexual preference categories. Nevertheless, erotic arousal while cross-dressed was reported less frequently by homosexual transsexed women.

Blanchard's suggestion that there are two types of transsexed women and that the nonhomosexual variety must be autogynephilic leaves little opportunity for individual differences in sexual preferences and behavior among nonhomosexual transsexed women. Those transsexed women who have been pigeon-holed as displaying autogynephilia are essentially similar to homosexual transsexed women, since both groups seek GRS to more closely match their genitals with their mindset.[39] It is interesting to note that Blanchard does not appear to have tested his theory with postoperative women. For example, do the symptoms of autogynephilia change following surgery? This issue is considered in chapter 10.

In a study of changes in sexual orientation among transsexed people as a result of their medical treatment, six heterosexual transsexed women, or 50 percent of the sample, reported a change in sexual orientation after starting hormone therapy. Estrogen, it seemed, reduced tension and offered a feeling of relaxation and a calming of emotional disturbances. Autogynephilia played no role in changes in sexual orientation among these nonhomosexual transsexed women.[40]

To evaluate a proposal that transsexed men have more in common with straight men than with lesbians,[41] semistructured interviews were conducted with 6 lesbians and 12 transsexed men. All the transsexed men had previously identified as lesbian and none had undergone phalloplasty, the surgical construction of a penis, due to its high cost and uncertain success rate. Most of the lesbians had been "tomboys" during childhood, playing boy's games and wishing to avoid appearing in public as a girl. Although they experienced parental pressure to conform to a feminine role, they did not like wearing dresses. Although they might look like a boy they did not wish to be mistaken for a boy in social situations, some preferring to appear androgynously as neither a boy nor a girl.

Transsexed men were similar "tomboy" types to lesbians in many ways. They were interested in boy's games and clothes but, unlike lesbians, they identified as boys and wished that they had not been born a girl. Transsexed men are averse to their developing bodies and reject both the values and ideals of womanhood. Young transsexed men prefer to hide their breasts and feel inappropriately attired when forced to wear a dress. The boundary between a "butch" lesbian and a transsexed man is both permeable and fluid. Despite this possibility, lesbians define themselves as women, whereas transsexed men affirm their sex as male.[42]

Of particular interest are differences in sexual behavior between lesbians and transsexed men. It had previously been suggested that transsexed men avoid self-stimulation of their sex organs, preferring to obtain sexual satisfaction from a partner, while feeling masculine during such activity. Although most transsexed men are friendly towards men, the opposite is true for lesbians. Sixty-seven percent of transsexed men report fantasizing that they are men, whereas none of the lesbians do so. Also, a greater number of transsexed men have experienced a same-sex encounter before the age of 18 than occurs for most lesbians. Few, if any, transsexed men experience sexual pleasure when their breasts and vagina are stimulated. They also exhibit a low level of masturbation and orgasm when compared to that reported by lesbians. It appears that sexual behavior is suppressed somewhat in transsexed men.[43]

Prior to their transition, many transsexed men identify as lesbian, although up to 50 percent were heterosexual at one time, and about 10 percent have been previously married to men. Forty-five generally well-educated transsexed men aged 37 were interviewed. Some identified as men but had not started their transition, whereas others had already completed their transition. Transsexed men undergoing hormone therapy had been doing so for about six years on average. Thirty-four of the transsexed men had undergone bilateral mastectomies, that is, the surgical removal of both breasts, and 21 had undergone hysterectomy, but only four had completed phalloplasty. Two chose metoidioplasty, a less-invasive procedure that takes advantage of the enlarged clitoris resulting from long-term testosterone therapy.

All except one of the participants were sexually attracted to women prior to transition. However, during sex they considered themselves playing the role of a straight man. The transsexed men either decided not to become sexually involved with women owing to perceived inadequacies, already had a partner prior to transition, or decided to start a relationship with a woman after starting transition. Having a partner that can validate a transsexed man's masculinity is very important for their self-esteem.[44]

The transsexed men's earlier heterosexual relationships with men were considered beneficial in teaching them how to behave like men during transition. In most cases, such liaisons were initiated to circumvent social stigma and to maintain family expectations. Their attitude toward men was based more on friendship than anything else, with only one of the transsexed men finding men at all attractive. For some transsexed men, a sexual relationship did eventually develop with gay men, but this took an average of seven years to occur. Confirmation that the transsexed men were indeed men was obtained more frequently when their previous female partner supported them both emotionally and otherwise during the transition process.[44]

An interesting issue is whether children raised by homosexual parents develop a gender identity consistent with their birth-sex and a later heterosexual lifestyle. Although there is a greater likelihood of such children engaging in same-sex friendships when compared with those raised by heterosexual parents, most children exhibit a heterosexual sexual orientation from adolescence onwards. It was clear that co-mothers, both members of the lesbian relationship, generally provide a more nurturing environment than do some fathers in a heterosexual partnership. Lesbian parents provide a supportive and warm environment for raising children. Importantly, heterosexual parents are not needed to ensure birth-sex appropriate gender identity development.[45]

A close relationship between sexual orientation and gender identity is the critical assumption underlying the proposal that autogynephilia characterizes older, nonhomosexual transsexed women when compared with their homosexual counterparts. Although some evidence supports the notion, there has been no definitive experiment showing that an obsession with one's image as a woman is a necessary accompaniment of gender identity atypicality in nonhomosexual transsexed women. There is no equivalent difference between homosexual and nonhomosexual transsexed men corresponding to autogynephilia in transsexed women. The sexual behavior of transsexed men, on the other hand, is clearly different from that of lesbians, with the transsexed men's role in any relationship being that of a man. The quality of homosexual relationships between women is such that children can be raised in a loving, supportive environment with no evidence that their likelihood of homosexuality or atypical gender identity development is any different from children raised in heterosexual families.

SUMMARY

Evidence from both chromosomal studies and genetic analyses of twin data supports the inheritance of both homosexuality and childhood gender nonconformity. Further evidence of a biological basis for homosexuality and gender identity is provided by differences between such people and their heterosexual counterparts in physical traits such as handedness, with homosexual and transsexed people being more frequently left-handed and having a leftward dermal ridge asymmetry. Evidence of a biological basis for transsexuality is provided by similar digit-ratio values for transsexed and natal women. Autogynephilia reflects a presumed fundamental difference in self-image between heterosexual transsexed women and their homosexual counterparts. Even if autogynephilia proves to be an inappropriate characteristic of transsexed women, it does suggest a close association between gender identity and sexual orientation.

Chapter Six

PSYCHOLOGICAL ASSESSMENT OF TRANSSEXUALISM

Since the psychological makeup of transsexed people is not fundamentally different from that of other people, the psychological assessment of the medical condition, transsexualism, based entirely on test scores is problematic. Nevertheless, there are some interesting aspects of a transsexed identity that are worth considering. This chapter examines personal identity and personality traits related to transsexuality.

FORMING A TRANSSEXED IDENTITY

Between the ages of two and seven most children progress through the stages of forming a coherent gender identity consistent with their natal sex. However, for a few, either gender identity development becomes stalled at an immature level, or the acquired gender is contrary to the child's natal sex, leading to enormous difficulties for the child and their family and friends. Some of these children will eventually live satisfying lives, possibly as homosexual men and women, while a small proportion will eventually transition to the other sex. Many transsexed people experience their first feelings of gender difference when they are young, so information about forming a transsexed identity is relevant to their subsequent choice of lifestyle.

Transgender describes "the community of all self identified cross gender people whether intersex, transsexual men and women, cross dressers, drag kings and drag queens, transgenderists, androgynous, bi-gendered, third gendered or as yet unnamed gender gifted people."[1] Transgendering processes can be classified into four styles: migrating, oscillating, negating, and transcending. [2] *Migrating* involves moving from one side of the male-female gender divide to the other on a permanent basis. *Oscillating* involves moving to and fro between male and female polarities, as illustrated by the part-time cross-dresser. *Negating* indicates processes that completely eliminate binary gender categories, a stance adopted by *gender warriors*. Finally, *transcending* presupposes going beyond binary gender categories towards a new experience involving an indeterminate number of gender possibilities. One way to visualize this process is to locate gender at any point within a sphere rather than at either end of a line representing woman at one end and man at the other.

In the early stages of their transition, some transsexed people fashion a new sense of self by socializing with members of support groups and others in the trans-community. This helps their adjustment by enabling transsexed people to tell their own story and listen to others' stories. For example, in one such group a transsexed person claimed to have a "girl-brain in a boy-body." Others reported feeling different for as long as they could remember. The most common evidence of transsexuality is cross-dressing, or fantasizing about cross-dressing, as a child. This process symbolizes the "true self" before it is influenced otherwise by authority figures such as parents and teachers. Most transsexed women report ineptness at sports from an early age, whereas transsexed men were generally admired for their athletic prowess as well as "tomboyish" behavior such as climbing trees.[3]

The media, including the Internet, books, television, film, and video, have played an important role in helping people realize their transsexed identity. The most common nonfiction media are scholarly books, Internet mailing lists and chat lines, book autobiographies, and television documentaries. Some people are helped by reading novels with a transgendered theme. Visual media play a significant role in facilitating the formation of a new transsexed self-identity, especially when people immerse themselves in its emotional, intellectual, and spiritual content.[4]

A transsexed person's identity is influenced by their own self-image, especially their own body satisfaction. Many transsexed people of both genders have an intense preoccupation with the aesthetics of their outward appearance, especially when in public. This obsession is centered on the shape of the body, secondary sex characteristics, and dress code. Perhaps a negative attitude towards one's own body, as indicated by discomfort when appearing in public, might result from problems in establishing adolescent sexual relationships. Many transsexed people who proceed to genital reconstruction surgery (GRS) ensure that the appearance of their physical self conforms with their inner sense of gender identity. By so doing they resolve the anxiety-provoking conflict between their own self-perception and their body representation as seen by others.

The body image of transsexed men and women has been studied using the Sensory Integration Body Imagery Test, which evaluates body-perception conflicts by measuring the time taken to perceive body parts. The neck area plays a prominent role in transsexed women's body image. There is also a high level of perceptual inhibition for the genital area in transsexed women, whereas transsexed men display a high level of perceptual inhibition for the breast area. There is emotional investment in body parts that are significant contributors to a transsexed person's gender comfort.[5]

PERSONALITY OF TRANSSEXED PEOPLE

Personality differences can be measured by conventional question-and-answer tests as well as by projective tests such as the Rorschach, or ink-blot, Test. Projective tests require the client to interpret ambiguous diagrams, the idea being that individual differences in such interpretations will reveal the operation of "subconscious" psychological processes that cannot be revealed so easily using paper-and-pencil tests. Rorschach scores tend to become more stable from adolescence to adulthood.[6] However, the subjective nature of projective tests makes such predictions unreliable.

Psychological tests suggested for evaluating transsexed people such as the Thematic Apperception Test (TAT), the Draw-a-Person test, the Body Image Scale, the Symptom Checklist 90-revised (SCL-90-R), the Crown Crisp Experiential Index (CCEI), the Bem Sex Role Inventory (BSRI), and the Rorschach Test fail to discriminate reliably between those diagnosed with the medical condition of transsexualism and those who show no evidence of the condition.[7]

Psychiatric diagnostic tests such as the Interview for Dissociative Disorders, the Dissociative Experiences Scale, and the Childhood Trauma Questionnaire do not discriminate between transsexed people and others. Nevertheless, dissociative experiences in those diagnosed inappropriately with gender identity disorder (GID) may result from a mismatch between their own self-image and that perceived by others. Psychological tests used to diagnose dissociative disorders have little practical value in assessing the medical condition of transsexualism.[8]

Gender-atypical people diagnosed with GID comply with cultural stereotypes of femininity without any uneasiness. Those not diagnosed with GID consist of two groups: those with a vague sense of maladjustment linked to a pronounced feminine identity, and those with only a slight feminine identity with no particular adjustment difficulties.[9] The personality profile of transsexed people indicates that only a few aspects measured by the Minnesota Multiphasic Personality Inventory (MMPI), a commonly used personality test, lie outside the normal range, suggesting only limited psychopathology for the group as a whole. Only the *MF*-scale, which measures masculinity-femininity, and the *PD*-scale, which measures personality disorder, exceed the expected range.

Transsexed women attracted to men and those attracted to women differed on some of the MMPI test scores, the latter scoring higher on hypochondria, depression, and hysteria, which suggests possible neuroticism.[10] When the MMPI was administered to young transsexed women seeking GRS, an absence of psychopathology was revealed. As expected, they scored higher than others on femininity.[10]

A special gender identity subscale (Gd) was derived from items contained in the MMPI test. The scale was evaluated using clients at a gender clinic and a matched comparison group of male psychiatric outpatients. The most diagnostically useful items included (in order of discriminative power and with the positive response attached):

> I have often wished I were a girl. (True)
> I would like to be a private secretary. (True)
> I like adventure stories better than romantic stories. (False)
> I enjoy reading love stories. (True)
> My judgment is better than it ever was. (True)
> If I were a reporter I would very much like to report sporting news. (False)
> I am very strongly attracted to members of my own sex. (True)
> I would like to be a nurse. (True)

Using an arbitrary cutoff score, 88 percent of the gender clinic clients and 92 percent of the comparison group were correctly classified as gender atypical and having a psychiatric condition, respectively. The major features of the *Gd* items include identifying with stereotypical feminine interests and denial of masculine interests, accompanied by excellent health.[11] Presumably the psychiatric comparison groups scored outside the normal range on many of the MMPI scales, suggesting that comparing gender clients with other than a normal comparison group is both ill-advised and discriminatory.

Twenty-nine percent of a sample of transsexed women and 26 percent of transsexed men reported substance abuse problems. Nine percent of all transsexed people report having been previously diagnosed with a serious psychiatric illness, mostly depression or borderline personality disorder.[12] Borderline personality disorder is characterized by problems with emotional control; sufferers experience intense episodes of anger, depression, and anxiety often accompanied by self-harm. Sufferers cannot easily change long-term goals, and the disorder influences friendships, career plans, and gender identity.[13]

Of 82 clients tested at the Monash Medical Centre Gender Dysphoria Clinic in Australia, 48 were considered transsexual, the remainder being pathologized with gender identity disorder of adolescence and adulthood, nontranssexual type (GIDAANT). This "diagnosis" was based on the now outdated DSM-III diagnostic criteria. The average age of clients was 34, with more of the GIDAANT (22 percent compared with 6 percent) candidates being married. The GIDAANT group exhibited more psychopathology than those diagnosed with transsexualism. Both groups scored above average on femininity, as well as on other scales measuring gender identity and interests. Eighty-five percent of the transsexed clients were rated as having a low level of psychopathology. On the other hand, nearly half of the clients labeled as GIDAANT were classified in the higher psychopathology category because they exhibited symptoms of depression, emotional distress, and chronic maladjustment. Borderline personality disorder was not associated with transsexualism for this carefully selected sample.[14]

When scores on Cattell's 16PF personality test are compared for transsexed people and a nontranssexed comparison group, transsexed people are lower in ego-strength, greater in emotional disturbance, and have difficulty coping with disappointments. In general, transsexed people tend to be highly sensitive and have rich inner lives, but they are also impatient and demanding, revealing both high expectations and a tendency to avoid responsibilities. Transsexed people tend to be low in self-confidence, rather inhibited, cautious, and socially introverted. Discomfort generated in response to a person's gender identity atypicality (GIA) affects one's sense of self, which under adverse circumstances may destabilize.[9] Alternatively, transsexed people might simply display an adaptive response to society's rejection of their transsexual lifestyle, including their therapist's search for pathology when there probably is none.

When assessed using the Draw-a-Person Test, transsexed women produce drawings that are more feminine than those drawn by others, including natal women. Drawings by transsexed women are rated higher on elaborateness and size but are similar to natal women's drawings on completeness. The overall quality of transsexed women's drawings is higher than those drawn by others, suggesting a potential use for the Draw-a-Person Test in the psychological assessment of transsexualism.[15]

A minority of transsexed women also tend to have more psychiatric symptoms, a more pronounced female gender role, and a poorer body image than do natal women. Nevertheless, there are no differences between the personality profiles of transsexed women and others on the Big Five Personality Inventory (NEO-PI).[9] Perhaps GIA produces a greater level of dissociation, implying that some aspects of a person's thoughts are removed from consciousness to minimize the emotional cost of dealing with them.

Transsexed women and natal men have higher scores on self-esteem and dynamic body-image than do natal women. Transsexed women differ from natal sex comparison groups in their sex-role identification, with 71 percent of a sample of transsexed women attaining high scores on both masculinity and femininity, suggesting an androgynous personality. These findings are consistent with postoperative women's positive adjustment to their new lifestyle, adopting a greater variety of flexible behaviors than do nontranssexed people.[16]

Since masculinity-femininity is a personality characteristic, the psychological representation of gender may not correspond exactly with people's views on gender. From the psychological point of view, masculinity and femininity constitute two separate personality characteristics rather than being at opposite ends of a single dimension. Masculinity, or instrumentality, is related to dominance and independence, whereas femininity, or expressiveness, is related to warmth and compassion.[17] Nevertheless, traits such as instrumentality and expressiveness are not associated exclusively with gender but also with other personality variables assessed using the Big Five Personality Inventory.[18]

Gender Diagnosticity distinguishes between masculine and feminine job interests measured by the relative likelihood that the interest is characteristically masculine rather than feminine. Women and feminine men are often more interested in people-oriented jobs such as personal care and counseling whereas men and masculine women tend to be more interested in object-oriented jobs such as engineering and industrial trades. Frequently, gay men have similar interests and hobbies to those of women, whereas some lesbian women exhibit masculine interests.[17]

Transsexed women are more feminine than natal men in gender-diagnostic jobs, gender-diagnostic hobbies, and self-ascribed femininity. Compared to natal men, transsexed women score lower in instrumentality and higher in expressiveness, a gender identity that is more like women than men. When compared with natal women, transsexed men provide more typically masculine responses on all personality measures except instrumentality and expressiveness. Although the instrumentality and expressiveness personality measures do not reliably distinguish between the transsexed and others, gender-diagnostic job and hobby interests do. The gender-diagnostic scores for transsexed women are intermediate between those for natal men and women, whereas the scores for transsexed men approach the masculine end of the scale. Transsexed women have similar gender-diagnostic interests to those of gay men, but with a greater level of ascribed femininity. Transsexed men have different gender-diagnostic interests from lesbian women, and a greater level of accompanying masculinity.[17]

Brain responses to stimulation differ between transsexed women and others. The P300 event-related expectancy response is detected about three-tenths of a second after the stimulus onset when auditory stimuli are presented during a memory test. Postoperative transsexed women have a reduced P300 amplitude in the left frontal and temporal-parietal regions of the brain when compared with natal women. There is also an increase in P300 delay at the central frontal brain region for transsexed women.[19]

Personality differences between the transsexed and others are difficult to discern. There are some differences in masculinity-femininity as well as in characteristics related to psychopathology such as depression and self-esteem. However, some of these latter characteristics may reflect adjustment difficulties during transition resulting from the stress and stigma imposed by intolerance rather than fundamental personality-trait differences between transsexed people and others. Perhaps the most salient differences relate to a reversal of gender role, especially in respect to transsexed people's job interests.

When compared to those who are psychologically well adjusted, transsexed women who experience more than their fair share of lifestyle difficulties tend to be more depressed and more sensitive to adverse events in their environment, and they suffer from a greater number of health problems.[20]

LIFESTYLE AND ATTITUDE DIFFERENCES AMONG TRANSSEXED PEOPLE

Lifestyle and attitude differences among transsexed and transgendered people, including transvestites, become prominent during the transsexed person's adjustment to living full-time in the opposite gender role. Owing to their greater prevalence when compared with transsexed women, transvestites provide a useful source of information on the development of gender identities that are at variance with their natal sex.

Docter and Prince[21] surveyed characteristics of transvestism using a convenience sample of 1,032 male cross-dressers. Although the 30 percent response rate is low for surveys in general, it is not surprising considering that responses were solicited using specialist magazine advertisements and by discrete contacts with members of transvestite clubs.

Committed transvestites exhibited higher sexual arousal, lower cross-gender identity, a greater prevalence of a heterosexual orientation, less propensity to feminize their body, and less motivation to live entirely as a woman than those with transsexual tendencies. On the other hand, the so-called marginal transvestites reported a stronger cross-gender identity, an eagerness to feminize their body, less sexual arousal when cross-dressed, a propensity for sexual relationships with men, and transsexual tendencies including a desire to live full-time as a woman.

Eighty-seven percent of transvestites were heterosexual, most being older than 40. Sixty-six percent started cross-dressing before the age of 10, 93 percent preferred complete cross-dressing, and 79 percent experienced orgasm while cross-dressed. In terms of socialization, 71 percent of respondents appeared cross-dressed in public, only about 25 percent having visited restaurants and used the ladies' toilet. Seventy-five percent of respondents had completed at least one "purge" of their entire wardrobe. Such dispensing with all their feminine attire is quite common among transvestites as they enter a periodic denial stage that is terminated quite abruptly when they realize their need to dress up cannot be so easily "cured."

Eighty-three percent of wives knew about their husband's cross-dressing, including 32 percent who knew prior to their marriage. Only 19 percent of wives completely objected to their husband's cross-dressing, with 28 percent being accepting. These findings should be interpreted cautiously, since the biased sampling of respondents might produce an overrepresentation of men in their late middle age, when the children might have left home.

The participants' transsexual inclinations were indicated by 17 percent of respondents feeling that they were a woman trapped in a man's body, 4 percent already using female hormones, and 43 percent desiring to begin hormone therapy at some later time. On the basis of these responses, the respondents were divided into two groups. Group 1 participants were classified as men who wish to express their feminine side occasionally. Group 2 participants felt like a woman trapped in a man's body. Thirty-nine percent of Group 2 participants desired GRS, with 29 percent preferring to live full-time as a woman.[21]

Transsexed people report long periods of distress with their natal sex and gender role, whereas transvestites, 87 percent of whom are heterosexual men, engage in periodic cross-dressing mostly for sexual and other pleasurable pursuits. Those who start identifying as transsexed women as adults precede their possible GRS with a long period of living in the opposite gender role.[22]

Docter and Fleming[22] examined four aspects of transgendered behavior: cross-dressing identity, feminization of the body, sexual arousal, and social/sexual role. A transgendered/transsexed sample was used, 88 percent of whom were transvestites who dressed fully as women part-time, the remainder having lived full-time as women. Fifty-one percent of the latter group had undergone GRS. Eighty-two percent of transvestites were married, whereas 71 percent of full-time transsexed women had been married previously. Forty-five percent of transvestites and only 9 percent of transsexed women were currently living with their wives. Forty percent of the full-time transsexed women had a female partner and 20 percent had a male partner, whereas 53 percent of transvestites had a female partner and 6 percent had a male partner. Most participants were better educated than the general population, suggesting a biased sample.

There are two basic dimensions of transgendered behavior in natal men. The first dimension is *Identity,* defined as self-perceived transgender identity as feminine. Full-time transsexed women score higher than transvestites on this dimension, especially for living full-time as a woman and aspiring to GRS.

The second dimension of transgendered behavior is *Role,* with full-time transsexed women scoring higher than transvestites. This dimension measures actual gender atypical behavior such as going out to restaurants as a woman and passing well. There are no age-related differences among full-time transsexed women on these dimensions. There is no suggestion of autogynephilia, the sexual arousal experienced when presenting as a woman, since nonhomosexual transgendered males report being less aroused by sexual stimuli the greater their reported level of distress experienced when adopting the opposite gender role.

The Bem Sex Roles Inventory (BSRI) has been used to examine the hypothesis that transsexed people adopt sex-typing behavior that is typical of the opposite sex. *BSRI* scores classify people in terms of low and high scores on both masculinity and femininity. People scoring high on one dimension and low on the other are defined as masculine and feminine, respectively. Those scoring high on both dimensions are androgynous, whereas those scoring low on both dimensions are considered undifferentiated.[23]

Most of the older transsexed women sampled were university educated and married, with an average age of 36, compared to the other participants, whose average age was 21. As expected, natal men scored higher on masculinity than femininity, the reverse being true for natal women. On the other hand, transsexed men scored similarly to natal men, whereas transsexed women, especially younger ones, scored even higher on femininity than did natal women. Both transsexed women and transsexed men were more androgynous than natal members of both sexes.[23]

A survey of 188 male cross-dressers indicated that 44 percent were transvestites (they never wanted to have GRS), 23 percent were transsexuals (they wanted GRS and appropriate medical treatments), and 33 were transgendered, defined as men who frequently cross-dressed and who had a more stable feminine gender identity than the transvestites. The average age of participants was 44, a majority being employed in high-paying jobs, with almost 50 percent being married. The partners of 90 percent of married cross-dressers were aware of their husbands' cross-dressing. Except for a slightly poorer body-image, the cross-dressers did not differ from other men on the personality measures evaluated, except that those with psychological problems obtained personality test scores consistent with their condition. Generally speaking, the transsexed women were more aesthetic and had a lower sexual drive and a more feminine gender identity than the other groups of cross-dressers.[24]

Although transsexed people do not usually exhibit any serious personality problems, transsexed women, in particular, differ from natal men by being closer to natal women in their personality profile. Some transsexed women's distress is indicated by their greater neuroticism and emotional disturbance and lower level of ego-strength. Transsexed women have occupational interests that are similar to those of natal women, and similarly, transsexed men prefer masculine occupations. Overall, the most adaptive personality style for transsexed women is probably an androgynous one that incorporates both masculine and feminine traits. The lifestyle of transsexed people is based on gender identity and gender role as assessed by various types of transgendered behavior.

ADJUSTMENT PROBLEMS EXPERIENCED BY TRANSSEXED PEOPLE

Despite the small personality differences between transsexed people and others, some transsexed people experience quite severe psychological distress. The following examples include rare cases of eating disorder concurrent with GIA.

Just like natal women, transsexed women are at a greater risk of developing eating disorders than are natal men. The prevalence of anorexia nervosa in adolescent and young adult women ranges from 0.5 percent to 1 percent. The prevalence of bulimia nervosa lies between 1 percent and 3 percent. Some men with eating disorder also have sexual inactivity and disturbed gender identity development. So femininity is considered a risk factor for eating disorders in both men and women.

Hepp and Misos[25] provided case studies of two transsexed women with eating disorders, one aged 36, the other aged 22. Both women had severe body dissatisfaction leading to anorexia nervosa and bulimia nervosa, respectively. The third case was a 43-year-old transsexed man with anorexia nervosa complicated by a lack of menstruation that was evident prior to starting testosterone therapy.

A rare case of anorexia nervosa in identical male twins, one of whom had early cross-gender yearnings but who lived primarily as a man, has also been described. The other twin lived full-time as a woman after being referred to a gender clinic for possible GRS. Both twins had developmental delays in language and motor skills and were diagnosed as eating-disordered.[26]

Anorexia nervosa in a 24-year-old transsexed man following mastectomy and hystero-oophorectomy to remove the internal sex organs has also been reported. Eating disorders are not uncommon in transsexed and homosexual people, particularly since such people aim to be sexually attractive. This client was unusual in having complications resulting from alcohol dependence and major depression as well as borderline personality disorder. The MMPI personality test revealed difficulties in interpersonal relationships, impulsivity, low frustration tolerance, depression, and anxiety, as well as high suggestibility and immaturity. Perhaps eating disorders are a risk factor in gender atypical people.[27]

A 25-year-old transsexed woman suffering from bulimia nervosa, a rare condition in natal males, expressed her eating disorder by maintaining a stable weight by excessive exercise. She had done this to maintain an ideal feminine shape so that she could attract male attention. This woman was marginalized socially with no regular employment except for her involvement in escort services. She had been sexually abused as a child and was now living away from family and friends.[28]

SUMMARY

An important basis for diagnosing the medical condition of transsexualism is an understanding of how the transsexed identity is formed. Although we do not understand exactly how this occurs, people can explore their transsexed feelings using support groups and by reading published information. Although personality tests as well as other psychological tests have been used to determine differences between transsexed people and others, there are no consistent findings. Nevertheless some discrepant scores on masculinity-femininity associated with occupational interests characteristic of the opposite sex, as well as deviations from normal scores on tests indicating psychological disorders, have been observed. Perhaps the most adaptive personality involves androgynous characteristics. Even though current psychological tests may be questionable for assessing GIA, psychological aspects should be considered, especially when there are other health complications, such as eating disorders.

Chapter Seven

TRANSSEXUALISM AS
A MEDICAL CONDITION

This chapter provides an up-to-date account of psychological diagnostic procedures for transsexualism and related medical conditions. Special attention is given to the requirements of young transsexed people. The terms *transsexualism,* as a medical pathologization of transsexuality, and *gender dysphoria* are not interchangeable, since *gender dysphoria* refers to the distress caused by a mismatch between born-sex and current gender identity. *Gender dysphoria* is a necessary but not sufficient condition for a diagnosis of *transsexualism,* or *gender identity disorder* as it is currently inappropriately named in psychiatric diagnostic manuals. In practice, only a small proportion of applicants presenting for assessment at so-called "gender dysphoria clinics" are diagnosed with transsexualism.

Save for medical complications, pregnancy is a natural variation of female sexuality. Being pregnant is usually a joyful experience unless the pregnancy is unexpected and abortion is desired but is not forthcoming because of cultural and religious restrictions. In such circumstances the distressed woman might experience "pregnancy dysphoria" resulting from external pressures that are beyond her control. Likewise, transsexuality is a normal variation of gendered behavior due to a mismatch between the transsexed person's genitals and their mindset regarding their affirmed sex. Any distress that might occur is most likely due to other people's adverse response to the transsexed person's situation. Unless there are accompanying psychological problems, there is no sense in which transsexuality is a mental illness. Yet, in order to obtain the desired medical treatment, most transsexed people must sacrifice their sanity to the likes of psychiatrists and clinical psychologists who are presumed to be experts in the diagnosis and treatment of "gender identity disorders." In many instances, these specialists are really just "gatekeepers" so that surgeons who perform GRS and other medical procedures for transsexed people will be legally protected.[1]

Trying to diagnose transsexualism in transsexed people is more difficult than diagnosing most other medical conditions. For one thing, some applicants consider that they have a right to hormone therapy and genital reconstruction surgery (GRS). They consider the various medical professionals involved as "gatekeepers," whose primary role is to select candidates for surgery using what appear to be arbitrary criteria.

The currently accepted prerequisites for transition include at least 3 months of psychotherapy before hormones can be prescribed, a minimum period of 12 months during which the candidate must live exclusively in the other-gender role (the real-life experience) and, finally, letters from two independent psychiatrists or clinical psychologists confirming that the client is a suitable candidate for GRS. Variations in this prolonged diagnostic procedure include increasing the minimum time for the real-life experience to two years and selecting only young, passable candidates who have never been married. Such candidates might be accepted as members of their affirmed sex without being detected as transsexed in most social situations. The diagnostic procedures differ from country to country and are somewhat more liberal in places such as Thailand.[2]

Many friends of the trans-community deplore the unnecessary pathologization of gender-atypical behavior by the medical profession.[3] Such pathologization of their normal gender identity atypicality (GIA) can have devastating effects on transsexed people's self-esteem, especially if their medical records are shared with other professionals. Nevertheless, it is important to diagnose and treat psychiatric complications when they exist.

PSYCHIATRIC COMPLICATIONS IN THE DIAGNOSIS OF TRANSSEXUALISM

Perhaps the most important consideration is the transsexed person's mental health. Those with delusional thoughts about "changing sex" should be routinely screened during psychiatric evaluation leading to either elimination from the gender program or else delaying their progress until the psychiatric problem has been resolved. Sometimes depressed clients are offered appropriate therapy leading to recovery and a resumption of their GIA treatment. HIV and genital disorders are not normally considered as contraindications for GRS. The situation can be difficult if the onset of depression during GIA assessment results from a feeling of "failed masculinity."[4] However in these cases the decision to perform GRS is solely that of the surgeon using medical advice from other experienced professionals.[2]

Gender identity problems occur in from 15 percent to 25 percent of cases of schizophrenia, with some patients exhibiting delusional thought about proceeding with a "sex change." About 5 percent of GRS applicants have some symptoms of schizophrenia.[5] When GIA results from delusions accompanying undiagnosed schizophrenia, caution is required, since once antipsychotic medication has had its positive effects on the client's thought processes, they may regret hormonal and other treatments for GIA.

Dutch psychiatrists are consulted by gender clients on average about once every four and a half years. In 39 percent of cases, the medical condition of transsexualism is identified as the primary condition, whereas for the remainder there is accompanying psychiatric illness. In 75 percent of these cases, transsexualism is a secondary condition, so once the psychiatric illness has been ameliorated, the client generally no longer exhibits cross-gendered behavior.[6]

Often the client has read widely on GRS procedures using Internet resources and books and has consulted with those who have already undergone GRS. Perhaps the client has already self-diagnosed her condition and is seeking confirmation from medical consultants so that hormones can be prescribed. The diagnostician's task is difficult, because clients might have learned the appropriate "script" for obtaining hormones after seeking advice from successful clients. Self-reference is rare in medical practice, and most clients only seek medical help when they are ill. With so much pressure placed on gender clinic personnel by eager aspirants for GRS, responsibility is required to minimize the regret following GRS. This is undoubtedly the reason for gatekeeping and the maintenance of minimum standards of care for those with GIA.[2]

Transsexed people are often offended by the medicalization of GIA and the implication that they are mentally ill. Their situation is often complicated by accompanying medical conditions resulting from social isolation and relationship difficulties during transition. These conditions include anxiety, post-traumatic stress, and depression, leading occasionally to substance abuse. About 10 percent of preoperational transsexed women have attempted self-mutilation of the genitals. Also, 2 percent of transsexed men have attempted breast mutilation. Since transsexed people try to present as disease-free to obtain hormones and surgery, instances of depression may be underdiagnosed. Nevertheless, GRS can be considered a life-saving procedure, as the suicide rate in transsexed women is about 20 percent prior to GRS and as low as 1 percent after surgery. Self-satisfaction, as measured by subjective reports, improves for most transsexed people following GRS.

HISTORICAL PRECURSORS OF CURRENT ASSESSMENT PROCEDURES

This section discusses the early ideas of Harry Benjamin and the proposal that there are two basic types of transsexed people, those who exhibit strong cross-gendered feelings and behavior during adolescence and early adulthood and those who begin their transition as middle-aged adults.

Benjamin,[7] a pioneer in the diagnosis and treatment of transsexualism as a medical condition, realized early on that sex and gender can be easily discriminated: sex is located below the belt and gender above it. Benjamin classified transvestites and transsexed people in terms of six categories. The *pseudo-transvestite* is interested in sporadic dressing, is mainly heterosexual, and is not interested in sexual conversion. The *fetishistic transvestite* lives as a man and dresses as a woman primarily for sexual enjoyment. He may request some counseling but is not interested in GRS. The *true transvestite* considers hormone therapy worthwhile and is heterosexual but may change sexual orientation when dressed as a woman. The *nonsurgical transsexual* frequently dresses as a woman, lives as either a man or a woman, has a low libido level, and requests hormone therapy to maintain a satisfactory quality of life. The *true transsexual (moderate intensity)* lives and works as a woman, if possible, after having obtained insufficient relief from cross-dressing. Hormone therapy and surgery are requested and often granted. The *true transsexual (high intensity)* requests immediate GRS and, if young, tends to live with a person of the opposite natal sex. The risk of suicide in a *true transsexual (high intensity)* is high if the request for surgery is denied. A *partial transsexual* has started the cosmetic surgical and hormonal aspects of the transition process but has not completed GRS.[8]

Benjamin distinguished between gender identity and sexual orientation by claiming that a transvestite has a social problem, a person diagnosed with transsexualism has a gender problem, and a homosexual has a sex problem. In early studies reviewed by Benjamin, hypogonadism, or a lack of fully mature sexual organs, was found in 40 percent of the people he saw. Of 246 male transvestites Benjamin treated in his clinical practice, 65 percent were diagnosed as transsexed. Eighteen percent of those who eventually underwent surgery were only-children, a rate well above the population average. Even in the 1960s, 86 percent of GRS outcomes were rated at least satisfactory in terms of both appearance and functionality.

For 90 percent of transsexed people, both male and female, conscious distress with their gender identity atypicality occurred before they were fifteen. Of the 207 cases reviewed by Jan Wålinder,[9] 185 of whom were natal men, 45 percent were true transsexed, 17 percent tended towards transsexuality, and the remainder were transvestites. Most clients were of average, or above average, intelligence, 37 percent suffered from parental disadvantages, such as divorce, death, etc., and 20 percent were dressed as children in crossgendered clothing by their parents. Transsexed women were found to have shorter arms in proportion to their leg length than do natal men.[9] Transsexuality has had three main characteristics since this early period: a strong sense of belonging to the opposite sex, disgust at one's genitals and secondary sex characteristics, and the desire for sex reassignment.

Benjamin suggested that psychoanalysis and psychotherapy cannot effect a cure, and such resistance to psychological intervention has been reiterated more recently by others.[10] So hormone, and possibly surgical, treatment must be the intervention of choice, especially for adults.

Chiland,[11] a French psychoanalyst, reported that the European Court of Human Rights considers GIA to be a self-diagnosed condition. Chiland hypothesized that people with GIA cannot experience love nor being loved unless they become the opposite sex. Chiland proposed three basic characteristics of the typical GIA client: identity, homosexuality, and transvestism. It is important, therefore, to distinguish the characteristics of young transsexed people, some of whom may be homosexual, from those of older transsexed people so that appropriate hormone therapy and surgery can occur. This is especially the case for older transsexed people. Chiland wondered what comes first, identification with the opposite sex or repugnance at one's own sex.

Gender dysphoria was first used as a diagnostic term in 1971 by Laub and Fisk.[12] Lothstein[13] studied psychological and sociological factors related to the medical condition of transsexualism, 80 percent of his clients being natal men, mostly in the 18 to 30 age range but with about 10 percent being over 50. Twenty-nine percent were married and 19 percent had children. The majority of clients were from higher socioeconomic groups and were highly educated, a bias resulting from cultural and financial circumstances. Several clients had various types of psychopathology including borderline personality disorder, latent schizophrenia, a tendency towards sadomasochism (now considered a normal variation of sexual behavior), and impulsive behavior accompanied by narcissism. These problems were attributed to impaired ego development, possibly caused by inappropriate mothering.

Some of Lothstein's clients gained their mother's support for both their cross-dressing and effeminate behavior, including a wish to remain emotionally close to their mothers. Any gender distress was characterized by conflict and defensive psychological strategies. "The mother-child relationship and the quality of parenting are the bedrock on which gender disturbances rest."[14] Lothstein suggested that a conflict between the "actual self" and the "true self," to which such people aspire, is a core feature of transsexuality.

Most of Lothstein's clients were socially isolated and lonely. They reported few socialization experiences as a child and few quality friendships. This led inevitably to an inability to form intimate relationships, with limited recourse to homosexual experiences. The desire for GRS increased under stress, older clients hoping they might be rescued from their isolation and alienation. Some transsexed men reported that they had learned that a woman's role was mainly to serve men so by becoming men themselves they could release themselves from this burden.

Projective tests showed that some transsexed people exhibit feelings of incompleteness, defectiveness, and depression.[13] Those who desired the genitals of the other sex were less anxious and impulsive, and less likely to contemplate suicide. Lothstein suggested that clients who were most fastidious about the surface accompaniments of femininity such as dress, makeup, and mannerisms might be helped psychologically and perhaps remain as transvestites. Reinstating the client's natal gender using psychotherapy might be risky if there is no accompanying self-image in that gender role. The more feminine exhibitionists desired both GRS and large breast implants. However, those transsexed men who requested both breast removal and vagina closure tended to exhibit high levels of psychopathology.

Lothstein[15] revisited the ideas of Edward Levine[16] by stating that "transsexuals seem to undergo a progressive role transformation from an extremely ambivalent, confused gender role during childhood and primary school years, to one involving homosexuality in post-adolescence, to that of drag queen (experimental cross-dressing) to that of self-declared, permanently cross-dressed transsexual." In the 1970s, some transsexed women clients were classified as schizoid, obsessive, having indulged in cross-dressing at a relatively late age, and having become isolated and less convincing in their opposite gender role, leading to depression and withdrawal. Transsexed men's adaptation was usually much more effective, possibly due to their prior association with homosexual communities. Unfortunately, many transsexed people limit their social relations to the transgendered community, leading to even greater social isolation.

Lothstein[17] examined the outcomes from psychological assessment of self-identified transsexed people consisting of 565 women and 134 men, a ratio of 5:1 in favor of transsexed women. Prior to GRS there was little evidence of severe psychopathology, especially after the person started living full-time in the cross-gender role. There was no serious psychopathology nor reality impairment in transsexed men. In general, transsexed men were healthier than transsexed women and were no different psychologically from natal men and women. Lothstein's review indicated that transsexed women were, on average, more psychologically disturbed than transsexed men. They tended to experience a lower sex drive and had less overall information on their own, and other's, sexuality.

A modern review of gender identity atypicality that supersedes much of the earlier views of Lothstein and others was sponsored by the Gender Identity Research and Educational Society in the UK in 2003. It was co-authored by a group of international experts in the field chaired by Milton Diamond.[18]

PRIMARY AND SECONDARY TRANSSEXUALISM

Clinicians who recognize two varieties of the medical condition of transsexualism—primary and secondary—use different evaluation criteria for these two groups. Primary transsexualism is distinguished by its early onset, with clients reporting memories of cross-dressing when they were young, as well as partaking in feminine activities such as playing with dolls from an early age. Primary transsexed women who often exhibit homosexual sexual preferences from adolescence onwards frequently enjoy greater success in transition than do their older counterparts.

Secondary transsexualism develops after a period of possibly fetishistic cross-dressing[19] when the client starts to assume a more permanent feminine self-identity around puberty. Often secondary transsexed women prefer sexual relationships with women. They seek initial assessment at an older age and some of them have been, or are still, married with a family. Some gender clinics consider secondary transsexed women as having poorer prospects for GRS, although there is little evidence to support such an assertion.[20]

The primary transsexed group tends to present earlier for assessment, show better social gender reorientation, have less erotic arousal when cross-dressing, and experience fewer postoperative regrets than does the secondary transsexed group. Transsexed women usually have a poorer postsurgical outcome than do transsexed men, although at present, successful genital surgery is not always possible for the latter. GRS outcomes are about 87 percent successful in transsexed women and 97 percent successful in transsexed men, even though final refinement is not technically possible, nor affordable, for all transsexed men.

Differences between primary (young) and secondary (older) transsexed people have some diagnostic value. Cross-gender identity was studied in male transvestites and transsexed women, 66 percent of whom were primary, as well as a comparison group of heterosexual natal men. Primary transsexed women preferred playing feminine games with female friends from an early age, as also did many of the secondary transsexed women. Such feminine behavior as children was not so evident for transvestites nor for the heterosexual group. Most primary transsexed women started cross-dressing before they were 7, whereas most secondary transsexed women started after they were 12. Nevertheless, there was scarcely any difference in the relative frequency of current cross-dressing between the two groups of transsexed women.[21]

Only transvestites engaged in fetishistic cross-dressing. Secondary transsexed women who were not fetishistic as adults tended to play with feminine toys and have more female friends when young. Most primary transsexed women preferred a heterosexual male sexual partner and, not surprisingly, a few secondary transsexed women had similar sexual preferences. Only the transvestites preferred mainly heterosexual female partners. Transsexuality for natal males may result from a conflict between competing masculine and feminine self-systems, with the feminine one winning eventually. This resolution occurs earlier for younger transsexed women.[21]

Seventy-four percent of respondents to a survey sent to readers of a transvestite magazine, compared with 25 percent in a U.S. national sample, were the eldest male child in their family, 40 percent had more than one sibling, and 19 percent, compared to 6 percent in a U.S. national sample, were only-children. Fifteen percent of respondents had one older sister, 86 percent reported a close relationship with their mothers, and 68 percent reported a negative relationship with their fathers. These parental relationships differed substantially from those revealed by survey respondents who were not transsexed.[22]

The survey showed that 97 percent of transgendered respondents reported cross-dressing experience before puberty. Seventy-eight percent of respondents had been covert cross-dressers, with their family not knowing about their activities, 21 percent reported having long hair as boys, and 78 percent reported that dressing up was sexually arousing when they were young. Slightly more than half were emotionally elated by cross-dressing when young, whereas 12 percent, mainly transsexed people, had neutral feelings, it being considered a "normal" activity for them.

A close relationship with the mother is more likely to be associated with being a true transvestite than a transsexed person, since the mother-child relationship tends to be somewhat negative for the latter, even though many transgendered people claim their mother was influential in encouraging their overt cross-dressing. Thirty-one percent of transsexed people had been in public dressed as a girl.[22]

Most nonhomosexual men with GIA present initially for assessment in their thirties, although new clients in their fifties and sixties are not uncommon. Although such clients say that the conscious wish to be a woman only materialized a few years previously, their initial cross-gender feelings started in early childhood or at puberty. The delay in becoming feminized is frequently due to marriage and children, complicated sometimes by an unwillingness to become divorced.

Thirty-one percent of a group of nonhomosexual men who desired to live permanently as women had never married, 48 percent had cohabited with only one partner, and the remainder had had a relationship with more than one woman. Those with an early cross-gender identity tended to have a low sexual interest in women as well as an earlier age of presentation for assessment. Each successive marriage delayed assessment by four years, with each child contributing an additional two-year delay. For example, if a transsexed woman had been married twice and had four children, the expected delay in seeking assessment would be 16 years. So a family man who first exhibits GIA in his mid-twenties might wait until his early forties before seeking medical help. This is a common age at which secondary transsexed women start their transition.[23]

Diagnosing transsexualism by psychological means is difficult, since there are few behaviors that distinguish transsexed people from others, except those who also suffer from serious psychiatric conditions such as schizophrenia and borderline personality disorder. The client should have some control over these conditions before being offered assistance for GIA. From the earliest days, professionals proposed two types of transsexed person: primary and secondary. The outcomes of hormone therapy and surgery are more positive for the primary transsexed, although there is insufficient evidence to deter secondary transsexed people from pursuing full transition.[24]

HEALTHCARE ISSUES FOR TRANSSEXED PEOPLE

Providing affordable health care for transsexed people is important. Issues requiring consideration include the problematic role of the gender professional as a gatekeeper, since many transsexed people feel they cannot always be honest in case they get excluded from the gender clinic program. A better alternative is a partnership approach in which the clinician assesses the client's capacity to provide informed consent after understanding the risks and benefits of medical interventions.

The DSM-IV diagnosis of transsexualism, now known as gender identity disorder (GID), as a mental illness contributes to prejudice against transsexed people and hinders their fight for human rights. The GID diagnostic criteria for children and adolescents are sexist in that they do not recognize that many young transsexed people are gay or lesbian. Also, a greater level of care of transsexed people who are suffering from HIV infection is urgently needed.[25]

One of the problems faced by transsexed people is some medical practitioners' inexperience in transgender care. Patient handouts for both transsexed men and women should contain advice on medical aspects of their transition. For all transsexed people the transition takes approximately five years, although the actual in-role living component is usually completed within two years. The risks associated with testosterone therapy for transsexed men include liver disease, diabetes risk, weight gain, and a decreasing level of high-density lipoproteins, as well as increased homocysteine levels leading to a cardiovascular disease risk. There is also a slight risk of breast and endometrial cancer, should there be any remnant malignant tissue following surgery. Common side effects of testosterone therapy include acne in about 12 percent of clients, increased skin oiliness, weight gain, fluid retention, and headaches.[26]

For transsexed women, the medical practitioner should be aware that, in view of potentially serious side effects, the lowest effective estrogen dosage should be used. Breast development is a gradual process taking up to two years. Galactorrhea, or release of breast milk, can occur in about 10 percent of those treated with estrogen, whereas hyperprolactinemia, an abnormal increase in prolactin, a hormone secreted by the pituitary gland, is common.

Spironolactone is a commonly used antiandrogen that reduces testosterone production and decreases the concentrations of both testosterone and dihydrotestosterone at the cellular level. In some cases, spironolactone allows feminization to occur more rapidly using a lower estrogen dosage. High potassium levels may become a problem as may low blood pressure, but generally there are few side effects from spironolactone treatment.

Regular medical checks should be conducted at three-month intervals during the first year of hormone therapy, and at six-month intervals thereafter. The primary-care physician should screen new transsexed clients for high blood pressure, ischemic heart disease, thromboembolism, cerebrovascular disease, liver dysfunction, kidney insufficiency, refractory migraine headaches or seizures, poorly controlled diabetes, obesity, hyperlipidemia (an abnormally high level of fatty substances in the blood), and psychiatric illnesses.[26]

DIAGNOSTIC OUTCOMES FOR TRANSSEXED PEOPLE

The standard diagnostic procedure for GID uses the fourth edition of the *Diagnostic and Statistical Manual* produced by the American Psychiatric Association. A diagnosis of GID for adults requires a strong and persistent cross-gender identification, frequent passing as the other sex, and a desire to be the other sex as well as a conviction of possessing the feelings and reactions of that sex. There must also be persistent discomfort with one's current sex, leading to a need to rid oneself of both the primary and secondary sex characteristics of one's natal sex and acquiring through hormones and surgery those of the opposite sex. There must be sufficient distress to impair the client's social, occupational, and other important aspects of her life.

The GID diagnosis is precluded if the client has an intersex condition. A diagnosis of gender identity disorder otherwise not specified sometimes applies when the client suffers from an intersex condition with accompanying gender dysphoria or when the client exhibits transient stress-related cross-dressing or has attempted sex-organ mutilation. The other diagnostic category, transvestic fetishism, is characterized by sexual arousal while cross-dressing, without any necessary desire for full sex reassignment. Occasionally, someone diagnosed primarily with transvestic fetishism will also exhibit gender dysphoria and a consistent desire to live full-time as the opposite gender, with or without hormone and surgical treatments.

There is a dearth of scientific studies of the reliability and validity of the diagnostic criteria for GID. For adults, the DSM-IV diagnostic criteria suggest that a candidate may not be suitable for sex reassignment when there is no evidence of distress in well-adjusted individuals. This is an unfortunate consequence of the pathologization of GIA.[27] Many people experiencing GIA do not suffer the degree and type of distress required for a DSM-IV diagnosis. Any social dysfunction they might experience is due primarily to the negative impact of others' attitude towards them. It is also debatable whether transvestic fetishism should be labeled as a psychiatric disorder and included in the DSM-IV classification, especially when there is no associated distress.[28]

Transvestic fetishism applies to a heterosexual man who has been sexually aroused by partaking in real or imaginary cross-dressing for a period of six months or longer. Although it is assumed that no such sexual excitement is present in GID, clinical observation indicates that some transsexed people indulge in fetishistic practices prior to hormone therapy, highlighting the importance of considering individual differences between applicants.

Questionnaire responses were obtained from heterosexual and homosexual male gender-clinic clients who responded positively to a question asking whether they had ever felt like a woman. Each heterosexual participant was classified by whether they only felt like women when cross-dressed (mild dysphoria; 15 percent of participants), sometimes felt like a woman when not cross-dressed (moderate dysphoria; 27 percent of participants), or felt like a woman at all times within the last year (strong dysphoria; 58 percent of participants).

Sexual arousal when cross-dressed was more common for the mild and moderate gender dysphoric participants than for the strongly dysphoric participants. Similarly, strongly dysphoric participants were least likely to masturbate during cross-dressing. However, at least 50 percent of the strongly gender dysphoric participants who were diagnosed with GID also exhibited symptoms of transvestic fetishism, suggesting that transvestic fetishism and GID are not mutually exclusive. Nevertheless, some applicants for sex reassignment deny their involvement in fetishistic behavior so as not to be misclassified and denied medical help.[29] These results suggest that the DSM diagnostic categories require revision.

A survey of 2,450 people between the ages of 18 and 78, 52 percent of whom were male, conducted in Sweden showed that 2.8 percent of men and 0.4 percent of women report sexual arousal when cross-dressed. Those reporting transvestic fetishism were more likely to be separated from their parents as a child, sexually abused, and easily sexually aroused, and to masturbate more often, have a same-sex partner when cross-dressed, use illegal drugs, and view pornography.[30]

Anne Vitale[31] recommended that the GID diagnosis be replaced by gender expression deprivation anxiety disorder (GEDAD). If left untreated, GEDAD leads to "confusion and rebellion in childhood, false hopes and disappointment in adolescence, hesitant compliance in early adulthood, feelings of self-induced entrapment in middle age, and if still untreated, depression and resignation in old age."

Vitale proposed three groups of GEDAD clients. Group 1 members are affected by insufficient androgenization of the fetus, leading to effeminate boys. Group 2 is similar to Group 1 and includes "tomboyish" girls who rarely marry. Group 3 contains feminine males who invest heavily in typically masculine activities and who are largely heterosexual. Frequently, they marry and have children, hold advanced educational degrees, and are employed in high-paying and prestigious jobs.

Some children, especially only-children, have no way of knowing that there is a physical difference between themselves and those of the opposite sex. They may be retarded in seeking medical and psychological help for their GIA, a difficulty that might extend into adulthood.

Group 1 boys with a feminine gender identity prefer to associate sexually with other boys during adolescence but also have peer girlfriends. Group 3 boys, who tend to indulge in excessive masturbation during adolescence, enjoy the company of girls but not necessarily for sexual reasons. A steady reduction in testosterone level with age relieves some of the distress experienced by those older Group 3 members who otherwise could not endure hormone therapy and surgery.[31]

Following a diagnosis of GID, and shortly after starting cross-sex hormone treatment, gender-atypical people experience a considerable improvement in their mental status, becoming less distressed and less anxious. With a proper differential diagnosis, a significantly long trial period of living in the new gender role, and a satisfactory surgical result, postoperative regret among those proceeding to GRS is unlikely.[31]

STANDARDS OF CARE FOR TRANSSEXED PEOPLE

The international standard for treating transsexualism as a medical condition is the Harry Benjamin International Gender Dysphoria Association's *Standards of Care for Gender Identity Disorders*, Sixth Version, published in February 2001. Medical staff should emphasize the flexibility of the standards of care (SOC) guidelines and adapt their treatment strategies to suit each individual client. The following summary is based on information contained in the original source.[32]

The SOC offer guidelines to professionals while recognizing that a flexible approach to diagnosis and treatment of GIA is advisable. The guidelines offer minimum standards, which can be relaxed depending on the client's needs. The standards offer reassurance that overseas candidates for surgery have followed approximately the same evaluation as locals. Departures from the published SOC used by individual gender clinics and professionals should be published in writing for the legal protection of all involved.

Before starting medical treatment, the client should have received at least three months of counseling, preferably performed by a clinical psychologist or psychiatrist with specialist skills in gender issues. Sometimes this stipulation can be waived if the client has been living for some time in the desired gender role, and most particularly if self-administered hormones have been used without medical supervision. Hormone treatment can be used as a diagnostic aid, since withdrawal of hormones can occur without lingering side effects within the first three months. This trial period enables clients to decide if they want to continue with the treatment after having experienced both the beneficial and undesirable effects of hormones.

A final evaluation occurs just before GRS when two independent professionals provide evidence that the client has successfully completed at least a year's real-life experience in the opposite-gender role. During this period, there should be improvement in the client's adjustment without contraindications such as serious medical complications, substance abuse, and exacerbated mental illness. Most surgeons also request medical reports on hormone levels and the level of general health.

Many gender clinic clients experience difficulty changing their name and sex on legal documents, gaining access to their children, and acquiring medical insurance for GRS and other procedures. Although most transsexed people want their condition to be depathologized, they simultaneously fear the consequences of being denied access to hormonal and surgical treatments if they do not have a recognized medical condition. On a positive note, the University of Michigan's Comprehensive Gender Services Program *accompanies* clients through their progress towards full transition rather than simply *working on* them. The program is supportive, consultative, and caring, its aim being "the non-destructive self-actualization of the client."[33]

Information on the client's current physical health and medical history, developmental factors, socioeconomic situation, and a family history going back at least two generations, if possible, should be available. Since many middle-aged clients regret not having transitioned when they were younger, consultation with their family due to the social consequences of transition is desirable. Although such clients have experienced many years of suffering, they have often considered the comfort of others, especially their family and friends, rather than themselves, and so deserve sympathetic consideration.[34]

Some clients seek only partial gender reassignment, as exemplified by men who live full-time as women without hormones and surgery and those requesting hormones to enhance their passability or to feel more comfortable as women. The counselor should recognize that some transsexed people are not interested in "passing," and have no intention of "becoming a woman," in the full sense. This situation complicates the evaluation process as many gender clinics assume that, except for medical complications, all accepted clients will eventually progress to GRS.[35]

The diagnosis of GID is governed by a combination of the DSM-IV criteria together with professional judgment adapted to each client's needs. Although distinguishing between GID and transvestic fetishism is challenging, for at least some clients these conditions occur together. Enlightened therapists question the validity of the GID label and suggest an alternative evaluation such as GEDAD that encompasses more of the psychological distress associated with GIA. Others believe that their clients should not be diagnosed with a mental illness as, in most cases, distress prior to treatment is often relieved after hormone therapy has begun. The client's progress towards GRS is governed by internationally approved standards of care.

EXAMPLES OF EVALUATION PROCEDURES IN SELECTED GENDER CLINICS

In the UK, gender services are concentrated in the southeast of England, the largest center being at Charing Cross Hospital's Department of Psychiatry in London. The Charing Cross Gender Identity Clinic, which employs SOC criteria, has a three- to nine-month waiting time. It receives about four hundred referrals annually, mainly from regional psychiatric services and general practitioners. New clients are interviewed to obtain a full psychiatric history, with emphasis on childhood cross-gendered behavior as well as subsequent personality and psychosexual development. Additional information is obtained at a second interview within the following three months. When possible, information from the client is usually corroborated by interviews with parents conducted with the client's consent. If the second interview confirms that the client is transsexed, and if no medical contraindications exist, treatment with cross-sex hormones is approved. Hormone therapy usually starts at a low dosage, with regular monitoring of liver function, blood pressure, and the lipid profile.

Assessments of the client's social, employment, sexual, and psychological stability occur every three months. Confirmation of employment, with the client's consent, is sought from employers. Physical changes following the start of hormone therapy are monitored, as are changes in sex drive. As time passes, greater attention is given to the client's welfare as it is affected by their family and significant others. Clients are required to change their name legally. They are encouraged to divorce their spouse if they no longer intend to live together. Partners, family, and friends may be interviewed, and clients are offered the chance to attend regular counseling groups. Clients who demonstrate long-term stability for at least two years, at least one year of which has been in full-time employment, are accepted as suitable candidates for GRS. Since the UK National Health Service waiting time for GRS is about three years, many clients seek private surgical arrangements.

The real-life experience is often accompanied by a reduction in anxiety and depression. Some transsexed women seek new partners following surgery, whereas transsexed men tend to stay with their current female partner if they have one. Following surgery, transsexed people often involve themselves in social and community activities and frequently enjoy better relations with their family and friends. They can now escape from a period of relative social isolation during the transition phase. However, satisfactory adjustment does not always occur, especially if the person cannot easily pass in their new gender role.

From 1976 to 1992 the Monash Gender Dysphoria Clinic in Melbourne, Australia, required unequivocal diagnosis of transsexualism, absence of psychiatric illness, single status, average or above average intelligence, at least 21 years of age, and a minimum two-year waiting period. Although successfully applied, these requirements exceed the minimum standards recommended by the SOC. Twenty-nine percent of 697 candidates presenting for evaluation progressed to GRS at an average age of 33 following an average waiting period of 2 years and 7 months. Based on psychiatric interviews, most candidates had an abnormal father relationship during their upbringing, were only-children or firstborn, and had left school before completing the final year. On average, they started cross-dressing when they were eight, began hormone therapy when they were 26, and started living permanently in their new gender role at 43. Most of the transsexed women had cross-dressed without sexual arousal and were now sexually oriented towards men. Many were blue-collar workers and attractively feminine.[36]

The gender clinics in the UK and Australia use stricter guidelines than those recommended by the SOC. Although there have been many reports of successful outcomes, no published data on success rates following GRS from these clinics exists.

After having satisfied a demanding assessment process and five years of full-time living in the opposite gender role, 68 percent of the transsexed women who attended a gender clinic in Sweden had an improved outlook on life, a positive self-image being associated with a successful transition. Only those diagnosed with borderline personality disorder experienced a relatively poor prognosis.[37]

Success in treating clients from the gender clinic in Toronto, Canada, who had experienced distress with their current gender identity was indicated by improved well-being and mood after cross-sex hormone therapy was begun. Following GRS, androphilic transsexed women were more likely to live with a man once they had completed facial electrolysis and had breast implants.[38]

DIAGNOSING GENDER IDENTITY ATYPICALITY IN CHILDREN AND ADOLESCENTS

Advances in the treatment of GIA in young people and adolescents have been made since the 1990s. Children and adolescents with GIA present with a long-term cross-gender identity that becomes more pronounced around puberty. Serious psychopathology must be absent, except for problems caused by living in the unwanted gender role under peer pressure to conform. Such adolescents must function socially without significant problems, as indicated by a supportive family and adequate school performance. The assessment team and family should maintain regular contact, especially if puberty-delaying hormones are used.[39]

Transition during adolescence invokes media and political attention, as illustrated by "Alex," a 13-year-old Australian born as a female who sought medical intervention to delay the development of secondary sex characteristics so that his transition to male upon maturity would be facilitated. Considerable intolerance and misinformation clouded the subsequent political debate on Alex's situation, both in Australia and elsewhere.[40] Legal authorization of appropriate treatment for "Alex" is not without its critics, since all young Australians with GIA who require puberty-delay medication must now have their cases considered by the family court rather than by medical experts as is the case in other countries. As Rachael Wallbank[41] has said:

> The net result of medicine's disorder perception of transsexualism, as expressed through law in *Re Alex*, is to add further delay and doubt, as well as increasing the monetary and personal costs of treatment by making treatment conditional upon the child passing through legal as well as medical gateways; in a predicament where the success of that treatment closely correlates with the promptness of its delivery. The decision turns upon the view that the diagnosis of transsexualism in young people is so unreliable that treatment (and its various stages) should only occur with court approval.

When consolidation of gender identity in a young person has not occurred, and because there is no definitive test for the medical condition of transsexualism, many clinicians warn against the prepubertal administration of cross-sex hormones. However, administering reversible puberty-delaying agents, such as slow-release forms of antagonists or luteinizing hormone-releasing hormone (LHRH) agonists or medroxyprogesterone, from Tanner stage 2 onwards is recommended for certain well-functioning young people. Tanner stage 2 occurs during early puberty when breast budding and pubic hair growth starts in girls and testes enlargement starts in boys. LHRH agonists delay puberty in both boys and girls so that cross-sex hormones may be administered later on if needed. This strategy should only be adopted when appropriate criteria are available to monitor the resulting physical and psychological effects of puberty delay. Such a procedure has the desirable effect of enhancing passability should these young people proceed to GRS as adults.

According to DSM-IV-TR criteria, children and adolescents can be pathologized with GID if they exhibit four or more of the following:

1. Repeatedly stated desire to be, or insistence that he or she is, the other sex.
2. In boys, preference for cross-dressing or simulating female attire; in girls, insistence on wearing only stereotypical masculine clothing.
3. Strong and persistent preferences for cross-sex roles in make-believe play or persistent fantasies of being the other sex.
4. Intense desire to participate in the stereotypical games and pastimes of the other sex.
5. Strong preference for playmates of the other sex.

It is worthwhile noting that these criteria might also apply to children who engage in extensive but normal cross-gendered behavior but do not feel any distress as a consequence.[42]

Kenneth Zucker has criticized the suggestion by Justin Richardson[43] and others that pathologizing "unusual" cross-gendered behavior in children using DSM criteria represents a concealed form of homosexuality prevention. Most gender-atypical boys become homosexual men in later life rather than transsexed women.[44] Diagnosing such children with a mental illness is worrisome when medical interventions might be considered an indirect "cure for homosexuality."

The primary therapeutic aims when treating young people with GIA include their nonjudgmental acceptance; minimizing associated behavioral and emotional difficulties; promoting collaboration among the evaluation team; and enabling the young person and their family to tolerate uncertainty in GIA.[45]

The prevalence of GIA in children lies between .003 percent and 3 percent for boys, and between .001 percent and 1.5 percent for girls. Children older than six or seven avoid expressing their cross-gender desire by either growing out of it or by suppressing their desire due to social stigma. Although the distress associated with GIA increases with age, gender-atypical boys are no different from other children in social and scholastic competence. About 60 percent of gender-atypical children become homosexual or bisexual,

30 percent become heterosexual, and approximately 7 percent become trans-sexed. GRS should be delayed until the child is at least 18 years old.[46]

Peggy Cohen-Kettenis and Friedemann Pfäfflin[47] provide assessment and treatment strategies for GIA in young people. Problems arise when as two-year-olds the children fail to label correctly their own, and other people's, gender. Such children have failed to develop an appropriate gender identity. Young boys insist on wearing female clothing and show no interest in rough-and-tumble play. These boys prefer playing with girls, but as they get older they risk becoming loners when their female playmates decline offers of com-pany, and when other children's bullying and teasing punishes their continuing friendship with girls.

Gender-atypical girls prefer comfortable clothes rather than dressing explicitly in boys' outfits. They often insist on wearing their hair short and avoid jewelry and other adornments. They associate primarily with boys and join in their rough-and-tumble play. In contrast to boys with GIA, these girls are rarely teased by their peers. However, they are distressed at not having a penis, fear the onset of menstruation, and try desperately to urinate in a standing position even by standing against a tree.

It is worthwhile noting that cross-gendered behavior occurs in 6 percent of 4- to 5-year-old boys and in 11.8 percent of 4- to 5-year-old girls. None of this behavior is considered sufficiently troublesome for the child to be referred for professional help.[49]

At adolescence, some gender-atypical children continue to behave like the opposite sex, facilitated by parents and teachers who allow them to attend high school dressed in their preferred clothes and with an opposite-sex name. These young people live full-time as the opposite gender and occasionally manage to have same-sex, or from their point of view, heterosexual friendships. Other children hide their opposite gender preferences from significant others but offer clues such as androgynous dress and appearance. They tend to cross-dress privately, mimicking the typically closeted behavior of adult cross-dressers.

The assessment procedure used in Utrecht, the Netherlands, involves five sessions, in the first of which the child and family are seen together and also separately. By so doing, the interaction between child and family can be observed and the child's cross-gendered behavior history obtained. In later sessions, each parent is interviewed separately to assess child-rearing practices, marital issues, etc.

The child is asked questions such as: "What are your favorite toys? Do you like to dress up? Do you like to take care of babies? If you look in the mirror, are there any parts of your body you are unhappy with? Suppose you weren't born yet and I, the fairy, asked you whether you would like to become a girl or a boy, what would you choose?"[48] Then follows a series of psychological tests such as the Draw-a-Person Test completed by the child, and the Child Behavior

Checklist completed by the parents. Younger children are also observed playing with a variety of toys.[47]

The Gender Identity Questionnaire for Children contains 14 items that are answered by parents covering such topics as the child's playmates, types of toys, role-play, etc. Gender-atypical children referred to a clinic were differentiated from an age-matched comparison group based on the total score on the test.[50]

Unlike the situation with adult clients with GIA, an attempt is made with child and adolescent clients to restore a natal-sex identification using counseling sessions with both the child and family present. For boys, a closer relationship with the father is fostered with some moderation of the commonly close relationship with the mother being attempted. Boys are encouraged to play more with other boys who are not aggressive and unlikely to be bullies. Ambivalent children might readopt their born gender role following such counseling.[47] Since it is more likely that cross-gendered children will become homosexual rather than transsexed, they should not be considered disordered as implied by DSM-IV.[27]

The Portman Institute in London, UK offers medical and psychological services to children and adolescents with GIA, as well as to their family and teachers. Psychosocial management of some intersex conditions and support for children whose parent is transsexed also occur.[51] Previous research in the United States, focused mainly on boys, had indicated that GIA is usually accompanied by behavioral problems, relationship problems with peers and parents, and, most notably, separation anxiety disorder.

Of the 124 clients who attended the Portland Clinic between 1989 and 1998, most were referred when they were 11 years old; 66 percent were boys, 32 percent were girls; and 2 percent were intersexed. Childhood GIA is disruptive to families; the proportion of intact families decreased from 84 percent upon referral to only 36 percent when the child completed the program. As a result, 48 percent of children were living with a single parent.[52]

Five percent of children with GIA were considered transsexed, and the rest were equally likely to become either heterosexual or homosexual. Some children present with complications such as separation anxiety, depression and emotional problems, learning difficulties, and refusal to attend school. Occasionally, GIA is associated with sexual abuse, the risk of suicide increasing in such cases during adolescence. The most common problems reported by young people with GIA involve relationships with parents, caregivers, and peers, depression, family mental and physical health problems, harassment, social isolation, and social anxiety.[49]

The concept of atypical gender identity organization (AGIO) has been proposed to describe the relative stability of young people's gender identity development. An inflexible gender identity results from atypical, possibly traumatic, events early in life that persist throughout childhood and into ado-lescence. Atypical gender identity derives from thought dissociation with feel-ings of persecution resulting from a childhood trauma. If depression is the only negative outcome from such developmental disruption, atypical gender development may respond to psychotherapy. However, puberty-delaying drugs should be considered for children who do not respond to such psychological intervention.[45]

George Rekers[53] proposed that psychotherapy should be used to treat child-hood and adolescent GIA rather than delaying assessment until adulthood when hormone therapy and surgery might be the only alternative. Rekers studied a boy named Wayne who had indulged in feminine play and cross-dressing from an early age. Wayne preferred the company of girls, avoiding contact with boys and any masculine activities. Rekers trained Wayne to play with masculine toys and change his speech habits so that they were more mas-culine. These "desirable" behaviors were reinforced by praise, while any femi-nine behavior was discouraged by forcing the child to be socially isolated and to read involuntarily as punishment.

Although Wayne's previous activity was primarily feminine, the therapy sessions gradually increased the frequency of his masculine play behavior. However, this masculine behavior did not generalize to situations in which no negative reinforcement was applied. So such unethical "brain-washing" did not result in any decrease in feminine activities when the child was alone.

Although most children with GIA who are younger than 12 do not request GRS as adults, those with extreme cross-sex identification from an early age risk devastating psychiatric problems such as depression, anorexia, and social phobia.[54] Their social and intellectual development may also be retarded as a result of their distress. In such severe cases, intervention to delay puberty is an appropriate strategy in preparation for hormone therapy and GRS when the child reaches maturity. By not developing inappropriate secondary sex charac-teristics, these young people will pass better in their affirmed sex.

More stringent eligibility criteria are required for young people com-pared with those for adults with GIA. Several years after surgery, these young people are well adjusted both socially and psychologically, with no regrets being expressed, and their social functioning was rated better than other adults at a similar stage following surgery.[45] A follow-up study of 15 young transsexed men and 7 young transsexed women whose average age was 18 showed that following GRS their gender distress had decreased considerably, their body satisfaction was higher, and their social life and social contacts had improved considerably. There was an increase in extra-version, that is, outgoingness, an increase in self-esteem and dominance, and a decrease in feelings of inadequacy. None of the adolescents had any post-surgical regret.[42]

A 16-year-old girl who sought sex affirmation as male had puberty delayed since the age of 13 using triptorelin, an LHRH-stimulating drug. Cross-sex hormone therapy started at 18, androgen treatment having a rapid effect both physically and psychologically. He felt much more outgoing and friendly. Before long he requested a mastectomy as well as ovarectomy and uterus removal. One year after these surgical interventions he reported no more gender distress. As confirmation of the effectiveness of his medical treatment, no one considered him to be, or have been, female owing to his convincing male presentation. He eventually underwent metoidioplasty, the surgical construction of a small penis from the enlarged clitoris that results from testosterone treatment, with positive results. Pubertal delay involves no irreversible procedures, as normal puberty proceeds should treatment with triptorelin be terminated.[55]

SUMMARY

Assessing GIA is complicated by the occasional presence of accompanying psychiatric conditions such as schizophrenia, which mimic some aspects of GIA. Assessment guidelines distinguish the medical condition of transsexualism from both transvestic fetishism and intersex conditions. There are different assessment requirements for adults and children as well as a default category to accommodate situations such as GIA accompanying an intersex condition. Unfortunately, these assessment proscriptions are not based entirely on published research, so dissension regarding their application exists.

The treatment of transsexualism involves application of the standards of care, a standardized protocol for managing the transition process that has been used successfully in many countries. Assessment and treatment of GIA in children and adolescents is controversial. The need to involve family in the assessment and medical treatments as well as the tendency for only a small proportion of young people to proceed to GRS demands caution when assessing young people with GIA.

Chapter Eight

PHYSIOLOGICAL EFFECTS OF HORMONE THERAPY

THE PHYSIOLOGY OF HORMONE ACTION

Hormones have a powerful effect on the basic physiological processes required for sexual development, growth, metabolism, and a number of other important body functions. Estradiol, a main form of the female hormone estrogen, and testosterone, the male hormone, as well as the stress hormone, cortisol, result from a complex series of chemical reactions starting with cholesterol, a common curse of people with a predisposition for heart disease.[1]

Atypical gender identity development in children may rely on prenatal hormone activity during brain development. For example, mothers who were administered an androgen-based progesterone produce girls who are male-identified, exhibiting tomboy behavior and preferring boys' toys. A similar masculinization occurs in daughters of mothers who took diethylstilbestrol during pregnancy to prevent miscarriage. Fraternal girl twins exhibit slightly more masculine behavior, such as improved spatial ability scores, when they have a male co-twin.[2] Perhaps there is a diffusion of testosterone from the male embryo to the female embryo as occurs in mice litters.[3]

The importance of sex hormones is illustrated when there is a sudden loss of hormone production following gonad removal. Castration in men, for example, produces a decline in sexual behavior with much reduced sexual activity two years afterwards. Rather than producing biological or behavioral effects directly, hormones' effects are mediated by metabolic enzymes, cellular receptors, and circulating binding proteins that facilitate the activity of hormones at the cellular level.[4] Hormones can only have their effects on body processes when appropriate receptors occur in body tissues. For example, a lack of testosterone receptors in people with the rare condition known as androgen insensitivity syndrome results in feminization even when the sex chromosomes are XY, that is, male.

Before puberty, girls and boys have similar estrogen levels. Although estrogen is more prevalent in women and testosterone is more prevalent in men, testosterone can be converted into estrogen as required. The enzyme aromatase converts androgens, such as testosterone, into estrogen. A large number of cells contain both estrogen and aromatase receptors. Aromatase in the placenta protects both the female fetus and the mother from any virilizing effects of testosterone and other androgens. Interestingly, estrogen plays an important role in skeletal maturation following puberty in both males and females, such as during the growth spurt around puberty. Estrogen also features prominently in carbohydrate and fat metabolism. Hypogonadism (smaller than normal gonads in both men and women) produces osteoporosis, a degenerative bone disease, if there are sex-hormone deficiencies. Hormone-replacement therapy is then needed to re-establish proper bone density.[5]

Tissues producing estrogens include the ovaries and testes, the placenta and fetal (but not adult) liver, bone cells, smooth muscle cells, and subcutaneous fatty tissue. Although aromatase expression is equally potent in men and women, in men it occurs mainly in fatty tissue. In women, aromatase activity is at least three times greater in the buttocks and thighs than in the abdomen and breasts. Aromatase effects occur in many regions of the brain. These include the hypothalamus and amygdala, the preoptic nucleus, the sexually dimorphic nucleus, the bed nucleus of the stria terminalis of the hypothalamus, and the medial amygdala, areas of the brain discussed in chapter 2.

There are two forms of estrogen: alpha and beta. In the brain, alpha estrogen receptors tend to occur in the hypothalamus nuclei, whereas beta estrogen receptors occur in the hippocampus and cerebral cortex. Some cancers in men secrete abnormal concentrations of estrogens leading to feminization as a side effect. Estrogens can also produce abnormal prostate gland growth, whereas estrogen deficiency produces decreased bone growth in men and women. In postmenopausal women, large amounts of fatty tissue provide residual estrogen, leading to some protection against osteoporosis.

The prostate gland, which generates seminal fluid in men, relies on testosterone for its proper development. Prostate volume is larger in anabolic-steroid users, and smaller in transsexed women who have been on estrogen therapy for an average of nine years, when compared with an age-matched comparison group. Compared with the latter, the testis in transsexed women is smaller (8 mL vs. 23 mL), total serum testosterone is less (1 nmol/L vs. 16 nmol/L), as also is prostate size (19 mL vs. 28 mL). Such results explain the relative lack of prostate problems in transsexed women.[6]

The pituitary gland, located in the lower-brain region, maintains proper hormonal balance throughout the body. The hypothalamus ensures that such a balance is maintained despite fluctuations in the body's biochemistry. Excess secretion of prolactin, the pituitary hormone responsible for lactation, results in gonadal failure, secondary infertility, and galactorrhea, the secretion of breast milk. Fortunately, pituitary tumors, or prolactinomas, are almost always benign. Since prolactinomas have an abundance of estrogen receptors, they produce elevated estrogen levels. Prolactinomas have been occasionally observed in transsexed women following estrogen therapy.[7]

For example, a pituitary gland lesion was reported in a 32-year-old transsexed woman with Klinefelter syndrome, an intersex condition resulting in feminization. She had undergone bilateral orchidectomy, the surgical removal of both testicles, as well as vaginoplasty, the surgical construction of a vagina during GRS. She had been taking a daily dosage of 1.5 mg of ethinyl estradiol and 150 mg of cyproterone acetate, an antiandrogen. She presented with headaches, weight gain, and general fatigue as well as slight galactorrhea, with her prolactin level more than 20 times the average level. She subsequently underwent surgery to remove a pituitary tumor. This is a rare condition in transsexed women, since no more than 7 percent have blood prolactin levels greater than 50 μg/L.[8]

EFFECTS OF HORMONES ON BODY CHEMISTRY

Estrogen affects blood-clotting ability. During hormone-replacement therapy (HRT), oral ingestion of estrogen reduces the levels of both tissue-type plasminogen activation (tPA) and plasminogen activation inhibitor 1 (PAI-1), leading to a reduced ability to absorb blood clots and an increased risk of thrombosis. The thrombosis risk is reduced when estrogen is administered using a skin patch, since the estrogen then bypasses the liver. Otherwise, about 60 percent of orally administered estrogen needs to be deactivated by the liver. Orally administered estrogen affects the levels of sex-hormone-binding globulin, corticosteroid-binding globulin, growth-hormone-binding protein, insulin-like growth factor I, and angiotensinogen; blood assays of these chemicals provide useful information on the risks associated with HRT.

Hormone-binding globulin attaches itself to hormone molecules and reduces their effectiveness, so hormone effects can be detected. For example, corticosteroid-binding globulin indicates how estrogen affects adrenal gland function, growth-hormone-binding globulin indicates how estrogen affects growth-hormone concentrations, and angiotensinogen is a precursor of angiotensin 1, a hormone responsible for an increase in blood pressure.[9]

For transsexed women receiving oral estrogen, tPA decreases during the first two months of estrogen treatment, after which it remains constant, indicating that estrogen reduces the risk of blood clots. However PAI-1 also decreases during this same period, resulting in reduced prevention of blood clots, a contrary result. For those transsexed women receiving estrogen using a skin patch, no changes from baseline for both tPA and PAI-1 occur, suggesting no increase in blood-clot risk. HDL cholesterol, triglyceride, and sex-hormone binding globulin increase after oral administration of estrogen, but not when skin patches are used. When estrogen is processed by the liver, as occurs with its oral administration, the concentration of fatty substances in the blood increases, an undesirable effect. So skin-patch estrogen administration has advantages.[9]

Oral ethinyl estradiol produces a higher thrombosis risk in transsexed women than do other types of oral estrogen, with the risk greatest when there is no accompanying cyproterone acetate. On the other hand, testosterone administered to transsexed men provides protection against thrombosis.[10]

Blood PAI-1 level decreases with an increase in estrogen level in natal women, whereas PAI-1 level increases with an increase in visceral fat level in both natal men and women. In transsexed women, testosterone; luteinizing hormone (LH), an ovulatory hormone produced by the anterior pituitary gland; follicle-stimulating hormone (FSH), an anterior pituitary hormone that prepares the ovaries (in natal women) for sex-cell production; and all the PA antigens, in particular PAI-1, decrease following cross-sex hormone treatment. Sex-hormone-binding globulin (SHBG) also increases following estrogen treatment. In transsexed men, estrogen, SHBG, and the PA antigens decrease following testosterone therapy.

Although estrogen treatment increases HDL cholesterol and triglycerides, potentially unhealthy fatty substances in the blood, estrogen may have a beneficial effect on atherogenesis, the dangerous buildup of plaques in blood vessels. This results from estrogen's antioxidant properties, which promote the expansion of blood vessels, inhibiting both the narrowing of blood vessels and the formation of blood clots. Although controversial, these beneficial effects suggest that estrogen therapy may reduce the chances of heart disease in transsexed women.

Before starting hormone therapy, fasting insulin levels, triglyceride levels, HDL cholesterol, and the amounts of visceral and abdominal subcutaneous fat in transsexed women are usually high. An initial increase in both PAI-1 and visceral fat are no longer evident after 12 months of cross-sex hormone therapy since oral, but not transdermal, estrogen reduces PAI-1. In transsexed men, HDL cholesterol decreases, as also does total body fat, especially in the abdominal region. So cross-sex hormones offer both advantages and risks that must be carefully considered prior to, and during, hormone therapy.[11]

An increase in intra-abdominal and visceral fat is associated with both an increased risk of cardiovascular disease and an increase in the likelihood of non-insulin-dependent diabetes. Estrogen deficiency is associated with impaired glucose tolerance, leading to insulin resistance. Insulin resistance, a precursor of diabetes, occurs when insufficient insulin is produced to absorb blood sugar after eating.

Increases in both SHBG and fasting insulin level occur following estrogen therapy in transsexed women, indicating that estrogen is a diabetes risk. Testosterone therapy in transsexed men causes an increase in both testosterone and DHT, as well as a decrease in SHBG, leading to a lower diabetes risk. So cross-sex hormone therapy can have opposite effects in transsexed women and men.

Prior to hormone therapy, transsexed men have a higher percentage of body fat than do transsexed women, whereas transsexed women have a greater amount of thigh muscle than do transsexed men. In transsexed women, hormone therapy produces an increase in body weight and subcutaneous body fat, especially in the hips and thighs, but also to a lesser extent in the abdominal region. The progestin action of the antiandrogen cyproterone acetate is responsible for redistributing fat from visceral to lower body regions. Thigh muscle decreases about 10 percent during the first 12 months of combined estrogen and antiandrogen therapy, transsexed women reporting a lower food intake during hormone therapy, possibly to stabilize their weight.

Transsexed men experience an increase in body weight, a decrease in hip circumference, and a corresponding increase in waist-hip ratio. Testosterone decreases abdominal fat and fat located in hips and thighs, but increases visceral fat and thigh muscle volume. A similar redistribution of body fat occurs in post-menopausal women.[12] Long-term estrogen therapy in transsexed women reduces their blood testosterone level to normal female values but has no effect on body shape, the waist-hip ratio being 0.87 for both natal males and transsexed women compared with 0.76 for natal females.

The effects of hormone therapy on body shape in transsexed people is modulated by differences in both body build and hormone levels prior to cross-sex hormone therapy. Compared with transsexed men, natal women have a lower waist-hip ratio (a critical value of 0.84 distinguishes the typical male-female body shape) and a lower waist-girth to body-height ratio. Transsexed men exhibit masculine body features in 6 of 14 body measurement indexes. They also have three times the testosterone level as well as higher levels of androstenedione, an androgen secreted by the adrenal gland, than do natal women. Transsexed men have a more masculine body shape, being somewhat plump with no particular deviations from a typically masculine shape in the shoulder and pelvis, characteristics that help them pass as men.[13]

Leptin regulates food intake and energy expenditure to help people maintain a relatively constant weight. Leptin level and body fat are positively related, with weight loss causing a decrease in leptin level.[14] Before hormone therapy, transsexed men have higher leptin levels than transsexed women do. Blood leptin levels and body fat increase following hormone therapy in transsexed women but decrease by about 60 percent in transsexed men after 12 months of testosterone treatment. The role sex hormones, particularly testosterone, play in body fat distribution is mediated by changes in blood leptin concentrations.[15]

Estrogen therapy prevents bone-density loss in transsexed women, leading to a lower risk of osteoporosis in later life. A decrease in bone-mass density occurs for transsexed men, whereas an increase in bone-mass density occurs in transsexed women, at least prior to removal of the testicles, a procedure known as orchidectomy. Orchidectomy reduces bone-mineral density unless accompanied by estrogen therapy.[16] Bone-mineral density increases steadily in preoperative transsexed women after at least two years of estrogen therapy.[17]

Hormones increase the risk of blood clots, cardiovascular disease, and diabetes, the amount of risk depending on how the hormones are administered. Estrogen therapy in transsexed women is beneficial when it produces higher levels of blood HDL cholesterol, a reduction in visceral fat, increased leptin levels, and a lower bone-loss risk. The effects of testosterone therapy in transsexed men are almost the opposite of those applying to transsexed women, with cardiovascular disease and bone loss being undesirable side effects.

HORMONAL EFFECTS ON HAIR GROWTH

Sex hormones play an important role in determining the hair types and distribution typical of men and women. The surface or epithelial cells of the sebaceous gland, responsible for the secretion of skin oil, as well as the developing cells of the hair follicle contain testosterone receptors. In the skin, testosterone is eventually converted to androstanediol glucuronide (Adiol G), an indicator of peripheral tissue androgen metabolism.

The effect of sex steroids on hair growth and skin oil production in transsexed women and men can be measured by the Ferriman and Gallwey method[18] using a number of skin sites: the lip, chin, chest, upper back, pelvic region, the upper and lower abdomen, arm, the back of the forearm, and the thigh and leg. All hair locations except the upper arm and the back of the forearm are considered androgen-dependent.

Following cross-sex hormone therapy in transsexed women, testosterone, Adiol G, LH, and FSH levels become almost undetectable. Male hair growth decreases from an average Ferriman-Gallwey score of 21 to 10 after 12 months of hormone therapy. The hair diameter decreases after the first 4 months of hormone therapy, after which it remains fairly constant. Hair growth rate and density decrease steadily on both the cheek and upper abdomen. A combination of estrogen and antiandrogen inhibits sebaceous gland activity except that responsible for beard growth. Facial hair width is reduced, but there is no change in facial hair length.

For transsexed men, the average Ferriman-Gallwey score increases from 2 to 16 after 12 months of cross-sex hormone treatment, with fairly rapid hair growth occurring during the first 4 months. The hair growth rate, hair diameter, and density increases steadily over the 12-month period. Some transsexed men develop acne on their face and back.[19]

HORMONE EFFECTS ON THE IMMUNE RESPONSE

Sex hormones affect the immune response, as evidenced by the greater incidence of autoimmune diseases such as rheumatoid arthritis in women, resulting from changes in white blood cell activity. Estrogen therapy in females, or castration in males, produces an increase in autoantibody levels, leading to an increased risk of autoimmune disease. The white blood cell count increases in transsexed women after four months of hormone therapy, whereas there is no such change in transsexed men. There is a decrease in natural killer cells as well as in immunoglobulin E levels in transsexed women after 12 months of hormone treatment, indicating decreased immunity accompanied by an increased proneness to female autoimmune disorders.[20]

The combination of estrogen and antiandrogen produces an increase in blood cortisol level leading to an enhanced stress response in transsexed women. Free cortisone excretion, a stress-related effect, increases in transsexed women, whereas no change in cortisol level occurs for transsexed men.[21]

HORMONE EFFECTS ON CARDIOVASCULAR FUNCTION

Nitric oxide plays an important role in reducing the risk of cardiovascular disease for those taking estrogen supplements, including transsexed women.[22] Antiandrogen treatment produces an increase in nitric oxide, a desirable outcome for cardiovascular disease prevention.[23]

High estrogen dosage levels in transsexed women increase brachial artery dilation when compared with natal men. The risk of cardiovascular disease is further reduced in transsexed women by estrogen's effect in reducing blood total homocysteine (tHcy) by about 30 percent. Lower levels of tHcy reduce the likelihood of blood clotting, a risk factor for cardiovascular disease. By contrast, there is an increase in tHcy levels by about 17 percent in transsexed men, increasing their risk of cardiovascular disease.[24] These changes in homocysteine levels are beneficial for transsexual women but hazardous for transsexed men.

The change in tHcy levels is positively related to changes in blood creatinine, a waste product of kidney action, for transsexed woman, and in albumin, a blood component required for proper fluid flow across cell membranes, for all men and women.[25] Oral and skin-patch estrogen are equally effective in maintaining low levels of homocysteine in transsexed women. Since estrogen decreases the concentrations of vitamins B_6 and B_{12}, dietary supplements should be considered during estrogen therapy.[26]

After four months of cross-sex hormone therapy in transsexed women, reductions occur in arterial diameter for both the brachial and femoral arteries, and in the compliance coefficient, an indicator of blood vessel wall flexibility. These effects are accompanied by an increase in heart rate. The initial increase in blood vessel stiffness decreases gradually during the first 12 months of estrogen therapy. These changes are affected by fasting insulin level, an increase in arterial stiffness with increased insulin levels occurring for transsexed women but a decrease in arterial stiffness occurring for transsexed men. The temporary increase in arterial stiffness in natal men and transsexed women undergoing high-dose estrogen therapy imposes a risk for those with prostate cancer and current heart problems. On the other hand, testosterone treatment for transsexed men does not affect blood vessel stiffness to the same extent.[27]

Endothelial cells on blood vessel walls regulate blood pressure and flow. Elevated blood levels of endothelin, a hormone that affects smooth muscle action, is a precursor of myocardial infarction and a cardiovascular complication of diabetes. Blood endothelin levels are higher in men than in women and are lower still in pregnant women due to higher levels of estrogen and progesterone during pregnancy. After four months of cross-sex hormone treatment, there is an increase in endothelin levels for transsexed men, whereas endothelin levels decrease for transsexed women. Although this finding indicates a reduced cardiovascular risk for transsexed women, high blood pressure remains a risk from estrogen therapy for about 2 percent of transsexed women.[28]

Long-term estrogen therapy in transsexed women produces greater endothelium-dependent and nitroglycerine-induced blood vessel dilation than in natal men. Although administering testosterone to transsexed men produces no change in endothelium-dependent blood vessel dilation, it decreases nitroglycerine-induced blood vessel dilation when compared with natal women. Endothelin-1, which stimulates smooth muscle function in blood vessels, increases in transsexed women in response to combined estrogen and antiandrogen treatment. By contrast, endothelin-1 is low in natal women, lowering their risk of blood vessel constriction. Although cross-sex hormone therapy in transsexed women enhances cardiovascular function, an opposite effect occurs for transsexed men.[29]

The percentage change in brachial artery diameter is greater for both transsexed women and natal woman than it is for men. Also, blood vessel dilation in response to nitroglycerin capsules being placed under the tongue is greater in both transsexed and natal women than it is for men. Triglyceride concentrations are greater and low-density lipoprotein cholesterol particle size, a possible coronary risk factor in men, is less for transsexed women than for natal men and women. So estrogen therapy provides cardiovascular benefits for transsexed women, although the increased blood vessel volume in transsexed women might also be due to androgen suppression rather than the increase in estrogen level.[30] The enhancement in arterial reactivity following long-term estrogen therapy is 222 percent for endothelium-dependent artery dilation and 145 percent for nitroglycerine-dependent artery dilation. Estrogen therapy also has a beneficial antioxidant effect on blood vessels.[31]

The risk of stroke increases in transsexed women on estrogen therapy. For example, a 46-year-old transsexed woman undergoing estrogen therapy suffered a dense left-side paralysis caused by a large stroke in the right hemisphere of the brain.[32] So far, only three such cases have been reported in the medical literature, suggesting that stroke risk is low during cross-sex hormone therapy.

The beneficial effect of estrogen therapy on cardiovascular function in transsexed women mimics that observed in natal women. This is achieved by lower levels of risk factors such as homocysteine, blood vessel stiffness, and endothelin level. Since most transsexed women also employ an antiandrogen, the latter's possibly beneficial effect on cardiovascular function is difficult to differentiate from that of estrogen. An antiandrogen might increase nitric oxide levels, leading to enhanced cardiovascular function.

HORMONE THERAPY AND FERTILITY

Cross-sex hormone therapy has deleterious effects on fertility, and most transsexed women become infertile after just six successive months of treatment. Infertility can occur even earlier in transsexed men.

Estrogen inhibits the effects of luteinizing hormone-releasing hormone (LHRH) and luteinizing hormone (LH) and reduces the number of LH or human chorionic gonadotropin (hCG) receptors in the testes, these being responsible for the production of sperm cells. Consequently, testicular activity is suppressed relatively rapidly within two to four weeks after commencing estrogen therapy. Transsexed women should have their sperm harvested and preserved by freezing prior to starting hormone therapy. Transsexed men should also consider ovarian tissue banking or embryo freezing if that is appropriate. Ovarian tissue preservation can be performed even after testosterone therapy has begun but most conveniently during oophorectomy, the surgical removal of the ovaries. Egg cell banking is not recommended due to the poor cell survival rate.[33]

Ethical considerations associated with the transsexed person's ability to reproduce using previously frozen sperm and embryos must be considered.

For some observers, the possibly deleterious psychological effects of the transition process might make raising a child a difficult prospect. However, there should be no difficulties provided the person adjusts well to their transition. Children with one transsexed parent usually develop normally and engage in a predominantly heterosexual lifestyle. So transsexed people must not be disqualified from assisted-reproduction programs.[34]

An Internet survey of transgendered/transsexed women revealed that about 40 percent, most often older people, had children from a previous relationship. Of those with no children, 40 percent would like to have a child and 40 percent reported that they would not. Of those with children, 50 percent did not want any more children, whereas 40 percent would like more children. Heterosexual transsexed women who wanted children preferred sperm donors, whereas lesbian transsexed women preferred to use their own sperm. Although at least 90 percent were not concerned about losing their fertility, 77 percent recommended that advice on sperm freezing be given to all transsexed women before hormone therapy begins. Of those under 40, 67 percent would have preferred to have frozen their sperm, whereas only 35 percent of those over 40 would have done so.[35] Since some transsexed people desire a traditional family life that includes children, we must anticipate this possibility by preserving reproductive tissue whenever possible.

HORMONE EFFECTS IN TRANSSEXED MEN

Hormone effects in transsexed men involve complications that require special attention. Some transsexed men have menstrual irregularities, mild hirsutism (excessive body hair growth), and polycystic ovaries in which the follicles fail to ovulate, leading to cysts that expand within the ovary. Transsexed men have higher levels of both testosterone and androstenedione, a testosterone derivative originating in the adrenal gland, than do natal women. Most transsexed men exhibit dysregulated production of ovarian steroids from the adrenal gland, a condition that occurs for very few natal women.[36] After three years of testosterone therapy, visceral fat in transsexed men increases by 47 percent. There is a 13 percent increase in thigh muscle bulk after one year of therapy.[37]

On a positive note, transsexed men are often better adjusted both socially and psychologically than transsexed women, since testosterone therapy provides a distinctively male appearance. This is evidenced by a deepening of the voice, the growth of body and facial hair, changes in skin texture, a reduction in subcutaneous fat, a redistribution of fat in the male direction, and frequently, male pattern baldness. Although transsexed men are often smaller in stature, they are seldom perceived as being visibly different from natal men.

Androgens and estrogens are involved in human bone metabolism, with the sex hormones found in bone cells for both men and women. Oophorectomy, the surgical removal of the ovaries, in transsexed men produces an estrogen deficiency that is associated with an increased risk of bone-mass depletion. Transsexed men who have had testosterone therapy but have not had their ovaries removed have a larger bone-mass density than those who have only had their ovaries removed. The latter have a similar bone-mass density to natal women. Postoperative transsexed men who are not on regular androgen therapy have lower bone-mass density than those who maintain androgen therapy, highlighting the benefits of androgens in preventing osteoporosis, a degenerative bone disease. Calcium supplementation can also be useful for those people who suffer bone loss.[38]

Prostate specific antigen (PSA), a blood indicator of prostate cancer when recorded at high levels, is also produced by female tissues, especially the breast, ovaries, and endometrium. Androgens enhance PSA's effects. PSA concentrations as well as urinary human glandular kallikrein (hK2) increase after 12 months of testosterone therapy in transsexed men. hK2 is expressed in the prostate in natal men as well as in breast cancer cells. The increase in PSA is most likely due to testosterone's effect on breast tissue.[39]

Potential complications arising from hormone therapy in transsexed men include excessive blood concentration of adrenal gland androgens, lower bone-mass density, and a higher level of PSA when compared with natal women. These effects illustrate the powerful influence of cross-sex hormone therapy on body functions.

SUMMARY

The physiology of hormone action provides useful information on the close biochemical affinity between the male and female sex hormones. It is not surprising that testosterone, for example, can be aromatized to form estrogen even in men, especially in fatty tissues. To better understand hormone effects on transsexed people, one must consider the responses of brain and other tissues to estrogen and testosterone, the role of the hypothalamic-pituitary-adrenal axis, and the differential effects of hormones on fat distribution, bone structure, and prostate gland function. Hormone therapy has differential effects on hair growth, the immune response, and cardiovascular function.

Chapter Nine

HORMONE THERAPY

Once a diagnosis of the medical condition of transsexualism has been made, most candidates for sex affirmation commence cross-sex hormone therapy, being prescribed estrogen for transsexed women and testosterone for transsexed men. According to the standards of care (SOC), the prerequisites for hormone therapy include being at least 18 years old, knowing about the health and social risks of hormone therapy, and having had at least three months of prior counseling. Occasionally, hormone therapy can be introduced almost immediately when a prior history of illicit hormone usage necessitates close medical supervision. Hormone treatment must only occur under medical supervision, preferably by an experienced endocrinologist.

Prior to starting hormone therapy, the client must undergo a full medical examination. Contraindications include a history of high blood pressure, heart disease, heavy cigarette smoking, and drug use. Most responsible medical advisors will not offer hormone therapy to those at risk, as the likelihood of a lethal pulmonary embolism is too great. In these cases, as well as for men over 40, estrogen administration using a skin patch (transdermal) is recommended.[1]

The positive effects of hormone therapy do not occur quickly but take two years or more to develop. In transsexed women, the desirable effects of estrogen therapy include breast growth, a redistribution of some body fat to the hips to more closely approximate a female shape, a decrease in upper body strength, a softening of the skin, a decrease in body hair, and a reduction in scalp hair loss. There is usually a decrease in libido, a reduction in testicle size, and a loss of spontaneous erections.

The medical risks include an increase in the possibility of blood clotting, the development of benign pituitary tumors, infertility, weight gain, liver disease, the formation of gallstones, high blood pressure, and diabetes. Fortunately, these are rare complications that can be prevented by regular medical monitoring of lipids, blood pressure, cholesterol, and blood sugar content. The medical advisor and client need to be aware of these risks and maintain regular contact.

Breast development starts almost immediately after cross-sex hormone therapy begins, followed by alternating periods of growth and quiescence.[1] Since androgens, such as testosterone, have an inhibitory effect on breast formation, estrogens are most effective when the testosterone level is low. This is achieved by administering antiandrogens such as cyproterone acetate or spironolactone. Breast development is satisfactory in 40–50 percent of clients, the remainder considering breast implants to enhance their feminine appearance. In a study of 69 transsexed women the average breast hemicircumference, the distance from one side of the breast to the other measured across the central section of the breast, increased from the male size of 3 cm to 15 cm after 18 months of estrogen therapy. Breast size stabilized after 18 months of hormone therapy.[2]

In a somewhat dated study, hormonal treatment regimes for transsexed people were surveyed in 20 gender centers, almost all of which treated both transsexed women and men. Six of the centers reduced the hormone dosage following gonadectomy, or GRS. Some centers used a progesterone supplement such as medroxyprogesterone, a combination no longer favored due to its deleterious side effects.[3]

Cyproterone acetate, an antiandrogen frequently employed in the UK and Europe but not in North America, is a progestin with marked antiandrogenic and antigonadotrophic properties. It decreases the blood levels of both high-density lipid (HDL) and low-density lipid (LDL) cholesterol. Since LDL cholesterol is a risk factor for heart disease due to its tendency to clog arteries, such a reduction is beneficial. However, the reduction in HDL cholesterol deprives the circulatory system of protection against potential atherosclerosis. Nevertheless, the reduction in HDL cholesterol is counteracted by an increase due to the effects of estrogen. Cyproterone acetate produces rapid feminization within three to five months without the need for larger estrogen dosages. The testicles are reduced in size, and testosterone levels reach those typical of natal women. However, cyproterone acetate can lead to depression and fatigue and is toxic to the liver in large dosages.[4] Although extended antiandrogen usage reduces testosterone level and libido, it does not necessarily interfere with a transsexed woman's ability to achieve a full erection.

Clients should be warned that some effects of estrogen, such as breast development, are irreversible upon discontinuation of the treatment. Also, estrogen has no effect on the male voice and musculature nor does it reduce facial hair growth, so ancillary treatments such as speech therapy and electrolysis are required to enhance passability. Interestingly, estrogen might lower the risk of Alzheimer's disease in transsexed women with elevated estrogen levels.[5]

The benefits of testosterone in transsexed men, administered every two weeks via a 250 mg Sustanon injection,[6] include a deepening of the voice, enlargement of the clitoris, an increase in body and facial hair, and male pattern baldness for those with a genetic predisposition. There is reduced fat in the hips, an increase in upper body strength, weight gain, and a dramatic increase in libido. On the negative side, fertility is reduced, acne occurs on both the face and back, and there is an increased risk of heart and liver disease. Transsexed men are also at risk of osteoporosis unless calcium supplements are taken.

After testosterone therapy begins, transsexed men experience an increase in clitoris sensitivity after about 9 days on average of testosterone therapy, clitoris growth after 22 days, a decrease in voice pitch after 23 days, and beard growth after 42 days. Transsexed men experience weight gain on average after 32 days, less body fat and increased muscular development after 35 days, and an increase in body hair after 42 days. Physical hormone effects occur faster in transsexed men than in transsexed women, resulting in a convincing opposite-sex appearance when compared with transsexed women feminized over a similar time period.[7] From both the emotional and social points of view, hormone therapy is beneficial for transsexed people, who generally experience relief from any distress they previously experienced, including a decrease in any pretreatment depression.

A short-term trial of low-dosage hormones is useful as a confirmatory evaluation of the medical condition of transsexualism. Clients who are not transsexed will suffer from an undesirable decrease in libido soon after starting hormone therapy. Perhaps these people are more accurately classified in terms of DSM diagnostic criteria as experiencing transvestic fetishism. They will stop taking hormones once they realize the deleterious effect on their sexual activity. People whose distress increases following hormone treatment might have a psychiatric problem such as borderline personality disorder, or else may not be transsexed. In such cases, hormone treatment can be terminated relatively safely after three months without irreversible side effects.[6]

The dramatic effects of cross-sex hormone therapy simulate those experienced during puberty by natal persons of the same sex. However, some body features cannot be changed, such as the skeletal structure in natal men. Other secondary sex features can be changed with difficulty and expense, such as removal of breasts, ovaries, and the womb in transsexed men, and facial hair removal and acquisition of a feminine voice for transsexed women.

RISKS ASSOCIATED WITH HORMONE THERAPY

Although the risks of hormone therapy are not usually life threatening, the endocrinologist should be aware of possible complications and explain these to the client prior to her consenting to hormone therapy. Estrogen therapy produces increases in prolactin level and elevated concentrations of liver enzymes. Androgen deprivation in transsexed women results in dry skin and brittle nails, whereas acne is an undesirable side effect of hormone therapy in transsexed men. Despite such problems, hormone therapy is reasonably safe for both transsexed women and men.

The mortality of transsexed women is no different from that of the general population except for an increased suicide risk for the 25–39 age group. There is also a higher incidence of AIDS irrespective of age. There is a 20-fold increase in the risk of venous thromboembolism, the risk being greatest during the first year of treatment.[8] Venous thrombosis and pulmonary embolism occur in from 2 percent to 6 percent of transsexed women treated with oral estrogens, its incidence being even less at 0.5 percent for life-threatening conditions. Thromboembolisms have an incidence of 2.1 percent in transsexed women younger than 40 but a greater incidence of 12 percent for those over 40.[9] Transsexed women in the over-forty age group as well as those with cardiovascular risk factors should be treated with skin-patch estrogens for which the thrombosis risk is low. The thromboembolism risk may decrease slightly with long-term estrogen use.[6] Even fewer transsexed women suffer from thrombophlebitis, a blood clot associated with inflammation of the vein wall, and arterial embolism.[1]

Estrogen therapy can cause potentially adverse effects on liver function as well as mild elevations in transaminases, chemicals involved in amino acid metabolism. One transsexed woman who suffered an autoimmune form of hepatitis provided an example of the potentially adverse effect of estrogen on liver function.[10] Liver function should be monitored every two months initially until the estrogen dose is stable; thereafter, a check every six months is sufficient.

Long-term hormone therapy increases the risk of hyperprolactemia, a disorder of the pituitary gland that results in an excess secretion of prolactin. This condition occurs in up to 50 percent of transsexed women after at least five years of estrogen therapy.[11] When recommended estrogen dosages are used, there is a negligible risk of developing pituitary tumors.

Only in transsexed women for whom progestogenic chemical castration is combined with feminizing estrogen therapy will full sac and lobe breast structures be formed. Hence, combined progestogenic antiandrogens and estrogens are necessary for the male breast to mimic the natural structure of the female breast. Orchidectomy, the surgical removal of the testicles, does not contribute beneficially to this process. Thirteen percent of transsexed women develop breast milk, and a third experience a decrease in blood hemoglobin, leading to the risk of anemia.[11]

In a rare case, a 41-year-old transsexed women developed breast cancer following orchidectomy, vaginoplasty, and augmentation mammoplasty, these surgeries having occurred 19 years previously when she was 22. During the intervening years she had been treated with cyproterone acetate (50 mg/daily) and ethinyl estradiol (100μgm/daily), a combination that produces breast development similar to that of a natal woman. There is a small cancer risk for transsexed women who develop full acini and lobular breast tissue when taking the progestogenic antiandrogen cyproterone acetate. Breast cancer was also noted in a 69-year-old man who was prescribed spironolactone as a supplementary drug to treat a prostate disorder.[12]

About 4 percent of transsexed women over 40 risk acquiring type 2 diabetes, since feminizing hormone therapy increases body weight and fat. This is about three times the U.S. average for the disorder. All such diabetes sufferers tend to be obese, with high blood pressure and excessive triglyceride levels.[13] Estrogen reduces the risk of prostate cancer in most transsexed women. However, a 63-year-old transsexed woman, following ten years of treatment with ethinyl estradiol and cyproterone acetate, developed prostate cancer after having undergone GRS.[14]

Hormone therapy might be responsible for a larger incidence of migraine headaches in transsexed women. The incidence of 26 percent is similar to that occurring in natal women but is substantially greater than the 8 percent observed for natal men.[15]

The risk associated with hormone therapy for transsexed people is not great. Except for a greater likelihood of thromboembolism in middle-aged transsexed women, transsexed people's mortality rate is no different from that of the general population. There is a slightly elevated risk of diabetes as well as hyperprolactemia in transsexed women, afflictions that can be controlled by careful monitoring by a clinical endocrinologist. Breast cancer is a serious but rare complication for transsexed women.

PSYCHOLOGICAL EFFECTS OF HORMONES

In adults, high levels of testosterone are associated with antisocial behavior, greater risk-taking, and poorer mental and physical health outcomes. In men, individual differences in testosterone levels are associated with dominance, aggression, violent crime, antisocial personality disorder, and negative emotionality and depression. The higher the level of testosterone, the greater the propensity to respond aggressively to threats, to dominate peer relationships, and to exhibit aggressive-destructive and sexual behavior.

Girls with higher levels of testosterone report high levels of depression, engage in more frequent masculine play, show a greater interest in sexual behavior during adolescence, and are more resistant to parental attempts to encourage feminine behavior. Interestingly, both low and high testosterone levels are associated with low levels of mood, there being an inverted-U relationship between testosterone level and mood. This implies that elevated mood is more likely to occur with moderate testosterone levels.

The positive effect of testosterone on risky behavior and its negative effect on depression are moderated by the quality of parent-child relationships, testosterone-related adjustment problems being less evident when there are good parent-child relationships. So social context moderates hormone effects on behavior.[16] On the other hand, high estrogen levels produce an increase in serotonin, leading to a reduction in depressive symptoms and an increase in well-being.

EFFECTS OF HORMONES ON COGNITIVE TASK PERFORMANCE

Since small gender differences exist in abilities such as verbal fluency, favoring women, and in spatial tasks, favoring men, perhaps cross-sex hormones produce performance changes in these gender-dependent cognitive tasks. Gender differences in personality and in cognitive performance measured before, and three months after, the administration of cross-sex hormones to transsexed men and women were evaluated. Comparison groups contained natal men and women who were not transsexed.[17]

Natal women scored highest on anger proneness as well as on various forms of anger expression, whereas natal men performed best on anger control. Transsexed women scored low on assault and irritability and were better able to postpone any anger they might have. By contrast, anger proneness increased over the first three months of hormone therapy for transsexed men. Feelings of sexual interest and arousability increased for transsexed men but decreased considerably for transsexed women.

Transsexed women exhibited greater verbal fluency at the end of the three months of hormone therapy, but there were no sex differences in spatial ability, as measured by the rotated-figures test in which people determine if two visual objects can be rotated to coincide. Transsexed women attributed more feminine behaviors to themselves than did the other groups, a finding evident before hormone therapy began.

Transsexed women reported more variable mood fluctuations over the three months of hormone therapy than did transsexed men. By contrast, transsexed women and transsexed men scored equally high on cheerfulness, liveliness, and feelings of satisfaction, with no evidence of depression for any of the participants. Overall, transsexed people did not differ in any important ways from natal people of their own sex.

An increase in testosterone level produces a decrease in verbal memory, which occurs for most people within two weeks of starting testosterone therapy. In men, the higher the concentration of follicle-stimulating hormone (FSH), the lower their ability on spatial tasks. Low concentrations of testosterone relative to estrogen are associated with poorer performance on spatial tasks.[18]

Transsexed people's verbal memory ability is similar to that of their affirmed sex rather than their birth-sex. The effect of estrogen therapy on cognitive function in transsexed women has generated conflicting findings, sometimes producing an improvement in verbal ability, sometimes not. Maybe there are differences between homosexual and nonhomosexual transsexed people in the way estrogen affects their performance on cognitive tasks.

A study of cognitive differences resulting from cross-sex hormone therapy was conducted using right-handed transsexed men and women who reported either a homosexual or heterosexual sexual orientation. The transsexed participants were tested one week before the start of hormone treatment and again fourteen weeks later. Natal women were tested either three to five days after their menstrual period or from seven to ten days before the next menstrual period had begun to control for hormonal differences during the month. The tests used to measure cognitive abilities included a verbal reasoning test, a line orientation test with good gender-difference discrimination ability, a two-dimensional rotated-figures test with moderate gender-difference discrimination ability, a three-dimensional rotated-figures test with good gender-difference discrimination ability, as well as the three-dimensional rotated-figures same-different test and a targeted throwing task, both with high gender-difference discrimination ability. Although no individual differences were found on the verbal reasoning and two-dimensional rotated-figures tests, the other tests revealed some gender differences.[19]

For the line orientation and targeted-throwing tests, natal males performed better than the other groups, implying that transsexed women were similar to both transsexed men and natal women on these tasks. Men performed better than women on the three-dimensional and same-difference rotated-figures tests, but there was no difference between transsexed women and natal males on these tests. There was also no effect of hormone treatment on visual-spatial ability for transsexed women when their scores were compared with those of natal males. Hormones had little effect on spatial ability in homosexual transsexed men. So, cross-sex hormone therapy has little effect on cognitive behavior.[19] Although estrogen might improve verbal fluency in transsexed women, three months is too brief a period to reveal any substantial cognitive change.

EFFECTS OF HORMONES ON THE EMOTIONS

Sex hormones influence emotional behavior in four different ways. First, sex hormones initiate behavior change in puberty, when attraction and emotional attachment to other people are desired. Second, sex hormones produce changes in brain receptors that indirectly cause mood changes by controlling the secretion of neurotransmitters such as serotonin, a brain regulator. Under such heightened levels of emotionality, a higher emotional sensitivity might produce irritation when negative life events occur, or well-being following positive life events. Third, metabolic processes can be modulated by sex hormones leading to mood changes. Finally, sex hormones directly influence the hypothalamus and the hippocampus of the brain, the areas involved in the emotional interpretation of sensory information.[7]

After three months of cross-sex hormone treatment, the sex-hormone levels of transsexed people lie in a range typical of persons of the opposite natal sex. After the start of hormone treatment and during the real-life experience (RLE), the emotional stability of transsexed women increases, a process that continues after GRS in most cases. This emotional readjustment is accompanied by decreases in both depression and anxiety, a direct result of estrogen therapy. In general, those transsexed people who have completed GRS are more content than those who are still undergoing the RLE, while the latter are in turn more emotionally stable than those transsexed people who have not yet begun hormone therapy.

Occasionally, shortly after hormone therapy begins, transsexed women experience increased feelings of emotional fragility and depression. This effect results from a rapid rise in estrogen levels during the early stages of hormone usage. In general, transsexed women tend to report more mood swings than do transsexed men, the peak effect occurring during the second month of hormone therapy. After stabilization, transsexed women experience an emotional adjustment to estrogen leading to less-extreme mood fluctuations.

Comparisons of expectations before and actual experienced feelings after a 14-week period of hormone therapy reveal changes in positive emotions as well as in both aggressive and sexual feelings for both transsexed men and women. Transsexed women experience more positive emotions, and transsexed men experience more aggressive and sexual feelings, than they had expected prior to starting hormone therapy. Transsexed women experience an increase in emotional intensity while transsexed men experience less emotionality over the 14-week period. Transsexed women demonstrate an increase in emotional expressiveness over time while transsexed men remain relatively stable.[7]

Both transsexed women and men change their mood in accordance with their expectations of experiencing feelings such as depression, tiredness, tenseness, and changeability. Transsexed women experience these and other negative emotions such as powerlessness, disappointment, and sadness more intensely than do transsexed men, both before and after 14 weeks of hormone therapy. Only transsexed women experience a higher than expected increase in positive emotions such as "easy to get on with," relaxation, and activity. This positive change during combined antiandrogen and estrogen treatment in transsexed women results in higher levels of positive emotions such as happiness and liveliness. For transsexed women, other aspects of emotional behavior, such as nonverbal emotional expressiveness, also increase over the period of hormone therapy.[7]

The emotional effect of hormones, whether as a general calming and initiation of well-being in transsexed women or else an increase in aggressive feelings for transsexed men, is a clear psychological sign that the transition is well underway. Although an increase in positive emotions is predicted by some transsexed women even before they start hormone therapy, others experience unexpected positive effects such as an increase in nonverbal emotional expressiveness. Sometimes transsexed women find crying difficult to control even after a few weeks of hormone usage. Although this would be the expected emotional response for those transsexed people who are experiencing difficulties in their transition, such traumatic events as loss of family, friends, and a job are also likely triggers of the feeling of helplessness that is responsible for emotional release.

SUMMARY

Once the medical condition of transsexualism has been diagnosed, the most common consequence is treatment with cross-sex hormones, estrogen, and an antiandrogen for transsexed women and testosterone for transsexed men. Over the next two years or so, hormone therapy promotes the development of some secondary sex characteristics of the assigned sex such as breast development and softer skin in transsexed women, and a deeper voice and facial and body hair in transsexed men. These body developments are accompanied by a complete reversal of sex hormone blood concentrations and, in most cases, feelings of well-being and achievement. For most transsexed people, acquiring secondary sex characteristics facilitates passing in their new gender role.

Despite these advantages, there are medical risks associated with hormone therapy such as thromboembolism, liver damage, and diabetes in transsexed women, and cardiovascular disease, bone-density loss, and acne in transsexed men. These complications can be minimized by regular monitoring by an experienced clinical endocrinologist and by maintaining a healthy lifestyle. Precautions required before starting hormone therapy, the risks associated with long-term hormone usage, and special issues of concern to transsexed men who are undergoing testosterone therapy are important considerations. Although hormone therapy has a minimal effect on cognitive-task performance in transsexed people, the emotional response can be quite dramatic, especially during the early stages of estrogen therapy in transsexed women.

Chapter Ten

SURGICAL PROCEDURES

For most transsexed people, genital reconstruction surgery (GRS) to more closely approximate the genital appearance of their affirmed sex is the final procedure in a long transition process. For many, it is a prerequisite for a new sex life and the fulfillment of a lifelong dream. Surgical techniques, especially for transsexed women, have advanced considerably over the last few decades, yielding results that are almost indistinguishable in appearance, and to some extent in function, from that of natal women.[1] The surgical results for transsexed men are not quite so impressive due to problems in constructing a functional penis. Nevertheless, technical advances continue so that surgical improvements for transsexed men can be expected.

The importance of GRS to the transsexed person is highlighted by the statement that "[d]emanding sex change [*sic*] is therefore part of what constructs the subject as a transsexual; it is the mechanism through which transsexuals come to identify themselves under the sign of transsexualism and construct themselves as its subjects."[2] Once surgery has been successfully completed, transsexuality reflects sexual normativity, and transsexed people can then start enjoying a normal life.

Before GRS can be contemplated, transsexed people are subjected to close medical supervision to ensure that their social, sexual, psychological, and employment status remains stable throughout their real-life experience. For the majority of those who undergo GRS, the outcome is positive. The incidence of postoperative regret is generally low, less than 1 percent for transsexed men and from 1 percent to 1.5 percent for transsexed women.[3] A regret rate as low as 0.1 percent for transsexed women has been observed in Germany.[4]

GRS is occasionally sought by transvestites over 40 who no longer experience erotic relief from their cross-dressing but who have been diagnosed with secondary transsexualism. GRS requests also come from clients who have suffered traumatic life experiences. The best prerequisites for successful GRS are mental and emotional stability, being younger than 30, undergoing a real-life experience lasting at least a year, and adopting a heterosexual lifestyle in one's affirmed sex, that is, a transsexed woman seeking a male partner and a transsexed man seeking a female partner. The minimum total consultation time prior to surgery, including prior counseling, is about three years.[5] However, some people are able to fast-track the process in not much more than one year.

During an earlier period, when the surgical procedures were not as sophisticated as they are today, a 70 percent satisfaction rate for transsexed women who had undergone GRS was typical.[6] Negative prognostic factors for GRS mainly relate to psychological dysfunction, family background, sexual orientation, disrupted social contacts, insufficient professional support during the "real-life test," and complications following surgery.[7] GRS is not a panacea for all transsexed women, especially when masculinization of the face and torso make passing as a woman difficult.[8] For such people, hormone therapy rather than surgery might be sufficient to relieve the distress of living one's life in the "wrong" sex.

The irreversibility of GRS requires a thorough medical and psychological evaluation to ensure that the transsexed person's motivation for GRS is based on their persistent need for such surgery rather than it being merely a whim. Nevertheless, those who manage well during their transition before surgery also manage well afterwards. Caution is required for those who exhibit medical and psychological problems prior to surgery, since their social adjustment after surgery might also be correspondingly poor.[9]

GENITAL RECONSTRUCTION SURGERY FOR TRANSSEXED WOMEN

The surgical procedures required to transform the male genitals into their female equivalent are complex. In this section, details of surgical innovations are described, together with some representative outcomes from currently available procedures. Information about individual surgeons and their procedures are contained in the appendix.

Similarities in the mature male and female external genitals at birth, such as the penis in males and clitoris in females, and differences, such as the closed scrotum in males and the opened labia in females, provide both the initial conditions and end-points for successful GRS in transsexed men and women.

A detailed description is now provided of one GRS procedure for transsexed women that forms a vagina (vaginoplasty) using both penile skin and a urethral flap.[10] The operation proceeds by first performing bilateral orchidectomy, the removal of both testicles, followed by the dissection of the penis into its anatomical components, the corpora cavernosa, which contains erectile tissue, the glans cap at the head of the penis together with the urethra, which carries urine, the neurovascular bundle, and the vascularized outer skin of the penis with its blood supply retained. The corpora cavernosa is then removed all the way to where it meets the pelvic bones, any remnants being destroyed to prevent erectile tissue from interfering with sexual intercourse postoperatively. The dorsal, or rear, part of the glans—the sensitive part of the penis—is used to form a clitoris, whereas the ventral half is relocated at the base of the vagina to form a cervix. The ventral, or front, half of the glans contains the urethra and urethra skin flap, whereas the dorsal half remains innervated by the neurovascular bundle for maximum sensitivity. The first part of the procedure is shown in Figure 10.1.

Figure 10.1
The Initial Stages of the GRS Procedure for Transsexed Women Leading to the Formation of a Neoclitoris, as well as Urethral and Penile Skin Flaps

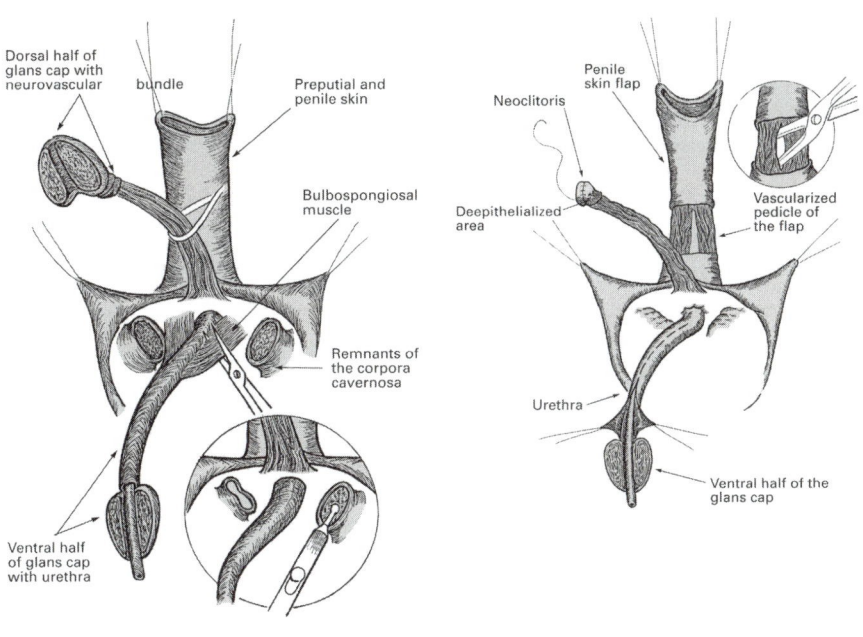

Source: Perovic, S.V., Stanojevic, D.D., and Djordjevic, M.L.J., (2000). Vaginoplasty in male transsexuals using penile skin and a urethral flap. *BJU International* 86:843–850.

As shown in Figure 10.2, the next part of the GRS procedure involves spatulating, that is, dissecting and flattening out the urethra to create a lubricated section of the vagina. This urethra skin flap is sewn on to the penile skin flap to increase the circumference of the vagina. The vagina is then closed off with the ventral half of the glans forming its base. Peritoneal space is constructed to enclose the vagina, which is attached to the sacrospinous ligament. The labia majora is constructed from remaining scrotal skin, any excess being excised. The remaining penile skin is used to construct the labia minora, which in turn acts as a hood to the clitoris. A perivaginal drain is left in for three days, and the urethral catheter as well as vaginal packing are removed after seven days. A vaginal stent, or dilator, is then used regularly to maintain the vagina's shape and depth.

Figure 10.2
Forming a Neovaginal Cavity during GRS for Transsexed Women

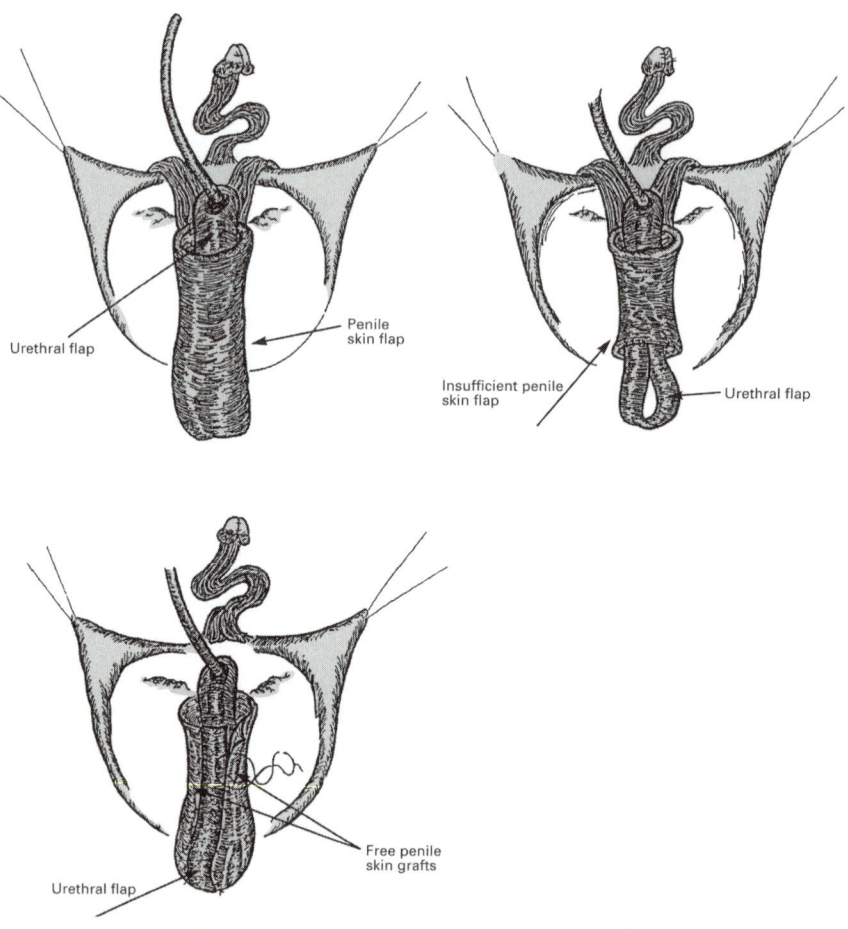

Source: Perovic, S.V., Stanojevic, D.D., and Djordjevic, M.L.J., (2000). Vaginoplasty in male transsexuals using penile skin and a urethral flap. *BJU International* 86:843–850.

Figure 10.3 shows the final stages of the complex GRS procedure. The final postoperative outcome indicates the close similarity of the surgical result to the genitals of a natal woman.

The outcome of the procedure was evaluated using the results obtained from 89 clients, whose average age was 28. The average follow-up time was four and a half years. The average vagina depth was 12 cm and lubrication of the vagina was considered satisfactory in 82 percent of cases. Six months after surgery,

Figure 10.3
The Final Stage of the GRS Procedure for Transsexed Women in which the Female Genitals Are Constructed

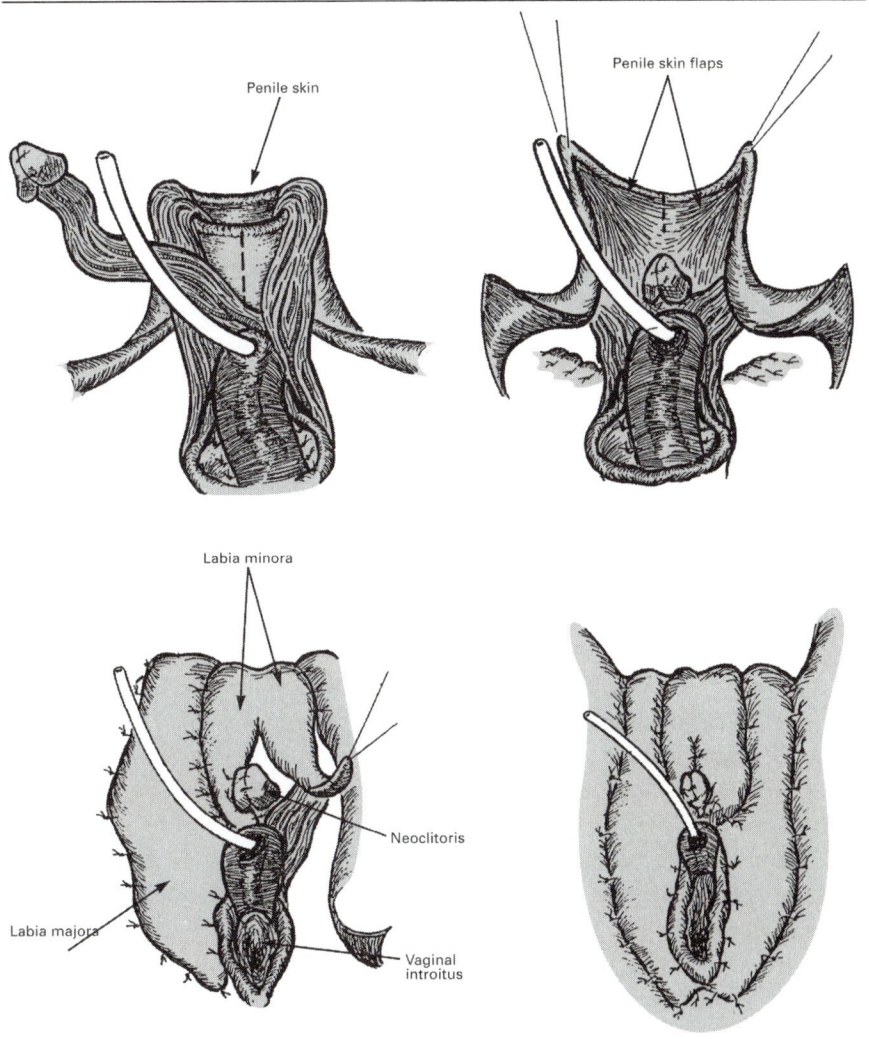

Source: Perovic, S.V., Stanojevic, D.D., and Djordjevic, M.L.J., (2000). Vaginoplasty in male transsexuals using penile skin and a urethral flap. *BJU International* 86:843–850.

79 percent of clients could enjoy normal sexual intercourse, 93 percent experienced good sensitivity, and 82 percent were orgasmic. Eighty-eight percent of clients were pleased with the aesthetic appearance of their new genitals.

Successful vaginoplasty depends on the amount of skin available. The possibility of orgasm requires the integrity of the urethra skin as well as the ventral glans cap being relocated to the vaginal base. Regular sexual intercourse prevents vaginal contraction and so should be started as soon as is practicable after recovery from surgery. Otherwise, daily dilation is required.

Another evaluation of GRS involved transsexed women who had experienced about two years of real-life experience and were on average 37 at the time of surgery. Most of the transsexed women underwent a two-stage GRS procedure including cosmetic enhancements to the original surgery performed eight weeks later. The minimum vagina depth of 12 cm provided a satisfactory outcome for most women. The average recovery period was eight days following initial surgery, which itself lasted an average of 6.3 hours. Complications were not usually major but nevertheless affected 36 percent of the 66 women, a figure that is about twice that obtained in some other studies.[11]

The success of the surgery was indicated by about 90 percent of women being satisfied with the surgical outcome, cosmetically, orgasmically, and also for sexual intercourse. An inflatable stent is useful to maintain vagina depth during the first six months following GRS.[12] The inverted penile flap and similar skin-grafting methods for vaginoplasty can sometimes produce complications such as vaginal stenosis, or closing up of the vaginal passage, as well as inadequate vagina depth and poor lubrication.

The surgical construction of a vagina in transsexed women can be performed in a number of ways. As we have seen, the most common technique involves lining the vagina with an inverted tube formed using skin from the penis. When there is insufficient penis skin and a skin graft is impractical, a section of sigmoid colon tissue can be used in a more complex surgical procedure. An advantage of intestinal implants is that, unlike skin, they do not shrink. The isolated sigmoid colon section is usually about 15 cm to 20 cm long. An adequate vagina formed in this way should be at least 12 cm long and 3.5 cm in diameter, and should remain suitable for sexual intercourse for from two to eight years.

Eighty percent of clients who underwent such a procedure were satisfied with their vagina, including 58 percent who were also satisfied with sexual performance. Only two transsexed women experienced difficulty with sexual intercourse, since one of the side effects of the sigmoid technique is a narrowing of the entrance to the vagina. Seven out of the 10 transsexed women were orgasmic, a proportion no different from that obtained using the penile inversion technique.[13]

Another evaluation of the success of vaginoplasty using the sigmoid-colon method revealed an average vagina depth of 13 cm with an average width of 4 cm. Excessive mucosal discharge and offensive smell were noted in only 8 percent of women. To facilitate sexual intercourse, 3 percent used lubricators and 6 percent used dilators for up to a year following surgery. Eighty-nine percent of women experienced orgasm during intercourse, suggesting that both the cosmetic and functional aspects of the surgery were excellent. The advantages of sigmoid-colon vaginoplasty include a lower risk of vagina contraction, sufficient vagina width and depth without the need for long-term use of dilators, spontaneous mucus production to facilitate sexual intercourse, avoidance of the offensive smells that occasionally accompany a skin graft, and an appearance and texture that closely match a natal woman's vagina.[14] A possible complication of the sigmoid-colon method is periodic contractions of the vagina, especially during dilation and intercourse.[15]

Medical-imaging techniques such as magnetic-resonance interferometry (MRI) can be used to check the outcome of vaginoplasty using the combined penile and scrotal flaps method. In one study, the images revealed an average vagina depth of 8 cm, about 50 percent shorter than what is considered acceptable. The vagina had a correct oblique inclination for four women, no inclination for five women, and an incorrect inclination for one woman. For seven women, remnants of the corpora cavernosa and the corpus spongiosum were detected. The average thickness of the rectovaginal septum, separating the rectum and neovagina, was 4 mm.[16] MRI can also be employed before surgery to determine the best outcome.

SURGICAL OUTCOMES IN TRANSSEXED WOMEN

Important aspects of GRS include the postoperative person's future quality of life and maintaining good health. Postoperative transsexed women should receive the same gynecological care as natal women, with special attention being given to previous conditions such as the health of their prostate gland. Since the vagina resulting from GRS is similar to a hysterectomized degenerated vagina in a natal woman, appropriate medical care is required.[17]

According to one report, 97 percent of 110 transsexed women undergoing vaginoplasty experienced a sensitive clitoris. An informal survey among potential surgery clients indicated that among the preferred characteristics of the vulva were a relative lack of pubic hair, a short clitoral shaft, a delicate labia minora, a small but distinctive clitoris, and a clitoral hood that when retracted reveals the glans. The main problem was a larger-than-acceptable clitoris.[18]

The most devastating outcome of GRS is postoperative regret. Although the incidence of regret is very low, factors contributing to gender-role reversal following GRS include doubts about the correctness of the evaluation, doubts about the feasibility of living permanently in their new gender role, and the quality of the surgery.

Factors contributing to regret were investigated in nine transsexed women and one transsexed man, whose average age was 46. They underwent GRS at an average age of 35. On the rare occasions when it occurred, postoperative regret occurred on average about one and a half years after GRS.[19] Risk factors for regret include stress-related late onset of gender identity atypicality (GIA), fetishistic cross-dressing, psychological instability, and social isolation. A survey of 28 postoperative transsexed women included one who was married and eight who were divorced. Although no postoperative regret was reported, continuing postoperative counseling was considered helpful.[20]

It is interesting to compare surgical outcomes in different parts of the world. For example, the first GRS procedure in Belgrade, Serbia, occurred in April, 1989.[21] To qualify for surgery, transsexed women had to receive an unequivocal diagnosis of transsexualism, successfully complete the requirements of the real-life test for at least a year, and be sexually attracted to men. GRS was not offered to transsexed women who preferred sexual relationships with women. Although none reported outright regret, 18 percent of 22 transsexed women were not satisfied with their body's appearance following surgery. However, all transsexed men were satisfied at least to some extent. After GRS, transsexed people were more satisfied with interpersonal relationships, had more sexual satisfaction, and were more likely to pursue an education and seek work. They were also more likely to have sexual partners and enjoy an increased ability to achieve orgasm.

A study of the psychosocial outcomes of GRS derived from quantitative studies published prior to 1983 indicated that improvements are more likely to occur in sexual satisfaction and relationships than in socioeconomic outcomes. There was an overall success rate of about 75 percent, with serious problems, including regret, occurring for 7 percent of postoperative women. Clearly, a more careful psychological assessment of GRS outcomes is needed.[22]

Another report[23] indicated that 55 percent of postoperative transsexed women were satisfied with masturbation, 67 percent with coitus, and 80 percent with oral sex, with even higher satisfaction being reported for same-sex activity. Only 19 percent reported dissatisfaction with heterosexual coitus. Of 14 transsexed women only 4 were orgasmic, a relatively low proportion. However, 9 of these 14 women reported good sexual satisfaction. Seven of nine transsexed men were orgasmic and eight reported an increase in sexual satisfaction after GRS. Following GRS, there was a 75 percent increase in sexual activity for the transsexed women and a 100 percent increase in sexual activity for the transsexed men.

Studies of postsurgical outcomes indicate that up to 97 percent of transsexed men and about 90 percent of transsexed women are satisfied with their surgical result. The small postsurgical regret rate of 1 percent results from diagnostic error, absence of the real-life experience, and unsatisfactory surgical delays and outcomes. Although surgical regret is more likely when the client is older than 30, the incidence is still quite small. Although prior to GRS at least 20 percent of transsexed women have suicidal tendencies, the suicide risk is considerably reduced to between 1 percent and 2 percent following GRS. Clearly, GRS can be a life-saving intervention for transsexed people.

Seventy-one percent of transsexed women and 83 percent of transsexed men get a job following GRS, despite some gender-related loss of job responsibility, especially for transsexed women. Presurgical androphilic transsexed women tend to fare better postsurgically than do their gynephilic counterparts.[13]

Major psychiatric disorders are seldom associated with the development of the medical condition of transsexualism nor are they likely to occur following GRS. For young transsexed people, there are increases following GRS in extraversion, dominance, and self-esteem as well as decreased feelings of inadequacy, all these changes indicating an improvement in psychological functioning.[24]

A study of post-GRS outcomes in 232 former patients of the well-known GRS surgeon Toby Melzer, M.D., indicated that their average age was 44 when they underwent surgery and 47 at the time of the survey, suggesting that the majority were so-called secondary transsexed women. In terms of sexual attraction, over half were gynephilic before GRS but only 25 percent were gynephilic following GRS, a result due to the substantial increase in androphilia after GRS from 9 percent to 34 percent. A similar increase in androphilia occurred for reported sexual experience. Those who changed their sexual orientation towards men tended to be both younger and unmarried, a typical situation for so-called primary transsexed women. About half of these people had one steady male partner.[24]

Following GRS, 18 percent reported exclusively female partners, 36 percent reported exclusively male partners, 18 percent reported both male and female partners (bisexual), and 29 percent reported no partners (asexual). The number of different partners was largest for the bisexual group. Frequency of sexual activity was similar for all groups except the asexual one, the latter also being less likely to masturbate. Of those who were married prior to GRS, 11 percent remained married thereafter. The most stable partnerships involved a liaison with a natal woman in an apparently lesbian relationship rather than one with a natal man. Nevertheless many post-GRS transsexed women find it difficult to form stable sexual relationships.[24]

Episodes of autogynephilic arousal were fewer following GRS than before, 87 percent of those who had female partners prior to GRS reporting at least some autogynephilic experiences. The group preferring male partners had considerably fewer autogynephilic experiences than did the other groups. About

85 percent of participants were orgasmic after GRS, with 67 percent considering their post-GRS orgasms to be more pleasurable than before. This finding is similar to that for natal women, 24 percent being unable to achieve orgasm at least some of the time. Problems with the study include the sample from just one surgeon, the predominance of older middle-class participants due to the high cost of surgery, and the relatively low response rate of 32 percent.[24]

Occasionally, older clients in their forties and well-educated transsexed women with college and postgraduate degrees opt for a much shorter real-life experience than the standards of care recommend. In this situation, surgery can proceed after about nine months of real-life experience pending the approval of the woman's medical advisors. Very few of these fast-track women regret GRS, with only the occasional client wishing that her real-life experience had been longer. The practical and subjective benefits from having a short real-life experience, or none at all, include maintaining necessary employment, pursuing significant relationships and leisure interests, avoiding difficulties with authorities, and achieving personal comfort.[25]

The physiological sexual response in 11 postoperative transsexed women and 72 natal women was investigated using vaginal photoplethysmography while the women looked at erotic video stimuli. In this procedure, a probe is inserted 5cm inside the vagina and its sexual response recorded. Androphilic transsexed women had a greater sexual response to male stimuli while the opposite result occurred for gynephilic transsexed women. The results were similar for subjective feelings of arousal for the transsexed women. However there was no correspondence between subjective and physiological indicators of sexual arousal for the natal women.[26] In this respect, transsexed women responded more like natal men than like natal women.

Follow-up studies of GRS for transsexed women suggest that the quality of outcome is enhanced when suitable clients are selected for transition, the client complies with the treatment protocol, and there is adequate social and psychological support during both the medical procedures and the subsequent recovery period. More favorable outcomes with satisfaction and no regret are associated with a younger age at surgery, childhood femininity, sexual attraction to men, compliance with the standards of care, absence of other psychological problems, and good family support. All except about 6 percent of transsexed women report high satisfaction with their GRS outcome, as well as a substantial improvement in their quality of life following surgery. None of the 6 percent report outright regret but just occasional feelings of regret. Age at surgery, recalled childhood femininity and masculinity, and self-rated adequacy of counseling are the only preoperative factors associated with regret.[27]

The outcomes following GRS for transsexed women are almost always positive. Provided the diagnosis of transsexualism is appropriate and a sufficiently successful real-life experience has occurred, the likelihood of postoperative regret is small. Nevertheless, outcome advantages often occur for young women who are sexually attracted to men.

SURGICAL COMPLICATIONS

Complications of GRS for transsexed women include any of the following: hemorrhage; hematoma, a solid mass of clotted blood; infection; rectovaginal, perineal, and urethrovaginal fistulas, that is, abnormal openings between the rectum and vagina, both within the perineum and between the urethra and vagina; and partial necrosis, or tissue death, of skin grafts used for lining the vagina. Later complications include stenosis, or narrowing, of the vagina; prolapse, or displacement, of the scrotal flaps using skin grafts; and a lengthened urethral opening.

Vaginal stenosis is a risk if transsexed women do not have frequent sexual intercourse or do not dilate regularly. Unless sexual activity is regular, some people recommend using an inflatable silicon vaginal stent continuously for 30 days followed by its regular daily use for about three months after GRS. Sometimes the vagina is too narrow due to the limited space in males between the two pelvic bones.[28]

Prolapse of the vagina can be fixed by attaching it to the back of the abdominal cavity using mesh and anchors.[29] Problems with incontinence have been noted in 79 percent of 24 transsexed men and in 19 percent of 31 transsexed women.[30] One possible fix for incontinence involves an injection of gluteraldehyde collagen around the perimeter of the urethra.[31]

Vagina collapse causes distress in postoperative transsexed women. In one case, a section of sigmoid colon was used to construct a vagina in a 39-year-old transsexed woman. A vaginal stent was used for four weeks to dilate the vagina and ensure that it did not close up. Two months later an abnormal narrowing of the entrance to the vagina occurred, leading to abdominal discomfort and vomiting. The vagina required considerable reconstruction with a stent being inserted continuously for 30 days. No further problems were experienced following release from hospital and for up to seven months thereafter.[32]

Other postoperative problems reflect prior conditions and are unrelated to the effects of hormone therapy and surgery. For example, a case was reported of a 60-year-old transsexed woman who was diagnosed with a benign prostate tumor 26 years after GRS. Normally the size of the prostate gland decreases by about 30 percent after antiandrogen treatment or castration. The risk of prostate cancer is usually negligible if castration occurs before age 40.[33] This is a rare complication.

Postoperative transsexed women should undergo a full cervical evaluation including an annual Pap smear because of the risk of vaginal cancer.

In women who have undergone penile inversion vaginoplasty with the glans of the penis retained as a clitoris, routine cytological examination of the clitoris is advisable since the glans is more prone to cancer than is the skin surrounding the penile shaft. Furthermore, intraepithelial cancer of the glans is more likely to progress towards a more invasive condition than is intraepithelial cancer in other penile skin. These factors make regular cytological examination of the glans-derived clitoris a sensible precaution for transsexed women.[34]

Although postsurgical complications can be annoying for transsexed women, they are rarely life threatening provided there is appropriate medical intervention. In rare cases, preconditions such as prostate and penile skin cancer can complicate what would otherwise be a complete recovery following surgery.

SURGERY FOR TRANSSEXED MEN

Since GRS for transsexed men is complicated, uncertain, and expensive, many are content to experience the secondary sex characteristics induced by testosterone therapy, as well as some cosmetic and gonadal surgery. Financial considerations and reports from others of poor surgical outcomes are the greatest deterrents reported by transsexed men.[35]

While GRS for transsexed women provides a satisfying outcome both cosmetically and functionally in most cases, surgical procedures for transsexed men involve an unreasonable degree of cost, risk, and compromise. Owing to technical difficulties and cost, only 3 percent of a sample of 70 transsexed men had undergone GRS, 16 percent were planning it, and 29 percent had decided against undergoing the procedure. On the other hand, only 9 percent of 23 transsexed women had decided to forego GRS. Nevertheless, many transsexed men are more than satisfied with the results of their surgery than are transsexed women. In any case, testosterone therapy and breast reduction surgery deliver impressive results and may be sufficient medical interventions for many transsexed men.[7]

The goal of phalloplasty, the surgical construction of external genitals in transsexed men, is to create a penis that has erotic sensation and is capable of both sexual intercourse and urination while standing. A common surgical technique for constructing a penis uses a bony skin graft from the underside of the forearm. Complications following phalloplasty include urethrocutaneous fistula, leading to urine leakage from disrupted skin wounds. This complication is somewhat common, with a 64 percent risk, 21 percent of these instances requiring additional surgery. Other complications include a 14 percent risk of abnormal narrowing of the urethra, a 5 percent risk of skin flap loss and radius bone fracture, and a relatively large 45 percent risk of donor forearm morbidity. Overall, such surgery is fraught with complications that impose considerable risks for transsexed men.

A three-stage GRS procedure for transsexed men consists of a hysterectomy (removal of the uterus) followed by oophorectomy (removal of the ovaries). Other surgical procedures include vaginectomy (removal of the vagina), mastectomy (removal of breast tissue), prefabrication of a urethra in the donor forearm to simulate the passage of urine in a penis, and tissue expander implantation in the lower abdomen. Removal of the vagina, uterus, tubes, and ovaries can be performed easily using laparoscopic surgery.[36]

In the second stage of the procedure, which occurs about three months later, microsurgical phalloplasty with a tubed forearm osteocutaneous graft flap is performed, resulting in the construction of a functioning penis during the final stage of surgery. The clitoris is usually preserved and moved to the junction between a constructed scrotum and the inner thigh of one of the legs. Finally, the forearm wound is covered with a preserved abdominal skin graft flap. In the third stage of surgery two to three weeks later, division of the abdominal flap and glans sculpting occur, leading to a more realistic and sexually sensitive penis. A stent must be placed just below the membranous urethra for six months to facilitate urination.[37]

Phalloplasty using a radial forearm free flap can also be performed in one surgical session lasting from 6 to 12 hours. The surgical outcomes include a normally appearing penis with both tactile and erogenous sensation. The penile shaft contains a urethra that extends to the tip of the penis to allow urination while standing. The penile shaft is sufficiently large to incorporate a permanent semirigid erectile prosthesis to facilitate sexual intercourse. Alternatively, a silicon implant can be placed inside the penis to achieve rigidity while also providing sufficient flexibility to permit the wearing of sporting gear and swimwear. The surgical outcomes allow 36 percent of men to experience erotic sensation in the penis, since clitoral sensitivity is preserved. Forty-one percent of men report satisfactory sexual performance following surgery. Since long-term follow-up studies of penis implants have not been conducted, the long-term outcome of this procedure is uncertain. The surgical scar on the forearm remains an unsolved complication.[38]

An alternative procedure for phalloplasty involves using innervated skin from the lower abdomen to produce the tube that constitutes the penis. The urethra, constructed using a fold of skin gathered from the labia majora, is placed in its proper position within the penis to allow urination while standing. Erogenous sensation is achieved by incorporating some of the head of the clitoris towards the tip of the urethra. Although satisfaction with the cosmetic outcome of the phalloplasty was reported by about 71 percent of 82 men, there was a surgical complication in the urethra in 75 percent of cases. Just under 50 percent of men could urinate while standing, and sexual intercourse was possible for 39 percent. When compared with the forearm flap method there is virtually no visible scarring.[39]

A little-known complication of phalloplasty for transsexed men is the proper formation of the urethra to allow for urination in the male manner. This complication occurs in half of the current surgical procedures. The main problems are due to fistulas and strictures in the construction of the urethra that interfere with the normal flow of urine and arise when urine flow is redirected through the clitoris.[40]

A new surgical technique for GRS in transsexed men uses a one-stage procedure lasting about six hours that is performed by two separate surgical teams.[41] Mastectomy and chest contouring are performed at the same time as oophorectomy (removal of the ovaries) and hysterectomy. The procedure concludes with phalloplasty, the penis being formed from a skin flap obtained from the anterior abdomen wall. In a final stage of the operation, testicular prostheses are inserted into the labia majora via an incision in the abdomen to avoid scrotal scarring. The men are discharged from hospital about 12 days after surgery, and there are few, if any, complications. Full healing is usually achieved within four weeks after surgery. Both transsexed men and surgeons considered the outcome to be aesthetically pleasing, with some penile response to both pressure and vibratory stimulation.

Metoidioplasty, an alternative surgical procedure for GRS in transsexed men that is not as complex as phalloplasty, creates a penis by taking advantage of the enlarged clitoris that results from long-term testosterone therapy. The surgical procedure is possible since the distribution and course of the neurovascular bundle is similar in both the clitoris and penis. Metoidioplasty aims to straighten and lengthen the clitoris. A penile body is then constructed using clitoral skin and labia minora flaps. Finally, the labia majora are fused to provide a scrotum into which testicular implants can be placed.

Metoidioplasty was evaluated in 22 transsexed men aged 26 who had been treated with testosterone for an average of 17 months.[42] All the transsexed men had completed hysterectomy and adnexectomy, or removal of tubes and ovaries. The vagina had been removed, with the abdominal wall being preserved for urethral reconstruction. The results at follow-up, an average of four years following metoidioplasty, showed that the penis was on average 6 cm long with a maximum length of 10 cm, a satisfying result for 77 percent of the men. They could urinate while standing and were satisfied with the appearance of their new penis. Figures 10.4 and 10.5 illustrate the surgical procedures for metoidioplasty. Necrosis, or tissue loss, can occur with metoidioplasty, suggesting that the simpler procedure may not always be the best alternative.

A few different GRS methods for transsexed men were outlined. One version uses forearm skin and bone to construct a penis, whereas another technique,

Figure 10.4
The Initial Stages of Metoidioplasty Leading to a Functioning Neophallus Constructed Using an Enlarged Clitoris

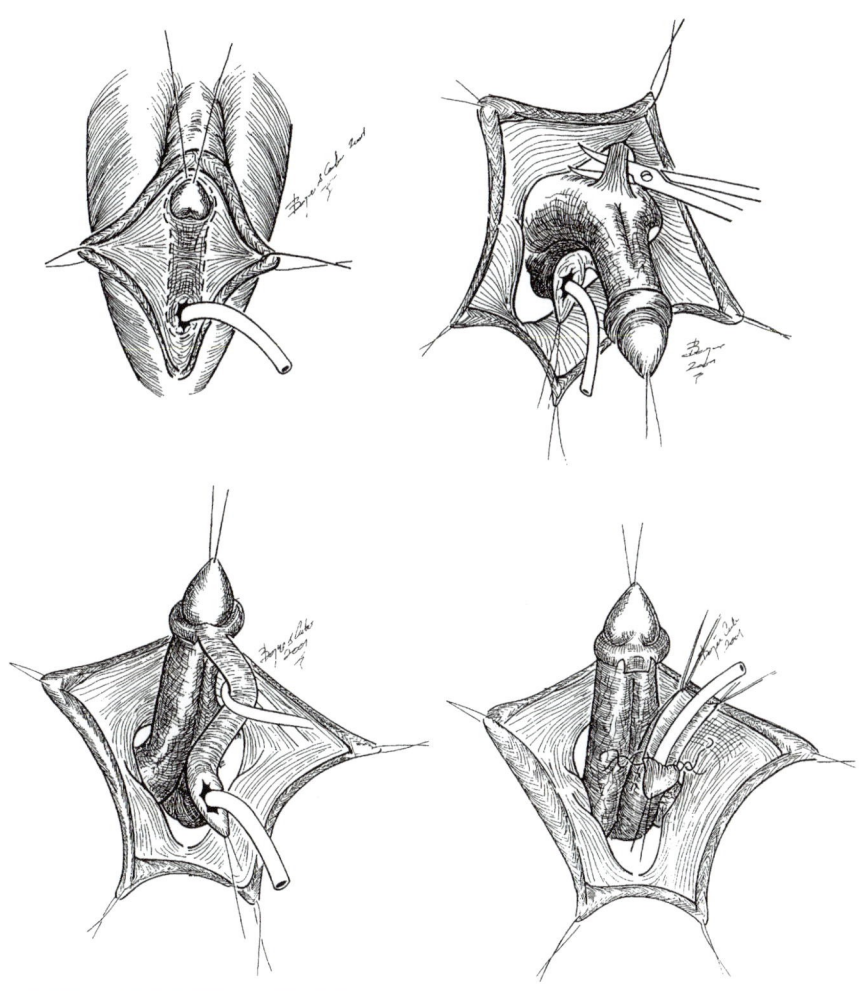

Source: Perovic, S.V., and Djordjevic, M.L. (2003). Metoidioplasty: A Variant of Phallplasty in Female transsexuals. *BJU International* 92:981–985.

metoidioplasty, takes advantage of an enlarged clitoris resulting from long-term testosterone therapy. Both methods have their medical complications, with successful surgical outcomes being less likely than current procedures for transsexed women. The relative merits of phalloplasty and the alternative, less complex metoidioplasty method that produces an erogenous but small penis, require further investigation.

Figure 10.5
The Final Stage of Urethra Construction in Metoidioplasty

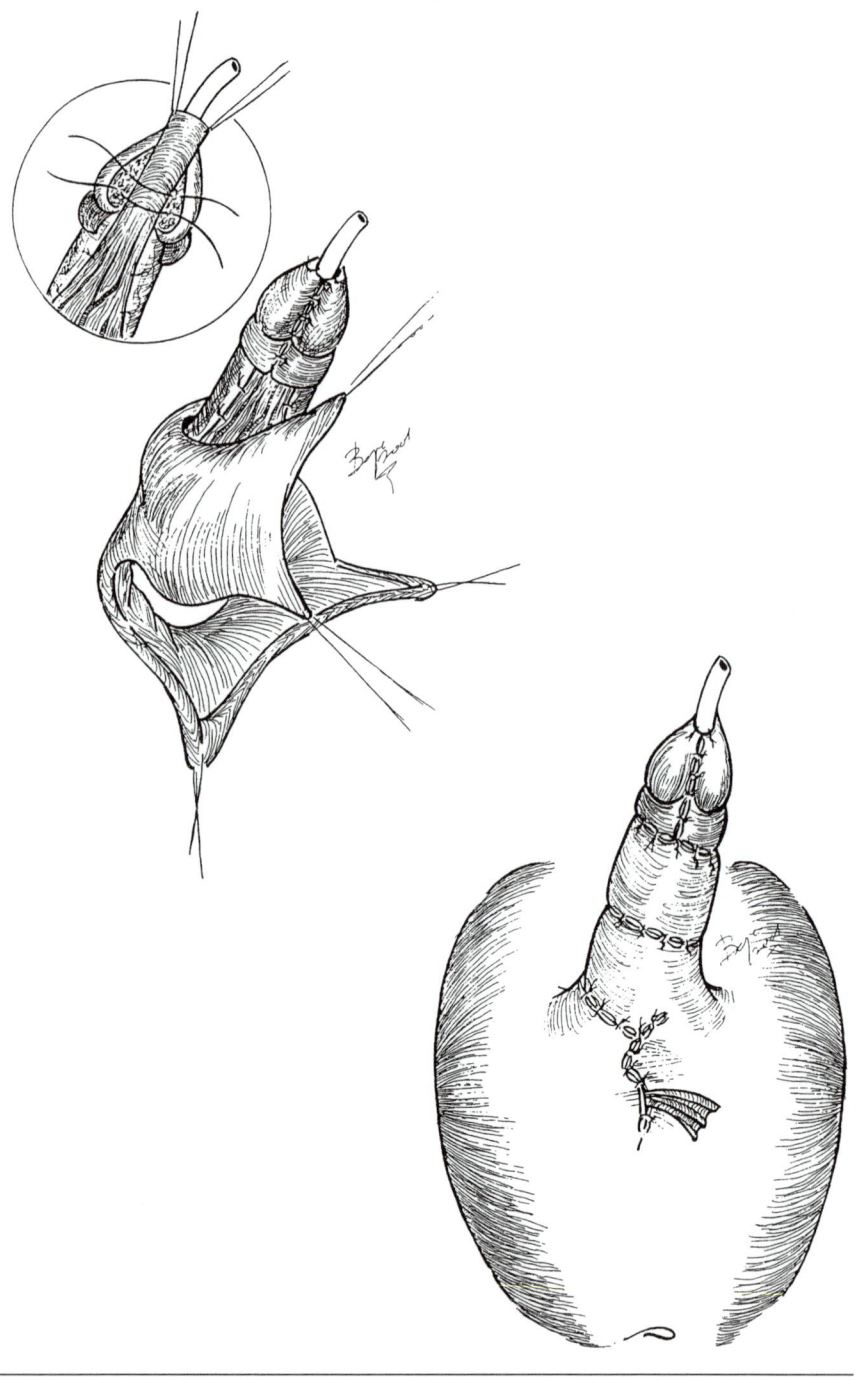

Source: Perovic, S.V., and Djordjevic, M.L. (2003). Metoidioplasty: A Variant of Phallplasty in Female transsexuals. *BJU International* 92:981–985.

SUMMARY

GRS is a successful, if complex, intervention to allow transsexed people to finally achieve reconciliation of their brain-sex with their external genitals. The surgical techniques have advanced considerably so that nowadays the procedures are safe and recovery from surgery is usually complete within a relatively short period of time. The GRS procedure for transsexed women has evolved to the point where several alternative procedures are available, the most common methods being the penile inversion procedure and the more invasive method using sigmoid-colon tissue to construct a highly functional vagina. Generally, the surgical outcome for transsexed women is positive, with only a small proportion of clients expressing distressing levels of postoperative regret. Nevertheless, postoperative outcomes are better on average for younger, androphilic candidates who did not experience any psychiatric or surgical complications.

The situation is still better for transsexed women than transsexed men, the latter enduring a much longer and complex procedure to create a penis without any promise of success in all cases. Such a situation occurs even when a simpler procedure using the enlarged clitoris resulting from long-term testosterone therapy is a viable alternative.

Chapter Eleven

ANCILLARY PROCEDURES

So that transsexed people can feel more comfortable in their new gender role, a number of ancillary medical treatments and support programs are available. These include speech therapy and facial hair electrolysis for transsexed women, since hormone therapy has no effect on voice pitch nor does it deplete facial hair. Other surgical techniques for transsexed women include augmentation mammoplasty, voice-box surgery, and facial feminization surgery.

SPEECH THERAPY

Speech therapy is undertaken mainly by transsexed women to feminize their male voice so that it more closely approximates that of a woman. To some extent, a convincing visual presentation can compensate for a deficient female voice. Clearly, interpersonal communication, primarily by means of voice and mannerisms, is important for a transsexed woman's acceptance into her feminine gender role.[1] A higher speech pitch does not guarantee that a transsexed woman will communicate seamlessly. For example, in social situations transsexed women need to relinquish their previous masculine habit of leading in conversational speech when with a group of men. Now they should wait their turn in the conversation, as many women feel obliged to do.[2]

The major difference between men's and women's voices is pitch. When compared with a typical woman's voice, the fundamental frequency and the resonant frequencies, or formants, are lower in men's voices. Whereas the fundamental frequency for men's voices lies between 107 Hz and 132 Hz, the female range lies between 196 Hz and 224 Hz, an increase of about 90 percent of an octave.[3] So that men can more adequately mimic female speech, the fundamental frequency needs to be raised to between 155 and 160 Hz.

Other aspects of feminine speech also need to be learned. For example, women differ from men in their pronunciation of the *TH* in words like *TH*is and *TH*in. Also their speech shows a more dynamic intonation pattern during the pronunciation of a phrase. Most people have noted, for example, the tendency for women to raise the pitch of their voice at the end of a phrase or sentence, a characteristic that only occurs in male speech when a question is being asked.[4]

When transsexed women who had received estrogen therapy for at least 18 months say sentences, first in a female voice then in a male voice, the average duration of isolated words is longer in the female version of the message. When speaking in a female voice, the fundamental frequency is higher and the pitch range is larger, but the loudness level is less. The central frequency of the third formant, produced by a reduced mouth cavity length, tends to be higher in female speech than in male speech. This effect can be produced by retracting the corners of the mouth, a characteristic feature of female speaking, as well as by appropriate placement of the tongue.[5] Female-sounding voices are correctly detected 99 percent of the time by naïve listeners, indicating that speech therapy for transsexed women is often successful.[4]

The fundamental frequency, or pitch, of speech determines whether transsexed women's voices are perceived as male or female. Fundamental frequencies less than 155 to 160 Hz are generally perceived as male, although an impression of femininity can be induced by including a larger number of upward inflections as well as greater pitch variability. To make their voices sound more feminine, transsexed women should pronounce consonants precisely and employ a softer voice tone. Transsexed women whose voices are most often perceived as female tend to be short in stature, with height less than 170cm, or 5' 7". So a desirable combination for passing as a woman based on voice is a high fundamental frequency and a short stature.[6]

Even when transsexed women increase their voice pitch so that it lies within the female range, good female voice quality is often elusive. Since male vocal cords have a greater mass than female cords, the laryngeal air pressure needed to start them vibrating is greater, leading to a generally lower pitch range. Also, since the male vocal tract is longer than that of women, the basic resonances are about 20 percent lower in pitch and have different resonance characteristics than those of the female voice. So, successful imitation of the female voice requires painstaking training to realign the formant resonances; no easy task. Speakers with higher vowel formants, important in aiding vowel identification, are more likely to be perceived as female even when the average pitch is the same. However, training the voice to produce appropriate formants is difficult for natal male speakers.[7]

At a more global level, male speech exudes competitiveness, whereas women converse in a more cooperative style.[8] Feminine speech style is characterized by the inclusion of empty adjectives such as *lovely, divine,* and *cute,* tag questions such as *don't you,* for example, "I think this is a lovely outfit, *don't you?*" as well as hedges such as *perhaps,* and *I wonder if.* Some commentators have suggested that the uncertainty associated with female speech reflects their lower status in society. However, the use of hedges might reflect women's superior verbal communication skills when compared with men. Whereas women's conversation is collaborative and built upon shared understanding, men avoid divulging personal issues and converse on factual topics such as sports and current events.[8] Successful passing by transsexed women requires use of language structures that are more characteristic of women than of men. They should be willing to listen to, rather than interrupt, another's conversation, move their mouths more when speaking, and smile more frequently.[9]

Social aspects of the communication skills of 47-year-old transsexed women when compared with those of a group of natal women of similar age indicate that transsexed women have more communication problems than do natal women. Such problems include the use of voice tone to communicate a message, prolonged conversations due to excessive talkativeness, listening skill problems, losing track of conversations when there is a lot of surrounding noise, and understanding what is being said in group conversations. Adequate communication depends on the transsexed woman's satisfaction with their voice.[10]

The most important strategy, at least initially, for using speech therapy to help transsexed women acquire female speech is to work on head resonance and voice volume while training the voice to have a lighter, more feminine character. Also important is intonation variability, with more upward intonations being required to approximate female speech. A delicate and light articulation, shortening of the vocal tract, and a lowering of volume are also needed to produce a convincing female voice. Possible changes in speech rate as well as coughing and laughing in a feminine manner are also important aspects of speech training.

Useful strategies for improving female speech quality include having the transsexed woman categorize her own voice in terms of masculine and feminine voice standards and minimize chest resonance by employing auditory feedback from listening to speech samples. The different effects of chest versus head resonance can be felt and heard by placing fingers of the same hand above and below the voice-box and then producing resonance by humming consonants such as *m* and *n*. Another effective strategy is to raise and lower voice pitch in a glissando or sliding fashion aiming always to increase the overall pitch of the voice. Vibrations are only felt above the voice-box when there is adequate head resonance. The female voice should be based on head resonance but with no falsetto, the latter being a male strategy to produce a false female voice.

Voice training should begin by using vowels formed by the front of the mouth, then progressing to words, and then to sentences, poetry, stories, and finally to spontaneous speech. Practice with phrases regularly used by women in normal speech is important so that confidence in speaking in real-life situations can be increased. Reciting poetry and children's stories in a highly modulated manner also helps produce a female voice tone. Learning appropriate feminine gestures to accompany the newly acquired speech is also important. Enunciating words by emphasizing initial consonants and learning to pronounce these words rather delicately is a worthwhile strategy. A slightly faster speech rate also makes the speech more feminine.[11]

In social situations, any deficiency in voice credibility can be overcome to some extent by a convincing female presentation in other ways, such as in appearance and mannerisms. Transsexed women are still more likely to be addressed as men over the telephone than in real life, indicating that physical appearance plays an important role in passing. One useful trick of course is to always introduce oneself with a female name when answering the telephone and prior to initiating a conversation. This strategy almost always works provided the fundamental voice pitch is reasonably feminine.

The measured average fundamental frequency of 14 transsexed women's speech ranged from 130 to 207 Hz. There was no difference in average fundamental frequency between the five who had experienced some voice training and those who had not, suggesting that voice training was inadequate for some of the transsexed women. The higher the fundamental frequency of the transsexed woman's voice, the higher was the femininity rating when only the voice was heard without seeing the person, as is the case over the telephone.[12]

The success of speech therapy has been evaluated using 10 transsexed women aged 45, 7 of whom had undergone GRS. They had received between 10 and 90 speech therapy sessions. Their current speech evaluated on average four years since their last therapy lesson indicated that the gains of 43 Hz on average following speech therapy were not maintained. Rather there was a reduction in fundamental frequency from 168 Hz upon discontinuation of speech training to 147 Hz at follow-up, this latter value being higher the larger the number of therapy sessions. This fundamental frequency was still higher than their pretherapy value of 126 Hz. Although the follow-up fundamental frequency was now slightly below the female range for seven participants, most were satisfied with their female voice. Perhaps they found other ways to present as a woman that more than compensated for any gender ambiguity in their speech.[12]

Transsexed men have fewer speech problems than do transsexed women, as testosterone therapy causes a steady decrease in fundamental voice frequency. In a survey of 16 transsexed men, none of whom had received any voice therapy, 14 reported a lower and heavier voice since starting testosterone therapy. For most, the change in voice quality occurred within three months of starting testosterone therapy. Transsexed men are pleased with their new voice, most indicating scarcely any difference between their voice and that of a natal male. Reassuringly, they are no longer addressed as a woman even on the telephone. Over a four-month period following the start of testosterone therapy, the maximum pitch decreased from 800 Hz to approximately 500 Hz in one man, and from 500 Hz to around 350 Hz in another. There were corresponding decreases in the fundamental voice frequency to around 125 Hz for both clients. However there was no increase in jitter (noisiness) and shimmer (relative weakness).[13]

Transsexed men pass more effectively if they adopt male conversation strategies such as telling people what they want rather than asking for it. A transsexed person's ability to pass requires the attainment of lexical, syntactic, and conversational skills over and above just mastering changes in fundamental pitch and fluctuations in speech dynamics. Transsexed men usually have an easier task in this respect than do transsexed women.

The goal of speech therapy in transsexed women is to increase the voice pitch as well as to acquire intonation and stylistic skills that mimic as closely as possible female speech. Although transsexed women's speech may not qualify as being distinctly feminine, when coupled with a convincing visual presentation few if any problems in passing in a female gender role are generally experienced. By contrast, most transsexed men start exhibiting a convincing male voice after a few months of testosterone therapy.

VOICE-BOX SURGERY FOR TRANSSEXED WOMEN

The voice is the most problematical aspect of adjusting to a new lifestyle following GRS for transsexed women, as unconvincing voice and speech create problems of social identity and assimilation. Since voice training does not always produce a satisfactory outcome for transsexed women, some resort to surgical techniques so that they can live more comfortably as women. Surgery to increase voice pitch is claimed to improve sexual identity, body image, self-esteem, and general well-being. A reduction of the laryngeal prominence (Adam's apple), known as thyroid chondroplasty or more simply, a tracheal shave, routinely performed either prior to the real-life experience, or during GRS, is also beneficial. Surgical techniques for raising voice pitch have generally involved reducing the vocal-cord mass, shortening the vocal cords, or increasing vocal-cord tension. Medical tests conducted preoperatively can be used to estimate the increase in voice fundamental pitch that might be reasonably expected from surgery.

Vocal-cord length is determined by the relative positions of the cricoid (lower) and thyroid (upper) cartilages, which lie in front of the larynx. The effect of surgery can be mimicked manually by pushing up the lower margin of the cricoid cartilage with the right index finger while simultaneously pressing down on the thyroid notch with the tip of the left index finger. If this manual procedure results in an increase in voice pitch, voice-box surgery may be effective. Such voice-box surgery is known as cricothyroid approximation surgery.

One voice-box surgical procedure involves increasing vocal-cord tension by inserting two mini-plates to connect the cricoid and thyroid cartilages using wire sutures. This procedure does not interfere with the internal structure of the larynx. If the surgery is unsuccessful, as indicated by no substantial increase in voice pitch, then the previous voice-box configuration can be restored by removing the mini-plates during follow-up surgery. The operation produces an approximation of the normal female thyroid and cricoid cartilage relationship leading to greater tension between them, and a subsequent increase in fundamental voice pitch.[14]

Reports were obtained from 28 transsexed women aged 44 who underwent cricothyroid approximation surgery in a German hospital between 1993 and 2001. Twelve of the transsexed women had undergone speech therapy prior to voice surgery. Over half of the women indicated their concern about their voice in public life, especially when using the telephone. Prior to surgery they had employed various strategies to make their speaking voice more feminine, such as raising vocal pitch, speaking more melodiously and softly, and speaking less often. Two-thirds reported that they felt less feminine if they did not adjust their voice, whereas 62 percent of the respondents reported that they were pleased with the voice surgery outcome. Satisfied clients were more likely to be accepted as a woman in public, including over the telephone. They felt more comfortable in social situations and did not relapse into a male-sounding voice except occasionally among their own family members. Even with successful voice surgery, follow-up speech therapy is desirable.[14]

Postoperatively, the fundamental voice pitch increased from merely a semitone to almost an octave. Whereas none of the women spoke in the female range before the operation, 28 percent could achieve this range immediately afterwards, with another 38 percent achieving some success a year later. Although the operation failed for four clients, the average improvement for 23 clients was just two to three semitones. On the other hand, good cosmetic results with only inconspicuous scarring were achieved for 90 percent of clients following the much simpler technique of thyroid chondroplasty, or Adam's apple reduction surgery, a procedure performed simultaneously with voice-box surgery.[14]

When transsexed women's speech is compared before and after cricothyroid approximation surgery, the average most common, or modal, frequency increases from 142 Hz before surgery to 186 Hz after surgery. There is about a 50 percent chance of one's voice being perceived as female when the modal frequency is 173 Hz, with 100 percent accurate identification occurring when the modal frequency reaches 238 Hz. Whereas prior to surgery the transsexed women's voice had two modes, one below 150 Hz and the other over 200 Hz, surgery removes the lower frequency mode, leading to less voice strain. Two of 14 transsexed women showed no change in voice pitch following surgery, indicating an 85 percent success rate overall.[6]

An evaluation of 21 transsexed women who had undergone cricothyroid approximation surgery indicated that the average increase in fundamental frequency was 71 Hz two weeks after the operation and a lower value of 57 Hz at six-months follow-up. There was a 10 percent increase in voice irregularity two weeks after surgery, which reduced to 3 percent at follow-up. Only 38 percent had a speaking voice in the female range six months after surgery.[15]

Another version of cricothyroid approximation surgery raises the voice pitch by using nylon sutures that join the cricothyroid and thyroid bones at four sites to reinforce the contraction of the cricothyroid muscle that joins the thyroid bone to the voice-box cover. It is prudent to decrease the cricothyroid distance more than would be required, as after surgery the sutures tend to loosen a little.

Medical imaging is a reliable method for evaluating the effects of cricothyroid approximation surgery. For example, when CAT scans were used to measure the cricothyroid interbone distance one week before and one week after surgery, the average cricothyroid distance was 10 mm prior to surgery and 4mm after surgery, resulting in a decrease in cricothyroid distance of 6 mm. The average voice pitch increased from 118 Hz prior to surgery to 226 Hz after surgery, resulting in a substantially closer approximation to female voice pitch.[16]

The success of cricothyroid approximation surgery as well as thyroid chondroplasty was investigated using as participants 42 transsexed women aged 39 who had undergone either or both surgical procedures within an eight-year period. Only four transsexed women had requested a repeat cricothyroid procedure to fix an unsatisfactory initial outcome. Overall, 81 percent were satisfied with the incision scar on the neck following surgery, and 86 percent of those having thyroid chondroplasty were satisfied with the cosmetic appearance of the surgical incision on their neck.

Following cricothyroid approximation surgery, 79 percent of the transsexed women reported an immediate improvement in female voice quality, whereas the remainder had a more prolonged recovery from surgery followed by a steady improvement in voice quality. Of those who undertook prior speech therapy without surgery, only 45 percent had experienced an improvement in their ability to achieve a female voice range. Cricothyroid approximation surgery had its maximum effect on the modal, rather than average, voice frequency.[17] This effect might result from the large variability in pitch during normal speech.

Voice-box surgery can reliably increase voice pitch from the male range to a fundamental pitch above 215 Hz, with fairly large individual differences within that range. Although intensive speech therapy also increases average vocal pitch into the female range, the resulting speech still lacks the quality of the normal female voice. Acquiring the appropriate formant frequencies as well as inflecting the voice appropriately are skills that must be mastered to more closely approximate female speech.

Unfortunately, cricothyroid approximation surgery is not without its problems. Surgical complications include difficulty in swallowing, sore throat, frequent throat-clearing, and vocal fatigue. Some of these problems persist a year after surgery, but fortunately at about half of their immediate postoperative incidence. Some people report an adverse effect of surgery on their singing voice. Ironically, successful surgery depends on the presurgical pitch range being within the masculine range with no evidence of voice strain resulting from long-term voice therapy. Since successful voice therapy relies on forcing the voice from its normal masculine range towards a more feminine one, the effort required to achieve this can sometimes produce severe voice strain.

In another study, the results from 20 cricothyroid approximation surgery clients aged 46 were reviewed during a follow-up investigation conducted on average 22 months after surgery. Whereas prior to surgery the fundamental pitch was between 134 Hz (the musical note D3) and 145 Hz (C3) for sustained vowel and reading tasks respectively, the corresponding follow-up values were within the range 185 Hz (F#3) to 202 Hz (G3). This amounted to an average pitch increase of about half an octave, following normal postoperative relaxation of the stretched vocal cords, compared with an initial octave increase in fundamental pitch immediately after surgery.[18]

The fundamental pitch when reading aloud was close to the 189 Hz value for natal women who performed a similar task. There was no change in hoarseness or in voice pitch range following surgery. Both the lower and upper limits of the voice range increased by about four semitones in each case. Fifty-eight percent of participants were satisfied with their voice and 33 percent were dissatisfied, whereas the remaining 9 percent were indifferent with respect to the outcome. Vocal output was rated as clear by 42 percent, rough or hoarse by 23 percent, and fair by 35 percent of participants. Forty-seven percent of participants still had their voice mistaken as masculine on the telephone occasionally, 31 percent reported that they were never mistaken, and the remaining 22 percent reported that they were often mistaken for a man. About 60 percent found an improvement in the femininity ratings of their laugh, whereas scarcely more than 40 percent reported that their coughing and throat-clearing were considered feminine after voice-box surgery. So, the overall success rate of cricothyroid approximation surgery in transsexed women in this case was just over 50 percent.[18]

In another study, success rates from cricothyroid approximation surgery were 79 percent and 72 percent as judged by both the transsexed women and their speech therapists respectively. The average postoperative gain in fundamental frequency was 11 Hz, a rather small improvement, suggesting that surgery be reserved for those who cannot acquire a feminine voice by just using speech therapy.[19]

Voice-box surgery is a procedure of last resort for those transsexed women whose voice pitch cannot be successfully feminized using speech therapy. Although the surgery is reversible if performed correctly, the success rate is scarcely 50 percent. So the procedure must be considered risky by conventional surgical standards. Even when voice-box surgery is successful, transsexed women still need to learn feminine ways of speaking, no easy task irrespective of their fundamental voice pitch.

AUGMENTATION AND REDUCTION MAMMOPLASTY

Hormonal treatment for transsexed women produces breast development that reaches its maximum extent after about two years. Although about 50 percent of people are satisfied with their breast development, others seek breast augmentation surgery using cosmetic surgical techniques similar to those used for natal women. The technical term for this type of plastic surgery is augmentation mammoplasty.

Of the 359 transsexed women who attended the Amsterdam Gender Clinic between 1979 and 1996, 56 percent underwent augmentation mammoplasty. The policy at this clinic was to perform augmentation mammoplasty during or after vaginoplasty so as not to produce women with both large breasts and a penis. Mammoplasty was performed simultaneously with vaginoplasty in 52 percent of the transsexed women, whereas there was on average a three-year delay between vaginoplasty and mammoplasty for the others. Seventeen transsexed women underwent a second mammoplasty operation, on average about five years after the first one. The average size of implanted breast prostheses was 254 ml, 75 percent being satisfied with their new breast size, which on average increased from an A to a B cup.[20]

Interestingly, the desired breast implant size increased from about 200cc in 1986 to an average of 280 cc in the mid 1990s, suggesting a preference for larger breast sizes during that decade.[21] Breast augmentation should not proceed until at least 18 months after the start of estrogen therapy, by which time the breasts have reached about the maximum size possible using hormones alone. Postoperative complications occur in about 10 percent of cases.[22]

Breast augmentation and other cosmetic surgery procedures without proper medical supervision are risky. For example, an infection due to *Staphylococcal aureus* bacteria occurred as a result of implants in both the right breast and the left thigh of a 36-year-old transsexed woman. The client recovered after two weeks of hospital treatment and had new transplants inserted at a later date.[23] Another case involved bilateral breast cellulites and polyarthritis in a 29-year-old transsexed women who had procured the illegal injection of silicone in her breast tissue over a period of eighteen months. Although the resulting *Mycobacterium abscessus* infection was treated successfully with anti-biotics, the case exemplifies the serious medical risks associated with unsupervised breast augmentation procedures.[24]

Lung disease following unsupervised injection of silicone to enhance the breasts of a 34-year-old preoperative transsexed woman has been reported.[25] A rather unusual case involved a transsexed woman in transition who used a pump device to increase her breast size. Presumably she could not wait the 18 months to 2 years required for maximum breast growth while undergoing hormone therapy. This intrusion caused inflammation and bruising in the region surrounding the breasts.[26] Perhaps such minimal self-harm behavior indicates an associated condition such as borderline personality disorder, a not-uncommon accompaniment of the medical condition of transsexualism.

Transsexed men request breast removal (mastectomy) as part of their transition process. Breast cancer was a rare complication for a transsexed man following bilateral subcutaneous mastectomy. Ten years after mastectomy, he presented with a painless left areola mass in the breast. It is worth noting that breast cancer tissue contains more androgen receptors than either estrogen or progesterone receptors. A long-term increase in circulating androgens increases the risk of breast cancer in natal women. The risk is not completely eliminated after mastectomy in transsexed men as not all glandular tissue is removed. The treatment for this client involved oophorectomy (removal of the ovaries), which had the extra advantage of inducing an artificial menopause as well as indirectly reducing the risk of subsequent endometrial cancer.[27]

Breast enlargement surgery is commonly employed by about 50 percent of transsexed women to enhance their passability as women. Indeed, the trend has been to seek larger breast implants. Side effects from the surgery are rare, provided breast augmentation is conducted under proper medical supervision. Breast reduction surgery is routinely performed for transsexed men with a high success rate.

HAIR REDUCTION AND FACIAL ELECTROLYSIS

Human hair grows in a cyclic manner with an anagen, or growth, phase being accompanied by a quiescent, or telogen, phase. There is also a catagen phase during which the hair is at an intermediate stage of growth. During the anagen phase, cell activity occurs in both the hair bulb and dermal papilla, causing the old hair to be pushed out and replaced by a new one. Anagen phase hair is most sensitive to the various hair removal methods, so multiple treatments are almost always required as only some hair is in this growth phase at any one time.[28]

Most hair follicles are present at birth, with just a few ceasing hair growth beyond 40 years of age. Rudimentary hair follicles start producing hair as early as the sixteenth to twentieth week of embryonic development. Hair contains keratin proteins, which constitute the main hair shaft. The hair shaft grows within the outer hair root sheath, a part of the epidermis. Male body and facial hair consists of terminal hairs that are longer, pigmented, and coarser in texture than vellus hair, the soft, colorless hair typically found on women.

The hair follicles form groups known as follicle units, each of which contains two to four follicles together with sebaceous glands and connective tissues. Men and women have the same number of follicle units, but men have more terminal hair than women. Terminal hair in women occurs mainly in the genital region but can occur elsewhere on the body. For scalp hair, the anagen phase may last from two to six years, whereas for body hair this phase may last only three to six months.[29]

Androgens such as testosterone cause hair follicles with vellus hair to produce terminal hair. Androgens also prolong the anagen phase of body hair but shorten the anagen phase of scalp hair. This leads simultaneously to robust body hair in men and baldness in those men with a genetic predisposition for the condition. Androgens also increase the oiliness of both skin and hair. This means that people with androgen insensitivity syndrome, a rare intersex condition, have mostly vellus body hair. High doses of progesterone and estradiol inhibit 5α-reductase activity (5α-RA) in human genital and pubic skin, leading to a decreased production of dihydrotestosterone (DHT) and a reduction of body hair in transsexed women. Hair growth over the forearm and lower leg is less sensitive to the effects of androgens than is hair growth in other body regions.[29]

Several drugs can be used to reduce body hair. Spironolactone (SPA) is an aldosterone antagonist structurally related to progestins. SPA competes with DHT for binding to the androgen receptor but it has only one-twentieth the binding affinity of DHT for the androgen receptor, so high dosages of SPA are needed to suppress hair growth. SPA has an inhibitory effect on 5α-RA in skin, a similar effect to that of estradiol. The main side effects of SPA treatment are excessive urination, especially at night, and low blood pressure with associated headaches and fatigue. These side effects are tolerated well after frequent use of SPA with few changes in blood electrolytes and blood pressure being observed with its long-term usage. SPA should not be used with an excessive potassium intake as there is a risk of potentially life-threatening hyperkalemia. Owing to a possible gastritis risk, SPA should be taken with food. Cyproterone acetate (CPA) is often used as a supplementary antiandrogen to enhance feminization in transsexed women. CPA is effective in reducing terminal hair growth in transsexed women.

Even when drugs are used to accelerate body hair loss in transsexed women, they have little effect on facial hair. Consequently, more conventional manual methods of hair removal are required. Although shaving is the most common method of hair removal, it has the disadvantage of only cutting the hair at the skin surface, leading to relatively rapid regrowth. Shaving has no effect on hair thickness or growth rate. Another popular hair-removal method involves plucking or waxing. Waxing removes the hair at its roots and can be effective for up to six weeks following treatment. The only minor side effects are ingrown hairs that can occasionally lead to irritation when regrowth occurs. Depilation creams can also be effective. Since they only dissolve the hair shaft using a chemical reaction, regrowth occurs within about two weeks. Occasionally skin irritation can result from the chemicals used in such preparations.

Electrolysis is a tedious, painful, and time-consuming procedure used for removing facial and body hair in transsexed women. A fine needle is carefully inserted into each hair follicle. A combination of applied heat and electrical current leads to the destruction of the follicular isthmus as well as the lower follicle. Galvanic electrolysis passes a direct current to the hair follicle, destroying it, whereas thermolysis relies on the heat generated by alternating current to achieve much the same result. Since there are approximately 40,000 hairs in the male beard and about 200 hairs can be removed per hour, at least 200 hours of electrolysis are needed to remove most of the facial hair. The process is complicated further by the fact that only hairs in their growth, or anagen, phase can be removed permanently. Other hairs will eventually return but with much less resilience, making the final few hours of hair removal much easier. It is generally accepted that permanent hair removal is possible using electrolysis. Skin irritation from electrolysis clears up within a day or two after each session.

Since testosterone is responsible for beard growth in the first place, any residual testosterone in transsexed woman will maintain a luxurious growth. Once the combination of estrogen and antiandrogen therapy has reduced testosterone sufficiently, the removal of facial hair is easier and less painful, since estrogen and antiandrogen decrease hair diameter but not its length. Starting electrolysis before the commencement of estrogen therapy is not recommended. If full-time living as a woman starts about the same time as estrogen therapy, several days of beard growth will be necessary prior to each electrolysis session. This means that passing adequately is not always possible for transsexed women until facial electrolysis is reasonably well advanced. Being a woman is not easy.

Facial electrolysis is one of the most expensive single procedures in a transsexed woman's transition process, costing approximately $10,000 over two years or more. Laser treatment is a viable alternative that destroys the hair bulb. Effective laser treatment depends on melanin in the hair shaft that can conduct light energy to the hair bulb. Laser treatment is not so effective with grey hair and can cause damage to skin with a high melanin content if care is not taken.

A typical treatment uses long-pulsed ruby laser applied monthly to the beard and chest hair. People with black hair require about seven relatively painful hourly sessions to clear the beard and chest hair. Although no guarantee of permanence can be given, no significant regrowth occurs up to six months following laser treatment. Unlike electrolysis, regular maintenance treatment is required.[30] A 90 percent average hair clearance rate occurs after about nine treatments. Laser's hair removal effectiveness decreases with both age and with the amount of previously experienced electrolysis.[31]

Absence of facial hair is important for a transsexed woman's ability to pass socially and to enhance her confidence. Electrolysis remains the best option for permanent facial hair removal. However for younger transsexed women who have no grey hair, laser hair removal is a viable option provided repeat treatments can be tolerated.

FACIAL FEMINIZATION SURGERY

To improve their ability to pass as women, some transsexed women undergo facial feminization surgery (FFS). This is a complex and expensive procedure to recontour the face, including nose, jawbone, orbital ridges of the eyes, and forehead so as to more closely approximate the female facial form. The orbital ridges above the eyes are more prominent in males than in females, leading to a strong impression of masculinity. By contrast, the bone surrounding the eyes is much rounder and relatively larger in females. The cheek bones are heavier and flatter in men and more prominent in women, leading to a clear facial impression of femininity. Since the female face is less muscular but contains more subcutaneous fat than the male face, it appears softer, more rounded, and more "friendly" than does the average male face. The forehead height is less in females, about 6 mm shorter than that of males. Since the male nose appears generally larger in males than females, some reduction and contouring of the nose is an important part of FFS.[32]

Facial feminization surgery at the Amsterdam Clinic involves various combinations of jawbone angle reduction, a smaller and more rounded chin, and an increase in the roundedness of the eye sockets. Although such surgery produces pleasing outcomes for transsexed women, more carefully controlled follow-up studies are required.[33]

SUMMARY

Ancillary medical procedures such as speech therapy, voice-box surgery, cosmetic surgery including breast augmentation, and facial electrolysis are important for transsexed women. Although the successful attainment of feminine speech habits often results from speech therapy, a few transsexed women undergo voice-box surgery, which has only about a 50 percent success rate. Transsexed women often endure 200 hours or more of painful electrolysis to remove facial hair, although an increasingly larger number prefer laser hair removal, which is much quicker although not guaranteed to be permanent. About 50 percent of transsexed women seek breast enlargement surgery either accompanying GRS or on another occasion. Transsexed men, on the other hand, request breast reduction as a necessary part of their masculinization. Facial feminization surgery is an expensive supplementary procedure used by transsexed women to enhance both their feminine appearance and passability.

Chapter Twelve

INTERSEX CONDITIONS

One of the most intriguing aspects of contemporary human sexuality is the fate of children born with intersex conditions. These include visually obvious departures from the normal sex organs in boys and girls as well as developmental effects caused by abnormal chromosomal configurations and abnormal physiological responses to sex hormones. People with such conditions are known as intersexed. Intersex conditions occur approximately once in every 2,000 live births, so they are not rare. Not only are such conditions distressing for the person, they are also upsetting for family and friends. In the remainder of this chapter, the term *intersex condition* is used in preference to the more archaic terms *hermaphroditism* and *pseudohermaphroditism*.[1]

Some intersex conditions result from biochemical onslaughts within the prenatal environment of the offspring. In animals, early exposure to anticonvulsants, for example, affects genital development, sex-dimorphic behavior, and reproductivity. In particular, male animals are prone to androgen deficiency. In humans, adolescent boys prenatally exposed to Phenobarbital have a smaller testicular volume, lower cortisol levels, and are significantly taller than unexposed adolescents. Their puberty is also delayed.[1]

Forming a gender identity is difficult for people born with genital anomalies. When one has ambiguous genitals, it is difficult to aspire towards a unique and consistent gender identity. The psychological world of the intersexed is a difficult one.

With some exceptions, until relatively recently the recommended treatment for those suffering from a physical intersex condition was to surgically remove any sexually ambiguous tissue so that sexual functioning during adulthood would be as normal as possible. This meant more often than not that babies born with an abnormally small penis, and possibly some hint of female sex organs, would be almost immediately assigned as female. It was assumed, somewhat unreasonably, that proper parenting would finesse the child into their adult female role socially, and eventually sexually. There is now clear evidence to suggest that such premature assignment can lead to considerable distress in later life. So nowadays, such premature surgery should be avoided.

Many pediatricians believe that people are psychosexually neutral at birth.[2] Their healthy psychosexual development depends mainly on the appearance of the genitals and, of course, correct legal sex determination is easily achieved for all but the intersexed. Some pediatricians maintain that there should be no doubt regarding sex assignment at birth. This of course places the family of an intersexed child in a difficult situation. Since it was generally assumed, based almost entirely on speculation and "clinical experience," that one's gender identity was fixed after two years of age, pediatricians believed that any surgery needed to make a child with ambiguous or malformed genitals sexually functional must be completed before the child was two years old.[3] Since attaining a stable gender identity takes longer than two years, the child might be erroneously assigned to a sexual identity that does not correspond with their ultimate gender identity.

In Milton Diamond's classificatory scheme,[2] a person's sex attribution consists of gender Patterns or practices, Reproduction, sexual Identity, sexual Mechanisms, and sexual Orientation, represented by the acronym PRIMO. Diamond's developmental model for gender identity change following surgery in the intersexed child involves several stages. In Stage 1, the child compares herself with others and develops an initial gender identity. In Stage 2, further testing of the child's own gender identity occurs assisted by a search for a niche within the gender identity spectrum. In Stage 3, the child becomes aware of his own gender identity, decides on an appropriate gender role, and then adjusts psychologically to the new circumstances. In the final stage, the child makes the psychological switch from one gender identity to the other, appropriating in the process society's accepted gender role and behaving consistently within that gender identification.

One's sexual orientation normally postdates a change in gender identity. This process is assisted by the child's need for a role model, either a transsexed, heterosexual, homosexual, or intersexed individual. As in many developmental processes, the peer group is often more influential than parents in helping the intersexed person attain these goals. Diamond's proposal for representing gender-change processes is rather different from the three-stage model for gender constancy discussed in chapter 3. This model assumes gender identity followed by gender stability and finally gender consistency.

Consideration of any intersex case should be based on the person's being psychosexually biased at birth—with psychosexual development being related to, but not determined by, the physical appearance of the genitals—and an open and full discussion of any doubt as to gender identity and sexual preference of a child or adolescent. Genital surgery should only be supported if it is the intersexed person's informed choice once they reach maturity.[2]

Tragic errors of sex reassignment are not limited to physical intersex conditions. For example, a detailed analysis of the "John-Joan-John" case concluded that premature sex reassignment to female is inappropriate for any natal male, or XY, baby with either ambiguous genitals or accidental damage to the genitals.[4] In this instance, a baby boy, "John," lost a large part of his penis due to a surgical error during circumcision. He was subsequently reassigned as a girl, "Joan," and underwent appropriate hormone and surgical treatments. However in adolescence, he reaffirmed his sex as male, made a successful gender reversal to "John," and was presumed to have lived happily with a family thereafter.[5] Sadly, this person, who is now identified as David Reimer, was anything but happy and committed suicide in May 2004.

Socialization is important for determining an appropriate sex affirmation in a child with an intersex condition. A desirable gender-assignment policy for such a child should consider reproductive potential, good sexual function, minimal medical procedures, an overall gender-appropriate appearance, a stable gender identity, and psychosocial well-being. However, not all clinicians emphasize the overriding need for the child to make an informed decision about possible surgical intervention once they reach maturity.[6]

Whether such premature surgical interventions provide positive outcomes for the client can only be determined by carefully conducted research. A review of the effects of clitoral-reduction surgery on sexual functioning in people with intersex conditions has been conducted. In most Western societies, being reared as female is common when there are genital ambiguities as well as physiological irregularities. This usually results in parents being advised that the child's future sexual functioning will be facilitated if the enlarged clitoris is reduced in size surgically. An alternative procedure that takes into account the unpredictability of the psychosocial effects of clitoral surgery and its uncertain influence on adult gender identity employs clitoroplasty, a dissection of the clitoral skin and removal of the paired clitoral corpora while preserving most of the clitoral sensation.[7]

Reassignment surgery for females with an intersex condition has been problematical. There is no evidence that surgery improves the person's psychosexual outcomes and promotes a stable gender identity. Indeed, the secrecy surrounding early surgical interventions can have a devastating effect when the intersexed person finds out exactly what happened. Clitoral surgery is characterized by a poor cosmetic appearance, with closing of the vagina being a perpetual problem, especially for young children. This means that more surgeries have to be undertaken later on, causing more physical and psychological trauma. Clitoral sensitivity is frequently compromised, leading to sexual dissatisfaction in adolescence and beyond. So the safest option is to not attempt surgery in infancy unless the condition is life threatening.[8]

Evaluation of 39 people with an intersex condition indicated that 56 percent suffered from congenital adrenal hyperplasia (CAH), 9 percent suffered partial androgen insensitivity syndrome (AIS), and the remainder had other, less-common intersex conditions. Seventy-two percent of the group had undergone clitoral surgery at an average age of 3.5 years. Those who had surgery reported sexual difficulties including a loss in sensitivity, communication difficulties with their partner, and a lack of orgasmic capability. Undoubtedly, feminizing clitoral surgery had a dramatically adverse effect on adult sexual function.[7] Interestingly, women with an intersex condition are frequently dissatisfied with surgical repairs to their vagina, whereas the opposite is true for most transsexed women.[9]

Any intervention to correct a genital anomaly in children with an intersex condition requires careful consideration by medical staff and the child's parents. These days it is considered bad practice to reassign the child's sex before an informed decision can be made by the child herself. Premature sex reassignment can do more harm than good.

CHARACTERISTIC FEATURES OF INTERSEX CONDITIONS

Intersex conditions have numerous presentations simply because sexual development in humans is such a complicated process. Hormonal abnormalities during early sexual differentiation may also be a precondition for developing gender identity disorder, so some intersex conditions are accompanied by medical complications such as transsexualism.

Normal and abnormal genital development is indicated by the seven-point Prader scale for quantifying the degree of virilization of female genitals. A Prader score of zero indicates normal female genitals and a score of 6 represents normal male genitals. Intermediate scores of say 3 or 4 represent the most ambiguous genital configurations.[10]

It is difficult to disentangle the effects of social environment and hormonal abnormalities on human intersex conditions. For example, female-to-male gender-role reversal beyond puberty occurs in several intersex conditions, especially in 5α-reductase-2 deficiency and 17β-HSD3 deficiency, both of these conditions resulting from rare genetic mutations.[11]

Sex-chromosome abnormalities produce various intersex conditions. Males with 47 XXY Klinefelter syndrome or with 46 XX male sex-reversal syndrome develop as infertile men and only experience endocrine abnormalities as they get older. Females with 45 X gonadal dysgenesis, or with 46 XY pure gonadal dysgenesis, often have ambiguous genitals. Males with 45 X or 46 XY mixed gonadal dysgenesis present in a similar manner to those with 5α-reductase 2 deficiency, or else with mutations to the androgen receptor leading to androgen insensitivity syndrome.

Disorders of androgen synthesis in males can appear as early as the eighth week of gestation. By contrast, the virilization effects of 21-hydroxylase deficiency in females may not appear until much later in the pregnancy. In both conditions, the internal urogenital tract is distinctly male, and the testes usually descend into the inguinal canals or labia majora. In this rare condition, what once appeared to be a clitoris grows to become a penis capable of erection after puberty.[12]

Some intersex conditions result from errors in biochemical processes that occur during early development. The 17β-hydroxysteroid dehydrogenase reaction is the final step in both the synthesis of testosterone in the Leydig cell in the testes and the synthesis of estradiol in the granulosa cell in the ovaries. The mutation of enzymes involved in these transformations leads to 46 XY children with internal testes and male Wolffian structures, but with female external genitals. These children are assigned as female at birth and raised as girls. They subsequently virilize and fail to menstruate at puberty. They exhibit low testosterone levels but normal blood testosterone to dihydrotestosterone ratios. The relative increase in testosterone level around puberty might result from the conversion of androstenedione in nongenital tissues. Beyond puberty, about 50 percent of such people seek sex reassignment as male.[12]

Children with 17α-hydroxylase deficiency have impaired adrenal function and incomplete masculinization. Inability to convert testosterone to DHT because of a 5α-reductase deficiency results in normally differentiated testes but deficient external genitals. There is also a clitoral-like penis and other severe genital abnormalities. Children with 5α-reductase deficiency undergo substantial masculinization at puberty and are commonly raised as men.[13]

An interesting example of 17β-hydroxysteroid dehydrogenase 3 deficiency, originally described by Stoller in 1970, involved a child born with female genitals being raised as a girl. After puberty she assumed a male identity, had genital surgery, and lived successfully as a married man.

The effect of 5α-reductase 2 deficiency is similar to that of 17β-hydroxysteroid dehydrogenase 3 deficiency in that virilization is impaired and most children are assigned and raised as females. The 5α-reductase 2 deficiency produces normal male levels of blood testosterone but low levels of dihydrotestosterone. Often there is virilization at puberty, leading to at least two-thirds of children with normal sex chromosomes exhibiting a male gender role thereafter. In some cases, the children are aware of their anomalous sex assignment from an early age. On the other hand, children born with complete testicular feminization are assigned and reared as girls, living their adult lives as women. However, those with only partial androgen resistance can live successfully as men.[12] Whether these genital assignments lead to happy and productive lives for these rare cases of biochemical sexual anomalies has not been verified.

Whereas the endocrine defects in Klinefelter syndrome, and in the 46 XX male with sex-reversal syndrome, become progressively worse with increasing age, men with 17β-hydroxysteroid dehydrogenase 3 deficiency, mixed gonadal dysgenesis, and 5α-reductase 2 deficiency tend to have normal androgen profiles. Most men with Klinefelter syndrome exhibit masculine gender role behavior, whereas 46 XY males with profound androgen resistance develop feminine gender role behavior. As in many intersexed conditions, sufferers are more likely to be reassigned from male to female than vice versa.[12]

Kallmann's syndrome results from a gene deficiency on the X chromosome accompanied by poorly developed gonads and a small penis without defects in scrotal fusion. Men suffering from Kallmann's Syndrome cannot reproduce due to delayed puberty and infantile genitals. They also have a high-pitched voice and a reduced sense of smell, as well as scaly skin, mental retardation, obesity, and undescended testes.[14]

Some males with a physical intersex condition exhibit a condition known as mixed gonadal dysgenesis characterized by disordered gonadal formation consisting of tissue-disordered testes and ovaries without normal follicles. In most cases, the Mullerian ducts remain intact, leading to incomplete, or delayed, masculinization and eventual assignment as female. More rapid than normal aging is also typical of the condition.[13]

Testicular feminization syndrome results in a female appearance with normal female external genitals even though there is a 46XY karyotype. Testes are commonly located in the labiosacral folds, and infertility is common. However, adequate female sexual function can occur after vaginoplasty. People suffering from Mullerian duct syndrome are 46XY males who possess a uterus and fallopian tubes in an inguinal hernia sac, combined with testes located in an abnormal position.

ANDROGEN INSENSITIVITY SYNDROME (AIS)

Complete androgen insensitivity syndrome (CAIS) results in insensitivity to the effects of testosterone. In this rare condition, androgen receptors fail to function in an XY fetus, leading to the birth of a female-appearing infant with internal testes that are usually removed surgically. Consequently, people with this condition are genetically male but have female sex organs. They also develop female secondary sexual characteristics during puberty.

Babies with CAIS are raised as girls, there having been no reported instances of gender reversal in later life.

CAIS has a prevalence of between 1 in 13,158 and 1 in 40,800, roughly the same range as earlier estimates for transsexualism, based on gender clinic data. Due to severe hormonal deficiencies, most women with CAIS undergo hormone-replacement therapy. Women with CAIS may have vaginal as well as clitoral underdevelopment, with 79 percent considering their vagina to be abnormal, and 64 percent complaining about a small, or nonexistent, vagina. For example, an average vaginal length of 8 cm is common in women with CAIS compared with an average of 11 cm in other women. Understandably, 66 percent of women suffering CAIS have infrequent intercourse.[15]

CONGENITAL ADRENAL HYPERPLASIA (CAH)

Girls with congenital adrenal hyperplasia (CAH), an excessive secretion of male sex hormones, most often have a female gender identity. However, due to the risk of developing masculine characteristics, a number of such girls are raised as boys. Cortisone treatment prevents hypermasculinization in CAH girls.[16] Women with CAH are more likely to have Kinsey scores of 1, indicating an extreme preference for sexual relationships with women.[17] The incidence of CAH is about 1 in 14,000.[18]

In CAH, impaired cortisol production upsets glucocorticoid feedback on the pituitary, hypothalamus, and suprahypothalamic centers of the brain, leading to an increase in both corticotrophin and androgen levels. In about 90 percent of cases, CAH results from a defect in the 21-hydroxylase gene; the greater the 21-hydroxylase gene mutation, the more severe the CAH symptoms. This genetic defect results in both impaired synthesis of cortisol, a stress hormone, and aldosterone, a steroid that facilitates electrolyte homeostasis and testosterone production. Cortisol secretion is governed by the adrenocorticotrophic hormone (ACTH) produced by the pituitary gland. An enzyme deficiency subsequently leads to increased levels of both ACTH and corticotrophin-releasing hormone.[18]

CAH was first recognized as a disorder in the nineteenth century and is observed most commonly in Hispanic and in some Jewish populations. There is a firm genetic basis for the disorder related to 21-hydroxylase activity, the carrier frequency ranging from 1 in 50 for the classical, or salt-wasting, form of CAH to 1 in 5 for the nonclassical or milder form of the condition. Clinical management requires a balance between two undesirable outcomes: excessive masculinization and excessive secretion of cortisol. The latter is characterized by Cushing's syndrome, the symptoms of which include obesity, short stature, osteoporosis, carbohydrate intolerance, and elevated blood lipids. Surgical removal of both adrenal glands is sometimes needed in the most severe cases of CAH.[19]

The excess androgen that is responsible for CAH is present during embryonic development. This leads to virilization of the external genitals in girls, resulting in an enlarged clitoris, fusion of the labia majora, and a common urethral/vaginal opening.[20] Treatment for CAH involves glucocordicoid and mineral-corticoid substitution therapy to suppress excessive androgen production. When severe virilization occurs these girls usually undergo surgical genital feminization.

About 75 percent of CAH sufferers produce insufficient aldosterone, an androgen-like compound, and so are unable to maintain proper sodium metabolism. This results in abnormal sodium loss via the kidney, colon, and sweat glands. The 21-hydroxylase deficiency condition can produce a salt-wasting crisis about 7 days postnatally that is sometimes life threatening. The most deleterious effects of CAH, such as a reduction in IQ—notably in verbal IQ relative to performance IQ—occur in the salt-wasting form of the condition. Such people risk an underdeveloped nervous system if appropriate medical intervention does not occur soon after birth. Other complications include lowered blood pressure and a loss of electrolytes due to salt depletion, also a life-threatening situation.[21]

A promising new treatment for classical CAH involves using an antiandrogen as well as an aromatase inhibitor and a reduced hydrocortisone dose. Treatment of the milder nonclassical form of CAH involves the use of a glucocorticoid—a birth control pill—as well as an antiandrogen. This regime reduces the likelihood of polycystic ovary syndrome, which is also a risk factor for transsexed men undergoing testosterone hormone therapy.

The mild form of CAH that occurs in 0.5 percent of the female population accounts for 5 percent to 10 percent of children with premature adrenarche, the physiological changes at puberty caused by the secretion of androgens from the adrenal cortex. It also affects between 5 percent and 10 percent of women with excessive male-like hair growth. In later life, children with CAH prefer to partake in masculine play activities and exhibit decreased parenting behavior. A similar deviation from expected feminine activities occurs in girls born of mothers who underwent prenatal progesterone treatment. When compared with other children, children with CAH tend to be more independent, sensitive, and self-assured.[22]

CAH sufferers are more likely to be left-handed than the general population. Most girls with CAH identify as female and tend to be heterosexual. They experience no notable neuropsychological abnormalities. Girls with CAH have gender identity scores intermediate between those of girls without CAH and tomboys. Only about 10 percent of CAH girls have gender identity scores outside the normal range, 6 percent of such girls being reared as boys due to their excess masculinization, especially if they are left untreated.[23] Girls with CAH tend to prefer transportation toys rather than dolls.

Only girls with salt-wasting CAH spend more time playing with masculine toys and less time playing with feminine toys when compared with a group of girls who do not suffer from CAH. Most of the salt-wasting CAH girls prefer playing with boys rather than girls, and they prefer typically masculine jobs. However, parents often wish that their CAH daughters would not partake in quite so many masculine activities, the extent of which depends positively on Prader score, that is, the degree of virilization resulting from CAH.

In terms of sexual preferences, 48 percent of CAH adolescent girls report same-sex imagery, and 22 percent prefer a same-sex partner. The corresponding values for AIS people are 15 percent and 10 percent respectively, probably resulting from a lack of androgen sensitivity that would bias their sexual orientation towards men.[24] Although girls with CAH score higher on masculinity in various gender-role tests compared with a comparison group of girls without CAH, they are equivalent on a gender identity interview and show no evidence of discomfort with their gender identity.[25]

SEX-REVERSAL SYNDROME

The SRY gene is responsible for testes formation. The SRY gene triggers the production of Sertoli cells, which direct a male's sexual development. On the other hand, organisms with XY chromosomes that have a duplicated short arm of the X chromosome and an intact SRY gene produce a male-to-female sex reversal.[26]

The sex-reversal syndrome, originally reported in 1964, results in a translocation of Y chromosomal material, including the SRY gene on the Y chromosome, on to the X chromosome. Sex-reversed 46 XX males have a masculine presentation, with small testes that do not produce sperm. Despite having XX chromosomes, such people do not have a properly developed uterus or ovaries. The incidence of sex-reversal syndrome is about 1 in 20,000 to 25,000.

The DAX1 gene might produce the abnormal conditions that generate the sex-reversal phenomenon. The DAX1 and SRY genes act antagonistically so that increasing dominance of the DAX1 gene leads to female sexual development, whereas increasing dominance of the SRY gene leads to male sexual development. So sex reversal is determined primarily by excess activity promoted by the DAX1 gene, as well as by the relative timing of DAX1 and SRY gene activity. This process might explain why testis formation in an XX DAX1:SRY embryo is retarded when compared with normal XY embryos. So DAX1 might be considered an anti-testis, rather than ovary-determining, gene.

46 XY females with complete androgen insensitivity syndrome have a pubertal growth spurt even though they have minimal testosterone. They eventually

grow taller than the average woman but slightly less than that of the average man. In such cases, both the testes and peripheral tissues produce sufficient estrogen to permit the accrual of a near-normal female bone mass.[27]

SUMMARY

Intersexed conditions, although relatively rare, produce difficult medical and social situations for both the sufferers and their loved ones. The surprisingly large variation in presentation of intersex conditions demands careful diagnosis together with a recognition that any intersex condition's effects might change over a person's lifetime. Whereas CAH commonly produces masculinization in women without any need for sex reassignment in most situations, AIS almost always produces sufficient feminization to warrant reassignment as female. The sex-reversal syndromes present unique complications characterized by infertility, with reassignment to the chromosomal sex being considered appropriate. All these intersex conditions offer a counter-example for the determination of legal sex by simply examining the external genitals.

Transsexuality has many of the properties of representative intersex conditions. Understanding the difficulties experienced by those with an intersex condition is important since it is now becoming evident that transsexuality is akin in some ways to an intersex condition. Any discrepancy between brain-sex and genital-sex is just as anomalous as the sexual ambiguities experienced by those with an intersex condition.

Chapter Thirteen

FAMILY AND SOCIAL ISSUES

One of the greatest fears transsexed people have is whether their immediate family, friends, and work colleagues will offer them support in what is a long and difficult process towards their own self-fulfillment and happiness. In many cases, those closest to the transitioning person find it difficult to cope, at least in the initial stages. This situation leads more often then not to shunning by family and friends so that the transsexed person has no further contact with their family, most particularly their children. Being denied their parental right to be with their children is heartbreaking and can lead to severe psychological difficulties. Sadly, this situation appears to be more common than otherwise, although there has been little research to inform counselors and the distraught transsexed person about appropriate remediation.

Five emotional stages experienced by families of newly outed transsexed people include denial, anger, bargaining, depression, and acceptance. The wives of transsexed husbands often report feelings of shock, horror, disbelief, anger, betrayal, self-blame, loss of self-esteem, and depression. It is clear that adjusting to the news that a loved one is "changing sex" is a traumatic experience for most people. Family counseling is needed so that loved ones can adjust to their changed circumstances and assist their transsexed relative. Such interventions should occur before the transsexed person and their family lose contact with each other.[1]

Marriage breakup is common when a spouse is transsexed, especially when a gender clinic refuses to help married clients. It is difficult to predict how tolerant the significant other will be once they discover their spouse's cross-gendered behavior. For this reason, many transsexed people find the revelation of their cross-gendered identity to be a traumatic experience.

Transition has a substantial effect on the transsexed person's children. Often the concern of courts adjudicating on divorce settlements is to minimize the conflict and trauma imposed on the child, possibly by terminating contact between the transsexed person and their children. Some transsexed people abdicate their parenting role because they fear their transition would be harmful to the child. When their former spouse is adamantly opposed to any further contact, the transsexed person believes that any legal fight is a lost cause. In more amicable circumstances, the transsexed parent continues to live with their family during the real-life experience, or else maintains frequent family contact while living apart.

The following interview vignettes illustrate the poignancy of children's thinking and their continuing love for a parent who is either transitioning or has already transitioned.[2]

Seven-Year-Old Boy with a Male-to-Female Transsexed Parent

"Linda wants to be a woman. Linda wants to start a fresh life. She likes living as a woman. I think that is happy for her. At first (when I was 4 1/2) I didn't quite understand. As I got older, I realized she must be happy living as a woman, so I'll just accept that."

Does Linda have a penis?
"She is going to have it taken off."

What is your worry?
"The thing I worry about is if he gets injections that the wrong amount would be given and something would go wrong. . . . Is there a chance he could die in the operation?"

Seven-Year-Old Girl with a Male-to-Female Transsexed Parent

Why does your daddy dress as a lady?
"It's a better life."

Ten-Year-Old Boy with a Male-to-Female Transsexed Parent

How do you feel about it?
"It's alright."

Why is your daddy doing this?
"He does not like being a man."

Eleven-Year-Old Sister

"My dad's having a sex change. He is turning into a woman."

Why?
"He feels like a woman."

How do you feel about it?
"I feel OK about it."

Fourteen-Year-Old Daughter with a Female-to-Male Transsexed Parent

"My mother's not happy in the body she is in. My mom is a lot happier since starting to live as who she wants to be. When I was 13, my mother said, 'I want to be a man, do you care? I said, no, as long as you are the same person inside and still love me. I don't care what you are on the outside. . . . It's like a chocolate bar, it's got a new wrapper but it's the same chocolate inside."

These vignettes demonstrate that transsexed people can remain effective and loving parents and that children can understand and empathize with their transsexed parent's situation. These cases demonstrate that gender identity confusion in the child with respect to their parent does not always occur. Any subsequent teasing the children might suffer from peers is no more of a problem than the teasing children get for a myriad of other reasons. The children's best interests are not served by the bullying tactic of trading off the children as scapegoats when the wife's need for retaliation results in her opposing any contact between her transsexed partner and their children. Although divorce is more or less inevitable in many cases, just as it is in most other situations of marital disharmony, it should not affect future contact between parents and their children, nor should be necessary so that married transsexed people can change the sex on their birth certificate. As Wallbank[3] has pleaded, "People with transsexualism and other intersexual people who have undergone irreversible sex affirmation treatment have only been permitted to correct or update the particulars as to their legal identity if they comply with such inhumane and strange conditions as the requirement they divorce their life-long spouse." The law purports to protect the mental health of married transsexed person's children by formalizing the anguish and despair experienced when the transsexed person is denied access to their children, often disregarding such children's wishes. The mother's adverse reaction to a transsexed spouse may reflect deficiencies in her own ability to adjust to change. Children with transsexed parents almost invariably exhibit no gender-atypical behavior themselves, but they are affected by the marital discord that arises between the transsexed person and their other parent.[4]

A survey of 10 gender therapists indicated that it is best for transsexed people to disclose their transition intentions to their children, the earlier the better. However, adolescent children might react adversely, so the transsexed person needs to be prepared for such a situation. Risk factors for the children include an abrupt separation, a spouse who is averse to the transition, parental conflict, and personality problems in both partners. Children fare better when they have a close emotional relationship with the nontransitioning parent, there is extended family support of the transitioning parent, and contact is maintained with both parents. Children manage best when they are younger or of mature age, with teenage children having the most difficulties contending with a transitioning parent.[5] It is interesting that parents who view transsexuality as a biological condition are more accepting of their child's situation. This finding accords with survey results from a broader sample of people described in chapter 1.[6]

The conflict between living a secret cross-gendered life and coming out to family and friends can lead to clinically significant levels of depression and anxiety. When a married man lives full-time as a woman most of the time but transgresses to being male when the situation demands it, problems of self-identity might arise. There have been no follow-up investigations to determine if temporary switching of gender roles is successful, or perhaps stressful, despite the maintenance of marital harmony.

Most cross-gendered men reveal their gender difficulties to their spouses before approaching a support group, although many access Internet support chat-lines during their exploratory phase and thereby maintain confidentiality. Concerns during the public outing phase include anxiety about how others will react to the news. Although many transsexed women are concerned about how their family and friends will react to their unexpected revelation, less than 25 percent report negative reactions. So some of their initial fears are probably unfounded. However, it is worthwhile providing close relatives with as much information as possible about transsexuality at the outset so that an informed discussion can occur.[7]

The main reason for telling family, friends, and work colleagues is the need to be responsible and inform people who might be affected by the transition. Sharing the news with a female friend may be ego boosting, since her reaction is usually less critical than that of male relatives and friends. For some transsexed women, outing themselves is based on a prior conviction that other people's love for them will be maintained and support will be forthcoming. It is preferable to come out face-to-face and provide significant others with time to absorb the news. Later on, a subsequent discussion might elucidate the likely consequences of the transition. To reduce the burden on the transsexed person, some relatives might offer to inform others, possibly encouraging them to be supportive as well.[8]

The conditions under which a transsexed woman's identity might be confirmed by her social interactions with family, friends, and others have been investigated. Whereas earlier reports had claimed that the majority of transsexed people suffer mental health problems derived mostly from adverse social reactions, interviews of mainly black transsexed women sex workers in New York City indicated that depression is less prevalent when there is good support from both family and friends. The benefits arising from such support are enhanced by being up-front about one's transsexed identity to close associates, by being successful in one's cross-gendered role, and by minimizing any conflict between one's transsexed identity awareness and social performance of the cross-gendered role. A transsexed person's self-esteem is enhanced when existing sexual partners negotiate a new role for themselves and their transsexed partner as well as when support is offered by parents, siblings, and more distant family members. Continued employment is a challenge that is both ego boosting and financially rewarding for the transsexed person.[9]

Occasionally, the relationships between various members of the transsexed community can be fickle. For example, it is not unusual for transsexed people to avoid contact with transvestites. In some organizations, passability becomes a status symbol, the more physically attractive members avoiding those who are not quite so fortunate. Eventually, transsexed people tend to leave support groups to live a life of their own, whereas transvestites thrive on the privacy these support groups offer. Some members of a group of transgendered people in Perth, Western Australia, that included 10 transsexed people reported going out in public as the opposite gender is about the most difficult challenge.[10]

The sexual preferences of transsexed people is an interesting issue. Frank Lewins[11] who interviewed transsexed women and men using opportunistic and probably biased sampling discovered that transsexed women in stable relationships tend to be sexually involved with women rather than men. After GRS these women indulge in what appears to be lesbian relationships.

Since 1997, representatives with a transsexual background have been elected to the board of the Harry Benjamin International Gender Dysphoria Association. This marked a turning point, since now consumers as well as gender specialists contribute to revisions of the standards of care. A greater number of so-called posttranssexed people have opted not to disappear into the world of women or men but to remain active in the various political movements for both transsexed and transgendered people.[12]

Perhaps the most difficult challenge for transsexed people is maintaining their family relationships. For those who have children, the reaction to their new lifestyle is often acceptable to the children but devastating for their partner. Because of the stressful situation that can often arise, proper care of the transsexed person is vital.

CARE OF TRANSSEXED AND TRANSGENDERED PEOPLE

Similarly to the homosexual community, transsexed and transgendered people occasionally experience prejudice and other negative responses from caregivers. This is an unfortunate situation since transsexed people, more than most, deserve the very best care. In nursing situations, accommodating a transsexed person in a gender-segregated hospital ward can be a problem, especially when inappropriate and abusive language is used by the nursing staff.[13]

Sixty percent of transsexed people experience some form of harassment or violence, and 37 percent experience economic discrimination. Drug and alcohol abuse by transsexed people often results from low self-esteem and a lack of both educational and job opportunities. Because of harassment and family difficulties, some transsexed and transgendered youth leave home and fend for themselves with inadequate resources. This leads to an increase in substance abuse, especially alcohol, cocaine, and methamphetamines.

Prejudice by health service providers prevents these young people from obtaining urgent help. Also, black-market hormone overdose is a further medical complication, especially when the client is too poor to afford the expensive hormonal treatments needed to treat transsexualism as a medical condition.[14]

The care of older transsexed people is problematic, since there is no guarantee that retirement communities will treat such people with dignity. Problems occur when religious senior citizen agencies reject transsexed people, and other agencies offer less than adequate medical care. This is an urgent issue for an aging transsexed population.[15]

THE SOCIAL LIFE OF TRANSSEXED PEOPLE

Most transsexed women value their feminine appearance as confirmation of their new identity. Such behavior reflects the cultural importance of women looking like women, the more attractive the better. A minority of transsexed women recall wanting to be a girl from an early age, many only experiencing such feelings during adolescence and beyond. Many transsexed women appreciate that transvestites can feel and look feminine occasionally, whereas for transsexed women the need to be feminine is perpetual. Although there was strong pressure to conform to gender expectations when they were young, some transsexed women recall feeling much more comfortable playing with girls and associating with a female group. When they were required to deal with boys, many transsexed women report feelings of anxiety, failure, and a loss of self-esteem. To tolerate this situation better, many tend to be loners.[8]

Further into their transition, some transsexed women resort to drugs and alcohol to conceal the mismatch between their true identity as female and the role expected of them by family and peers. In desperation, a small number mutilate their genitals to reinforce their affirmed sexual identity. As has been frequently observed, 44 percent of a group of transsexed women had engaged in hypermasculine activities such as serving in the military to compensate for, and possibly obliterate, their transsexed feelings.[8]

As transsexed women become more immersed in their own culture and identify increasingly more often as female, they start to question their own sexual orientation. Although most react cautiously to advances by men, they also realize that validating their womanhood might require having sex with men. Many transsexed women consider this aspect of their transition to be rather problematic, probably because very few middle-aged women report being gay prior to their transition. Nevertheless, many want to experience the thrill of being treated "like a lady" should the opportunity arise.[8]

Since Benjamin's[16] early work on transsexuality, adopting as complete a feminine lifestyle as possible during the real-life experience is important. In a study of experiences of passing, four transsexed women and eight transsexed men who were undergoing treatment for gender issues were interviewed. Five of these transsexed people had begun their transition after an acute emotional crisis. One of these, a 56-year-old transsexed woman, decided to transition because she felt increasingly unattractive due to aging (undoubtedly a risky justification for full transition). Most of the transsexed women had served in the armed forces, which provided an opportunity for them to prove their masculinity in the hope of "curing" their gender issues. Most had experienced physical or psychological abandonment by their same-sex parent during childhood, few had cross-dressed as children, and most were chronically depressed and anxious.[17]

An assumption, especially among the medical establishment, is that transsexed people will want to have GRS, pass as a man or woman, and thereafter live their lives by being as indistinguishable as possible from natal people of their affirmed sex. Transsexed people also need to acquire legal and social documentation appropriate to their new gender role. However, difficulties can arise irrespective of whether a transsexed person wishes to pass. Those who pass but live in stealth must hide their past life, often leading to confusion for others and stress for themselves. A transsexed man or women living in stealth is much less likely to serve as a confidant for other transsexed people, especially those who are in transition and who cannot pass easily. On the other hand, those who do not pass may have difficulty obtaining employment, their ambiguous appearance prejudicing their own safety as well as their relations with family and friends. A division of the transsexed community based on passability leads to distressing disagreements that prejudice any cohesive attempt to obtain justice for all transsexed people. Generally, the passing transsexed, especially those who are postoperative, aspire to, and acquire, a higher status than many others within the transsexed community.[18]

The need for transsexed people to pass is relaxed in many "progressive" transsexed and transgendered communities to provide space and acceptance of androgynous and gender-ambiguous people. Katrina Roen[18] refers to the binary gender status quo as "either/or" and compares this with a more flexible gender presentation as "both/neither." "Either/or" transsexed people frequently aspire to a life of stealth, even isolating themselves from other transsexed people. This occurs despite people such as Kate Bornstein[20] proclaiming that such behavior is politically incapacitating, especially when the transsexed person suffers stigma. Bornstein claims that passing represents shame, capitulation, invisibility, lies, and self-denial. Perhaps the gender diversity represented by "both/neither" is just as acceptable and as liberating as is racial and religious diversity.

Roen interviewed transsexed and transgendered people to obtain information on the importance of passing. One who presented as "both/neither" could not obtain a position in a college course even though she had the necessary qualifications. Some transsexed women maintained a "both/neither" orientation in private and in their everyday thinking, especially during transition, but felt some pressure to conform to an "either/or" presentation in public. Some of the transsexed participants reported that their medical advisors would consider a "both/neither" presentation as politically radical, leading to problems in obtaining approval for GRS. A majority opinion was that a transsexed woman's "goal was to live as an ordinary woman . . . and ordinary women don't mix in transsexual circles."[19] By contrast, most of the transsexed men had no trouble passing as male, so the "both/neither" category had little relevance for them.

In an anonymous note written in response to a query as to why a non-operative transsexed woman would consider herself to be "transsexed," it is claimed that one can be a woman despite having residual male genitals.[21] She noted that passing is unrelated to the existence of male or "neo-female" genitals, these being generally hidden from public view. The critical event for such a person is the decision to live full-time as a woman with hormonal assistance rather than feeling obliged to undergo GRS. Provided one can live comfortably as a woman, an important concern is the advisability of undergoing surgery that may compromise quality of life thereafter. Successful living full-time as a woman is the primary qualification for being "transsexed," so "sex," as represented by external genitals, is irrelevant.

When transsexed women start their real-life experience they should be perceived as a woman rather than as someone in transition. Often initial outings in public are carefully planned, being limited to relatively safe places such as gay bars and driving their own car to avoid exposure in public transport. Support groups are important at this stage despite the anxiety that is occasionally engendered by intolerance from "seasoned" transsexed women. In addition to socialization at support groups, transsexed women enjoy receiving advice on makeup, hairstyle, and the other accoutrements that enhance passability.[8]

The coming-out phase allows transsexed people to transform themselves so they can live as convincingly as possible as their "true selves." Many transsexed people agree that "passing . . . is the most important aspect of the whole thing. If you can't do that, I don't see the point of living this way."[22] Once passing is mastered to their satisfaction, many transsexed women no longer require transsexed community support and live as women, perhaps in "stealth" mode. For such people, being seen in public with an obviously transsexed or transgendered person risks revealing their own background. An alternative view from a so-called gender radical is that ". . . passing is more a fear that has to be overcome and when I overcame that fear to be nonchalant about it, I didn't care that I passed or not."[23] Nevertheless, people who maintain an androgynous appearance are often ridiculed and stigmatized and run the risk of suffering emotional and physical abuse. Hence many transsexed women strive to be passable and live anonymously in society as women.

Many transsexed people experience problems when outing themselves at work. For some, this leads to demotion, harassment, and eventually either dismissal or voluntary resignation. For those requiring the most social support, the loss of professional identity and their previous level of income is further exacerbated by the loss of family and close friends. Most transsexed people are challenged by their initial attempts at living full-time as their "true selves."[24] The reactions of their employer as well as the wider community determine whether their public acceptance is tolerable. For some transsexed people, passing is paramount, whereas for others just being themselves is more important. Interestingly, the transsexed community itself can be a source of distress, especially when passing postoperative transsexed people establish themselves at the peak of a transsexed hierarchy.

RELIGIOUS AND ETHICAL ISSUES

Acceptance into society's establishments, such as organized religions, is important for transsexed individuals. Considerable harm can result from institutionalized prejudice by a majority directed against an already disenfranchised minority.

Ethical issues of concern to Christians in their dealings with transsexed people include questions of gender, the impact of gender status on an individual's participation in religious events, the acceptability of GRS, and whether the church should solemnize marriages involving one or more transsexed people. Like the community in general, many religious people were initially exposed to transsexuality when media reports of successful GRS first appeared. Christians often oppose such surgery since it does not relate to procreation, nor does it solve a psychological, rather than a biological, problem. This is a common attitude among the religious that is inconsistent with the presumed biological basis of transsexuality.[25]

Some Scriptures stipulate that cross-dressing is as inappropriate a behavior as genital mutilation, the implicit assumption being that no one can interfere with one's preordained gender or sexual identity. This modern interpretation of Scripture ignores the elevated position accorded castrated males, or eunuchs, in many ancient societies. For example, by accepting the following edict in Mathew (19:12), a Christian should welcome transsexed people into all religious activities, including the sacrament of marriage.

> For there are some eunuchs, which were so born from their *mother's* womb: and there are some eunuchs, which were made eunuchs of men: and there be eunuchs, which have made themselves eunuchs for the kingdom of heaven's sake. He that is able to receive *it*, let him receive *it*.

Of particular significance is maintaining a legally valid marriage between a man and a woman when the man has transitioned from male to female by mutual consent of both parties. According to many religions, it is clear that no outside agent can separate those who have been formally united by the acquiescence of a God. This would imply that such an apparently same-sex marriage cannot be annulled.

Religious people fail to understand why anyone would want surgery to alter a healthy body especially when the long-term benefits of such a procedure have not been fully researched and documented. Their reservations are reinforced by the occasional incidents of postsurgical regret as well as accompanying dysfunction such as depression and prostitution. The lack of well-established facts on the impact of GRS on family life cannot ameliorate a critical onslaught from religious people.[26]

A Christian marriage involving at least one transsexed person remains valid provided it involves a union between a man and a woman. However, a problem arises when the legally accepted sexual designation of the transsexed people involved is based on biological criteria, rather than on social aspects of gender expression as recognized by relatives and friends. For example, a preoperative transsexed woman might wish to marry a natal man but for health reasons cannot endure GRS and subsequently change the sex on her birth certificate. Such a union might be considered same-sex, leading to the marriage being not recognized in many jurisdictions.

The theological status of a reconstructed sex organ, as opposed to a "God-given" one, is an interesting issue. It has been stated that "human sexuality is an artifact, and that artifactual sexuality is real sexuality."[27] So is a surgically constructed sexual organ an artifact? The extent to which the sexed nature of such an artifact can constitute the transsexed person's "true" sex is an interesting question. Maybe the resolution of such a dilemma might itself become a criterion for sex affirmation. However, when legislating sexual relationships within a marriage, society should really play no role in documenting a person's "real sex," since this is a private matter between the partners. As the general public infers a person's sex based on one's gender expression, everyone should have a right to express themselves in whatever way they feel most comfortable.

SUMMARY

Transsexed people often suffer debilitating hardship and distress upon informing their family, friends, and workmates of their impending transition.

Of particular concern is the effect of a transsexed person's transition announce-ment on their partner and children, and how they all cope following such a rev-elation. Unfortunately, this situation is often a precursor to marriage breakup, sometimes even demanded by the transsexed person's professional advisors, with the real prospect of her never being allowed to see her children again. This devastating situation, which occurs even when the children report few prob-lems with the transition, is the precursor to ill health for the transsexed person. Once the transsexed person has dealt with family and friends, they adjust to their new lifestyle by expressing their affirmed sexual identity in society.

In Western society, transsexed people contend with religious and ethical challenges that castigate them for being their "true selves." Such harassment, whether implicit or explicit, alienates some religious teaching from the realm of human rights and stretches the limits of ethical behavior towards another human being. An institutionalized and sanctioned form of such bigotry and prejudice occurs in societies that routinely punish transsexed and transgen-dered people as if they do not deserve to exist at all.

Chapter Fourteen

LEGAL ISSUES

The law has made life difficult for transsexed people. Not only is the social stigma suffered by them legitimized by law enforcement agencies, but institutions that most people take for granted have not made a transsexed person's life any easier. For example, marriage is difficult for many transsexed people. Gaining appropriate employment and social security rights also present many challenges.

A person's legal sex in most countries is based on genital appearance as determined by medical staff at birth. This sex designation is recorded officially by the state on the person's birth certificate. For transsexed people, their birth certificate contains the wrong legal sex until it can be changed following GRS.

MARRIAGE LAW

Legal aspects of marriage recognition when there is at least one transsexed person involved present difficult problems for all concerned. Sir Roger Ormrod, the presiding judge in the British case that challenged the marriage between April Ashley, a transsexed woman, and a natal man, asserted that one's sex is determined by the chromosomes, which in April's case was XY or male.[1] Nevertheless, in his reply to correspondence between Judge Ormrod and Henry Finlay, an Australian lawyer, over a decade later in 1988 and 1989, Judge Ormrod suggested that a marriage between a transsexed person and a person of the same biological sex might be recognized irrespective of whether

GRS had been performed, since it is important to "recognise and define the legal incidents and consequences of cohabitation and forget about the genitals."[2] So attitudes can change.

In *Christine Goodwin v. UK* (2002), a case involving a British transsexed woman who sought legal redress for employment discrimination, social security payments, and marriage, the court recognized the increasing social acceptance of transsexed people, in particular formal recognition of the new sexual identity of postoperative transsexed people. Since it is inappropriate for such people to live in a sexual "limboland," recognition of a transsexed person's right to marry should occur under all circumstances. Unlike in the UK, consummation is irrelevant to the legality of a marriage under Australian law, leading to the possibility that same-sex marriages might be validated, at least in principle. However, in a retrograde step, amendments to the Marriage Act to ban same-sex marriage by defining marriage as only occurring between a man and a woman became law in Australia in 2004.

Recognizing transsexed people as intersexed at the brain-sex level should lead to similar legal rights to those won for intersexed clients. However, this argument failed in the UK *Bellinger v. Bellinger* case, in which a transsexed woman sought legal recognition of her marriage to a natal man after appealing a previous negative verdict. This negative outcome resulted from a lack of scientific consensus of the brain-sex concept. Professor Green, an expert witness, emphasized that in any intersex condition, appropriate sex affirmation must consider psychological issues that can only be confirmed in later life. The biological sexual status of an individual was assumed not to be fixed at birth. Mr. Terry, a GRS surgeon, stated that the client's chromosomal makeup is irrelevant when considering a person's lifestyle and rights. However, the court was not convinced that such evidence had a firm scientific basis and so rejected the idea that sex determination involves processes other than chromosomal identity.

Lord Reed stated that "[i]f a society accepts that transsexualism is a serious and distressing medical problem, and allows those who suffer from it to undergo drastic treatment in order to adopt a new gender and thereby improve their quality of life, then reason and common humanity alike suggest that it should allow such persons to function as fully as possible in their new gender."[3] Also, Professor Gooren suggested that "[it] is reasonable to require from the law that it makes provision for those rare individuals in whom the formation of gender identity has not followed the course otherwise so reliably prognosticated by the external genitalia."[4] Human rights and natural justice require the law to be flexible enough to accommodate individual cases rather than adhering to biological misinterpretations deemed appropriate for all.

Andrew Sharpe[5] recognized the destabilizing possibilities when transsexed people dispense with legal aspects of their sex designation. In law, sex is defined in two different ways, one emphasizing psychological and anatomical gender harmony, the other based on social and cultural gender consistency. Much of the law relating to sex is affected by a disguised form of homophobia as well as by strict adherence to the sex categories, male and female. Some legislators believe that transsexed people are homosexual, an attitude that also pervades some of the medical profession, many lawyers and doctors basing their professional judgments on heteronormativity.[6]

Much of English law following *Corbett v. Corbett* emphasized the critical importance of the moment of birth as the final arbiter of assigned sex since "sex is determined at birth and by a congruence of chromosomal, gonadal and genital factors."[8] So any marriage between people of opposite genders but of the same birth-sex is rendered illegal. Legal and medical recognition of preoperative and nonoperative transsexed people is not well developed, such people being generally categorized as homosexuals. Most law reform has concentrated almost exclusively on postoperative transsexed women, thus alienating transsexed men for whom complete GRS is both risky and expensive. The law is probably more lenient towards "passing" transsexed people.[7]

Judge Ormrod limited his ruling regarding the legal definition of sex to the context of marriage. Although April Ashley, one of the protagonists, possessed a "constructed vagina," Judge Ormrod considered that it allowed unnatural sexual intercourse. He did not discriminate between sexual intercourse using a "constructed vagina" and anal intercourse, thereby providing strong evidence of institutionalized homophobia.

In another English case, *S.Y. v. S.Y.* (otherwise known as *W.*), a request to annul an unconsummated marriage was denied because surgical procedures could have corrected the wife's vaginal problem. However, vaginal intercourse following GRS did constitute consummation of a marriage for legal purposes, indicating the contradictions and institutionalized prejudice within English case law.[7]

Legal judgments regarding marriage involving at least one transsexed person depend on whether sexual penetration is necessary for a legitimate union. Otherwise there is no reason why marriages involving preoperative and nonoperative transsexed people cannot be legally validated. Reliance on fundamental biology such as the chromosomes pathologizes the transsexed person's body, which has been altered, at least hormonally, at great personal cost.

Assigning sex based on hormonal determinants occurring prenatally or at birth might resolve this problem. In *W. v. W.,* a case in which a transsexed woman who was born with partial androgen insensitivity syndrome was sexually assigned as female, the judge ruled in favor of the woman, since a mistake was made on her birth record. In this case, GRS "naturalizes" the body, in contrast to the "unnaturalization" occurring erroneously in transsexed women without a physical intersexed condition. It is important that lawmakers recognize transsexuality as an intersexed condition so that an enlarged corpus of case law can apply. The law should recognize the considerable relief from suffering that occurs when there is concordance between the physical and psychological aspect of sex and gender for postoperative people.[9]

In those jurisdictions that do not permit same-sex marriages, a transsexed woman may not remain legally married to her wife even though the medical condition of transsexualism is not a prerequisite for annulment of a marriage. In Australia, for example, annulment can only result from either the death of a spouse or divorce. In the UK, however, same-sex marriages by proxy between a transsexed person and their spouse are null and void.

Nevertheless, successful legal judgments such as *MT v. JT* in the United States, which approved a marriage involving a postoperative transsexed woman, contradict the biological determinism of *Corbett* since "sexual identity can be determined, for marital purposes, by the congruence of the transsexual's anatomical features with his or her psychological sex ... coalescence of the physical ability and the psychological and emotional orientation to engage in sexual intercourse was the crucial factor."[10] Procreation ability played no role in this verdict. Perhaps unenlightened jurisdictions view transsexualism as a disorder that can be cured by psychological intervention, thus invalidating other legal claims based on postoperative sexual affirmation.

THE *RE KEVIN* CASE IN AUSTRALIA

In 2001 in the family court of Australia, the landmark verdict by Judge Chisholm in *Re Kevin,* a case involving the validity of a marriage between a transsexed man ("Kevin") and a natal woman, dispensed with the *Corbett v. Corbett* chromosomal criterion for sex determination. In arriving at this decision, the judge referred to the canonical law of marriage that existed in England during the Middle Ages. By such a law, an intersexed person can act sexually as a male or female provided they remain permanently in their chosen sex, a situation that occurs for almost all postoperative people.

In the summary report of proceedings,[11] evidence confirmed the status of a postoperative transsexed person with respect to both their sex affirmation, and their human rights. In his conclusions, Judge Chisholm quoted from Thorpe to ask "[if] there [is] not inconsistency in the state which through its health services provides full treatment for gender identity disorder but by its legal system denies the desired recognition."[12] Further in paragraph 174, Judge Chisholm states that "if the law of marriage were to insist on treating Kevin as a woman, it would be taking a course that would seem to be inconsistent with virtually every other indicator of the way transsexuals are considered in our community." Indeed, as noted in paragraph 173, "a society which allows reassignment operations to proceed has a moral obligation to give full recognition to the effects of such surgery." The judge had rightfully adhered to principles of natural justice and human rights, as well as adding a generous dose of common sense.

The legal system cannot recognize any sex that is not exclusively male or female. So legally, intersexed individuals as well as transsexed people must be classified in an arbitrary way. Judge Chisholm defined legal sex more gener- ally as "the person's biological and physical characteristics at birth (including gonads, genitals and chromosomes); the person's life experiences, including the sex in which he or she is brought up and the person's attitude to it; the person's self-perception as a man or a woman; the extent to which the person has functioned in society as a man or a woman; any hormonal, surgical or other medical sex reassignment treatments the person has undergone, and the consequences of such treatment; and the person's biological, psychological and physical characteristics at the time of the marriage, including (if they can be identified) any biological features of the person's brain that are associated with a particular sex.... [P]ost-operative transsexuals will normally be members of their reassigned sex."[13] This definition is based on current scientific knowl- edge, which extends the legal definition of sex to include both psychological and lifestyle aspects.

As noted in paragraph 189 of the *Re Kevin* judgment, following sexual affir- mation Finnish people, for example, can be recognized as their assigned sex for marriage, without surgery being a prerequisite. To obviate a possible critique of marriage involving at least one postoperative partner, European law recog- nizes that procreation ability is not required for a marriage to be legal. Judge Martens of the European Court provided dissent in the unsuccessful *Cossey v. UK* (1990) marriage case to the effect that hormone therapy and surgery are needed to bring the transsexed person's outward physical sex in line with their psychological sex. Most importantly, this new sexual identity must be recog- nized legally.[14]

Judge Chisholm in *Re Kevin* stated that "failure to recognise the sex of post- operative [transsexed people] raises serious issues of human rights, such that the question arises whether the failure can be permitted on the basis of the margin of appreciation allowed to States under the [Australian] Constitution. It is clear that a decision in favour of the applicants would be more in accord with international thinking on human rights than a refusal of the application." Consequently, Judge Chisholm ruled that "postoperative transsexuals should be treated as members of the sex to which they have been assigned."[15]

In Paragraph 223 of the *Re Kevin* judgment, Professor Gooren advised that transsexed people cannot determine if their sex was wrongly specified at birth until they have experienced living in their preferred gender role. How much life experience is really needed is an interesting question, as some transsexed people claim that they know they were born into the "wrong body" almost from their earliest memories. In paragraph 239, Professor Gooren emphasized that transsexed people are biologically intersexed. Dr Walker in paragraph 240 indicated that whether a person is male or female depends on their own perception and the perception of others. Consequently, there can be a sexual inconsistency between brain-sex and body-sex (paragraph 253), leading to transsexuality being considered an intersexed condition.

Rachael Wallbank reviewed the implications of the successful Australian *Re Kevin* case for how transsexuality is viewed in contemporary society. Wallbank defined various terms related to "transsexualism" without claiming that a consensus exists. Brain-sex is often confused with "psychological sex," both of which do not correspond to physical aspects of sex such as the external genitals. So, "[i]n the absence of mental health, an individual's brain sex is the sex which the individual perceives the individual to be[, that is,](self-perception, or knowing, of one's innate sex)."[16] Brain-sex determines how a person functions at all times.

Although brain-sex is difficult to verify in practice, for legal purposes it should only be necessary to rely on the person's knowledge of their experienced sex when evidence is required by a court of law. Although transsexuality might be considered a biological rather than a behavioral phenomenon based on the evidence presented in chapter 2, there is no methodology for evaluating this proposition scientifically in living people. So it is difficult to deny transvestites a biological basis for their condition based on current knowledge.

Human rights, prominently featured in the judgment of *Re Kevin*, can also be violated unless care is taken. Recent UK legal "reforms" require applicants for "gender recognition" both to be diagnosed with "gender dysphoria," and to terminate any existing marriage. The former condition requires the transsexed person to be labeled as "mentally ill." The latter condition ignores the emotional anguish a transsexed person and their family suffer when a marriage is dissolved under duress.[17]

In *Sheffield and Horsham v. the United Kingdom*, Kristina Sheffield claimed that both her psychiatrist and surgeon required that she be divorced before undergoing GRS. This led to the former wife obtaining a court order preventing Sheffield from contacting her daughter. Also any marriage she might wish to engage in as a woman would be illegal under British law. In response to this ruling, the European Court upon appeal stated that "[i]t is no longer possible . . . to justify a system . . . which treats gender dysphoria as a medical condition, subsidises gender re-assignment surgery but then withholds recognition of the consequences of that surgery thereby exposing postoperative transsexuals to the likelihood of recurring distress and humiliation."[18]

DOCUMENTATION AMENDMENT AND EMPLOYMENT DISCRIMINATION

Perhaps the physician made a mistake in completing the original birth certificate for a transsexed person. This results from an inability to accurately predict the ultimate "congruence of psyche and soma" when the "psyche" is so immaturely developed at birth. To this extent, a revision of legal documents, such as a birth certificate, reflects not so much the "sex change" following GRS but the correction of a documentation error, admittedly a rare one, committed soon after the child was born.

The legal categorization of sex is based on the idea that the "true transsexed" cannot be forced by any psychological or medical means to accept their natal sex on any official documentation. Their transsexed condition is "an immutable state."[19]

In many jurisdictions it is not possible for a previously married transsexed women to change her birth certificate to read female if she insists on remaining within her marriage contract entered into as male. Neither the law nor society are willing to recognize what now appears to be a same-sex marriage in jurisdictions where such a marriage is illegal.[20]

Legal consideration of claims for employment discrimination by transsexed people requires eliminating prejudice, much of which is based on the mistaken belief that transsexed people are homosexual. This common misconception is even evident among those viewers who believe that Tinky Winky, the effeminate TeleTubby in the children's television show of the same name, is gay. Generally, transsexed and transgendered people are not protected by employment antidiscrimination legislation, except in a few inspired jurisdictions. Moreover, such people are not always included in the gay, lesbian, and bisexual campaigns for equality. Sometimes prejudicial judgments arise not from being affirmed surgically as male or female but merely from changing one's gender presentation. Some employers get away with such illegal discrimination by claiming that transsexed and transgendered workers adversely affect their customers' confidence, and of course their bottom line. The situation is much worse in those jurisdictions that prosecute anyone who cross-dresses in public.[21]

Sometimes it is difficult to determine a transsexed person's gender status, especially if they pass well. This has produced difficulties in sexual harassment cases when defendants claim they were misled about a person's "true" sex. For example, if a court determines that harassment was based on a *change* in sex, rather than sex itself, then the protection afforded by sex antidiscrimination legislation may not apply. In some situations, such harassment may even be legally sanctioned. Of course, the basic requirement in employment is competence on the job, and this should not be compromised by discrimination based on a cross-gendered presentation.

Receiving medical benefits is often problematic, as some courts refuse to recognize transsexualism as either a disability or a medical condition. However, some enlightened jurisdictions recognize any DSM-diagnosed psychiatric condition as a disability, resulting in assistance being offered. This situation is one of the very few ways in which transsexed people might benefit from the pathologization of their condition.

The relationship between discrimination based on sex and that based on transsexuality is interesting, especially when the transsexed person can avail themselves of sex discrimination legislation. For example, in *P v. S and Cornwall County Council* a transsexed woman won her case in the European Court of Justice based on direct sex discrimination when legal sex prevents a person from taking advantage of opportunities available to others. Such discrimination occurs when legal sex limits a person's physical characteristics including clothes, makeup, jewelry, and hairstyle, as well as access to toilet and changing-room facilities. Such violation of individual rights might involve the allocation of childcare and other female jobs exclusively to natal women, sexual harassment, discrimination against transsexed and transgendered people, and discrimination against people who violate sex-delineated dress codes.

Dress codes are usually more restrictive for men than women, leading to awkward situations at work should a man decide to wear female attire. A distinction is often made between sex discrimination that can affect the majority of people, such as advertising jobs for one sex rather than both, and sex discrimination that affects minorities for whom universal legal support is more difficult to obtain. Restricting the application of law in such a way is itself a type of discrimination instituted by the majority to undermine a beleaguered minority.[22]

Sex discrimination might occur if, say, a woman can wear a ponytail to work whereas a man cannot. Indeed, conventional standards of dress at work are different for men and woman, leading to possible harassment and discrimination should a man contravene these standards. A case for sex discrimination might apply if men are allowed to wear male clothes, and women female clothing, whereas cross-gendered dress is not allowed.[22]

The major forms of discrimination against transsexed people include sanctions towards those who are on hormone therapy and who are considering GRS; restrictions on the use of single-sex locations and activities; and importantly, their inability to change their legal sex following GRS. One of the problems in using sex-discrimination legislation for transsexuality is that there is no natal woman who is using hormones and surgery to affirm her physical sex, so there is no comparison group with respect to which discrimination can be proven. Nevertheless, the use of hormones and surgery to affirm one's sex is protected under the European Convention on Human Rights.[22]

An "intra-sex" comparison for determining the existence of discrimination involves "a chromosomal male who acquires or intends to acquire (through hormones and surgery) female physical sex characteristics [being] treated less favourably than a chromosomal male who complies with the aspect of his social sex role that requires retention of male physical sex characteristics."[23] A corresponding 'inter-sex" comparison for determining the presence of discrimination must show that "a chromosomal male who acquires, or intends to acquire, (through hormones and surgery) female physical sex characteristics is treated less favourably than a chromosomal female who already has female physical sex characteristics and is permitted to retain them."[23] Both types of sex comparisons might be used in a sex-discrimination claim.

In *Goodwin v. UK,* a case considered in the European Court of Human Rights, the court recognized the socially constructed nature of sex categories as well as one's right to choose a gender identity. The inability of transsexed people to conceive was not a deterrent to a legally binding relationship. "[T]he fundamental dynamic in the discourse around transsexualism is sexuality rather than gender, in essence a logic of heterosexuality, with the consequent practical and strategic problem, that gains for postoperative transsexuals are at the expense of further shoring up the construction of homosexuality as *the* fundamental deviation."[24]

Before changes to the legislation in 2004, the UK government had refused to change a postoperative transsexed person's national insurance record to indicate her affirmed sex. For example, a contrary argument in the *Sheffield and Horsham* case stated that "[n]o concrete or substantial hardship or detriment to the public interest has been demonstrated as likely to flow from any change in the status of transsexuals and, as regards other possible consequences, the Court considers that society may reasonably be expected to tolerate a certain inconvenience to enable individuals to live in dignity and worth in accordance with the sexual identity chosen by them at great personal cost."[25] Thankfully, this particular violation of human rights was ameliorated in the 2004 UK Gender Recognition legislation.

Legal strategies likely to enhance a transsexed person's chances of winning her case include describing a preoperational transsexed person as ill and in need of state-sanctioned health care and a successful postoperative life free from aberrant sexual behavior, having community respect, and behaving similarly to heterosexuals of the same gender. This latter criterion is a problem for "gender warriors," while simultaneously satisfying the gender patriarchy so admonished by feminists.[26]

The medical standards required for GRS are more stringent than those applying to informed consent in irreversible, and potentially risky, elective procedures such as sterilization, organ donation, and radical cosmetic surgery. There is always the fear that the client will change his mind after proceeding with irreversible medical procedures, a situation that can deter a judge from authorizing even a name change as an initial step towards GRS. The medical and legal communities serve as gatekeepers for society's disapproval of something as radical as a "sex-change." In a poignant quote, Anna Kirkland suggested that "transsexuals wanted to have more and better information about their condition; to dispel ignorance about transsexualism among gender professionals and the public; to obtain better services; to lessen the financial burdens of surgery; and finally, to be treated with the same level of respect as patients with other conditions."[27] That such a situation is more the exception than the rule represents a travesty of justice.

It is ironic that transsexed people must present themselves as ill, or distressed, to qualify for and obtain GRS. Yet, following surgery, they must present as well-adjusted people to convince a court that they are a "real" man or a "real" woman. In many instances, being a postoperative transsexed person is equivalent to relegating one's parental responsibilities following separation and divorce. It is also clear that those transsexed people who wish to win benefits from living appropriately as their affirmed sex should not violate society's binary gender norms but instead be perceived as "acceptable" in a patriarchal society. Interestingly, the strategies required of transsexed women to be successful in legal matters are those decried by feminists.[26]

VIOLENCE AND THE VIOLATION OF HUMAN RIGHTS

The rights of transsexed and transgendered people are often compromised by institutionalized violence instigated by various countries and states. Transphobia is deeply entrenched in society's institutions, leading to prejudice based on a presumption that the transsexed and transgendered are health hazards, a threat to public morality, as well as evidence of a decadent Western culture. Even greater hazards for transsexed and transgendered people exist in non-Western societies where state-sponsored violence is rife. In many places, transsexed and transgendered people are denied public-sector jobs, dismissed from them once their lifestyle is discovered, and frequently singled out for harassment. Much of this antagonism has been eulogized in the interest of maintaining the nuclear family against possible disruption.[28]

Semilegal police violence directed at transsexed and transgendered people is difficult to stem due to vaguely worded regulations and arrest procedures in which police interpret the law as they see fit. Particularly distressing has been the targeting of transsexed and transgendered people by police forces in Latin America, leading to torture and killings in holding cells. Privileged transsexed people can avoid the ingrained state-instituted violence meted out to their less-fortunate counterparts due to their better bargaining power with corrupt officials.[28]

Violence towards transsexed and transgendered people risks damaging their physical and mental health, a situation that must be addressed by their medical advisors. Surprisingly, schools are hazardous places for transgendered students, those suffering harassment leaving voluntarily to minimize the adverse effects of bullying.[29] As an indication of universal prejudice, "homosexuality and transgenderism is (sic) considered un-Christian, un-Islamic, against Judaism, a plague, a white man's issue, un-American, un-African, and part of bourgeois decadence."[30] Many societies believe that men who are gay or transgendered threaten male privilege and the social order and so deserve retribution.

Violence against transsexed and transgendered people, as documented worldwide by Amnesty International, violates the international covenants on both civil and political rights as well as that on economic, social, and cultural rights. In particular, both the UN Human Rights Convention and the European Convention on Human Rights forbid discrimination against transsexed and transgendered people. Also, organizations such as Amnesty International have campaigned against using "reparative therapy," a type of psychotherapy that attempts to cure or prevent homosexuality.[31]

An international survey of some 300 transsexed and transgendered people revealed that such people were more likely to suffer violence and victimization than others in the community. Unfortunately, transsexed and transgendered people are also less likely to receive supportive medical care and counseling. Despite legal protection, transsexed people receive insufficient medical and legal intervention following physical and sexual attacks. Transsexed women also suffer from misogynist crimes perpetrated usually by men, thus doubling their burden of stigma and fear.[31]

SUMMARY

Legal constraints that prevent transsexed people from enjoying a lifestyle similar to that taken for granted by others are based on the inflexibility of the law when something as fundamental as sexual identity is involved. Perhaps the most vexing problem affecting all transsexed people is the difficulty they experience in changing their designated sex on identity papers such as their birth certificate and passport following GRS. For those who are already married, or who wish to marry after GRS, the legal system's reluctance to reassign legal sex so that such marriages can be officially recognized has resulted in several notable instances of court action. Despite some initial disappointments in such cases, recent judgments such as *Re Kevin* in Australia offer hope to transsexed people that their human rights are finally being recognized. However, in areas such as discrimination at work and elsewhere, transsexed people still suffer from legal inconsistencies that encourage violence towards, and harassment of, transsexed and transgendered people.

Chapter Fifteen

CONCLUSIONS AND FUTURE PROSPECTS

Scientific research on the intricacies of transsexuality is in its infancy. Although there have been some interesting studies examining virtually all aspects of the condition, there is much that we do not understand. Clearly more research is needed, assisted by a substantial increase in research funding. Applying appropriate research methodology is difficult because of the small number of transsexed people, the difficulty of obtaining information from postoperative people who live in "stealth," and the need to obtain representative samples from such a small population. Some people of transsexual background have been mistreated by their specialist advisors and society in general, and so may not be willing research participants.

Despite the difficulties of conducting research, a wealth of interesting data has been acquired. There is sufficient evidence to suggest a biological basis for transsexuality even though the data were acquired from a relatively small number of postmortem brain samples. Understanding transsexuality as a biological condition, and one that is not based exclusively on psychological considerations, is particularly important. In Australia, for example, at least one court case confirmed the legal validity of a marriage between a transsexed man and his natal woman partner. Although human rights and a fully established male lifestyle were important, so was the evidence that transsexuality has a firm biological basis. Interestingly, several surveys have now shown that those who believe transsexuality has a biological basis tend to be more tolerant of transsexed people, their needs, and their role in society.

Some commentators have proposed that transsexuality is a type of intersex condition in which there is an ambiguity between the genitals at birth and the transsexed person's brain-sex. Such a definition might be considered a conflation of the original idea of intersex, which assumes genital ambiguity, whether this be the result of physical or physiological anomalies. Nevertheless, there is at least some merit in the proposal, since rehabilitation for selected intersexed and transsexed people requires hormone therapy and genital reconstruction surgery (GRS). However the proposal is controversial given that in almost every case an intersexed condition is diagnosable at birth, whereas the medical condition of transsexualism is usually not considered until gender-atypical behavior becomes evident in childhood or beyond. A recent survey[1] suggested that people are more lenient towards state-sponsored medical treatment for intersexed rather than transsexed conditions. It would be interesting to see if respondents are more supportive of free medical treatment for transsexed people after convincing them that transsexuality is an intersex condition.

Perhaps the most anguishing situation for transsexed people and their supporters is the inclusion of transsexualism (or gender identity disorder) as a mental illness with symptoms defined in the diagnostic manuals used by psychiatrists and clinical psychologists. Unless the transsexed person is suffering from a physical illness such as diabetes, or a mental illness such as schizophrenia, there is no sense in which a transsexed person is suffering from a disorder of any kind. More often than not, the diagnosis is imposed on unsuspecting transsexed people to protect surgeons and other medical specialists from being sued if treatments such as GRS, for example, lead subsequently to regret. Surely the surgeon only needs reassurance that the person is a suitable candidate for surgery.

In cosmetic procedures such as breast augmentation, which can be at least as risky as GRS, the surgeon only requires consent from the client in order to avoid postoperative litigation. So why must transsexed people be labeled as "mentally ill" in order to begin their medically supervised transition when we know that the incidence of postoperative regret is so low, even lower than regret rates for breast removal for breast cancer patients, and castration for men with prostate cancer?

All diagnostic categories related to gender identity atypicality must be removed from psychiatric diagnostic manuals. Those who do not adhere to society's gender norms must not be denigrated and typecast as disordered. All that transsexed people want is recognition that they represent a normal variation of gendered experience. A pregnant woman, and one experiencing the initial throes of menopause, request medical assistance to enhance their quality of life during critical phases of their lives. In no sense do we label them as physically ill just so they can obtain the temporary medical help they need. Similarly, transsexed people need not be "disordered" in order to access the medical help required to effect sex affirmation over a two- or three-year transition period.

Many transsexed people endure medical "gatekeeping" in order to qualify for appropriate medical treatments. In some cases they employ learned scripts to ensure that they are not rejected by the stringent standards of some publicly funded gender clinics. By so doing, it becomes impossible for the transsexed person and their psychological advisor to achieve a rapport that permits the honest rendition of the transsexed person's needs. Understandably, those who have been scared away from gender clinics by a combination of excessive evaluation, unrealistic demands, and uncertainty will inevitably seek out sympathetic expertise elsewhere. Arlene Istar Lev[2] provides a comprehensive account of the kind of professional relationship that enhances, rather than deters, progress of transsexed people in their quest for sex affirmation leading to a happier and more productive life.

If the prevalence of gender identity atypicality is as high as recent estimates have suggested, then there will be plenty of work for properly trained professionals in the field. Ignorance of the critical signs by parents, teachers, doctors, and others who maintain close contact with gender-atypical children only leads to undesirable consequences such as bullying, inexplicable adjustment problems, and a loss of self-esteem.

The solution of course is to improve the education and training of psychiatrists, psychologists, endocrinologists, social workers, speech therapists, and all the other specialists who deal with gender-atypical clients. Although the standards of care offer minimal but flexible guidelines for caring for transsexed people, there are no national or international bodies to accredit those who help gender-atypical clients. For example, full membership in the Harry Benjamin International Gender Dysphoria (sic) Association only requires evidence of experience in dealing with gender-atypical clients. There is no requirement for specialist training in the field. In particular, there are relatively few graduate courses in the counseling of transgendered clients.

The medical help received by transsexed people is primarily clinically evaluated rather than scientifically researched. Hormone dosages have been determined by a combination of trial-and-error and clinical experience. In general, the recommended dosages are relatively safe, but for some people with predisposing medical complications such as heart disease, high blood pressure, and diabetes, the risks associated with hormone usage increase accordingly. Some compromise must be maintained between using a sufficient dosage to produce desired secondary sex characteristics and ensuring that minimal ill effects are obtained. Regular blood monitoring and maintaining a healthy lifestyle are necessary. The least-known aspect of hormone usage is their long-term effects in elderly transsexed people.

Surgeries of all kinds are important for transsexed people. In all cases only those surgeons who have an established good reputation in working with gender-atypical clients should be considered. Although some idea of the techniques and outcomes from the various surgeons can be gleaned from the Internet, it is crucial that people seek information from those who have undergone procedures with these surgeons. Even then, complex surgery such as GRS depends on many variables, not the least of which is the transsexed person's presurgical anatomy and their general state of health. So reports from others, usually successful, can be misleading when individual cases are considered.

Social and family support for transsexed people has scarcely been researched in any systematic way. There are numerous obstacles that must be overcome once a person outs themselves as transsexed. At this time, counseling from experienced people is important, including of course the generous support offered by other transsexed people. The number of different demands can be overwhelming, including the impact of divorce proceedings for many married transsexed people, prejudice and shunning by family, friends, and work colleagues, the loss or downgrading of career, and the large investment in time and money, in many cases, needed for medical and other treatments.

Many transsexed people seek comfort, information, and help from support groups and online communities. Transsexed people must learn new ways to express themselves socially during the real-life experience. For those who have little experience with the gender norms for their affirmed sex, living full-time can be traumatic, if not a little exciting. For those transsexed women who have difficulty passing (and want to) their first few public outings can be daunting and risky. Even those transsexed women who do pass well must now experience the dangers that all women face in a society that can be violent and disrespectful of women. Although the dangers for transsexed men are no less, they do have the advantage of belonging to the dominant group in a patriarchal society.

A NONLINEAR EXPLANATION OF TRANSSEXUALITY

Most people are intrigued about how a mismatch between genital sex, or birth-sex, and brain-sex can arise. They recall their own consistent feelings of concordance between their gender identity and the shape of their external genitals. In fact, most people would never give the possibility of such an inconsistency a second thought.

A possible outcome of gender identity atypicality is inadequate formation of a consistent gender identity around the time the child starts elementary school. The gender-atypical child will shun gender-typed toys and dress. They prefer playing with opposite-sex children and find it difficult to socialize with members of their own sex. In some cases, such behavior will persist throughout childhood and adolescence, leading to problems in adjusting to a world that expects and rewards gender-consistent behavior. It is as if the child has become "fixated" on a gender identity that is different from that of other children of the same birth-sex. This situation can be alarming to the child's family and friends.

Paul van Geert[3] proposed a dynamic theory of cognitive development in children. He was fascinated by the sudden changes that occur when, for example, children are finally able to appreciate the concept of conservation of quantities around the age of four. Whereas previously they would only use the heights of containers to judge which one contained more water, now they could consider the width of the container as well so that containers with different heights and widths can contain the *same* amount of water.

Continuous processes, such as walking along a mountain track, can be simply represented by the rule that as one foot is placed in front of the other and the body moves forward, the distance to be traveled is correspondingly reduced. Much of this linear progress towards the goal is outside of the walker's awareness (unless she is becoming very tired). However, when she reaches the summit a feeling of euphoria overwhelms her emotions and she screams in delight. This latter experience occurs suddenly. Steady linear processes such as walking cannot explain such a change in emotional experience. Only complex, nonlinear ideas can do so.

Similar nonlinear processes work in physical disease when a person who has been exercising regularly and looks pretty fit suddenly succumbs to a heart attack and has to be rushed off to the emergency room. What his family and friends have not realized (nor himself) is that his heart function was becoming steadily more regular and less efficient. It is the sudden nonlinear change that transforms the man from an apparently healthy adult to a person with a life-threatening illness.[4]

So perhaps the formation of a consistent gender identity occurs relatively suddenly once the child has acquired sufficient information from both biological and environmental processes. There may be two mountains that can be climbed from a similar starting point just as the embryo before week six is sexually undifferentiated. These mountains are covered in deep forest and it is only possible to see whether you are heading towards the "correct" mountain when you get close enough to the summit. Even then, visibility can be reduced due to fog and clouds.

As the testosterone concentration increases due to the effects of the SRY gene, the male starts diverting from the common pathway to head towards the summit of Mount Boy. His progress is assisted by biological processes, especially those operating in the brain, as well as environmental influences from the womb, and after birth from family, peers, and others. A lack of testosterone causes the female to continue heading towards the summit of Mount Girl.

Since the forests on both mountains look very similar it is not possible for the person to be sure of their gender identity until they are close to the summit. When they reach the summit after about four years of traveling, they are delighted to be there and celebrate the occasion by receiving a "male gender identity certificate" at the top of Mount Boy, or a "female gender identity certificate" at the top of Mount Girl.

The constant push of testosterone will always direct a male to the summit of Mount Boy and a female will always end up at the summit of Mount Girl by default. Once a person has reached the summit of one of these mountains the other disappears for all practical purposes. There is no way the nonlinear process, unlike a linear process, can be reversed so that for example Mount Boy can be descended and then Mount Girl climbed.

If forming a consistent gender identity is a nonlinear process then small discrepancies in the initial position below the mountains might on rare occasions direct the person towards the summit corresponding to the opposite gender. So the final gender identity is simply the result of biased initial biological processes that direct the person towards the summit opposite to their predicted chromosomal, gonadal, hormonal, and genital configurations. Things can go wrong and the person who everyone thinks is male ends up at Mount Girl and vice versa for natal females. These rare individuals obtain a "male gender identity certificate" to go with their "female birth certificate," or else a "female gender identity certificate" to go with their "male birth certificate."

For such a transsexed person their gender identity is opposite to their genital sex but consistent with their brain-sex. Because this nonlinear process is no different in principle from the biological processes that form lungs, the skeleton, and the nervous system, for example, the final gender identity is an affirmed part of a person's embodiment. Although they cannot acquire the opposite brain-sex and get to the top of the other mountain, thanks to modern medicine they can at least alter their body, especially the genitals, to match.

A similar explanation can be used to account for gender identity in people with an intersexed condition. In this case the "mountain climbed" will depend on the biological processes that are likely causes of the condition. In certain conditions, such as androgen insensitivity syndrome, there may be concordance between genital-sex and gender identity. However, in many other conditions, especially those that produce ambiguous genitals, the eventual gender identity is unpredictable. It is obvious that one cannot terminate a nonlinear process in mid-track and arbitrarily reassign sex and hope that the environment will then take care of which summit is reached—the person's eventual gender identity. Perhaps the analogy of getting lost walking through the forest in the fog is not a bad one given some current pediatric practices. Just like many nonlinear processes, it is almost impossible to predict very far into the future. So the optimal strategy in many intersex cases is to wait until the child is mature enough to make her own decision.

In terms of this considerably simplified nonlinear analogy, there is no difference in principle between the developmental dynamics of transsexed and intersex conditions. Both involve departures from the usual initial biological precursors of sexual development. The path taken towards eventual gender identity development is in both cases unpredictable but often produces a discrepancy between birth-sex and brain-sex, leading to a gender identity that is inconsistent with genital-sex. The main difference between the two conditions relates to the visual difference in initial conditions for those intersexed people with ambiguous genitals, and the lack of initial visible clues to their genital-sex brain-sex discrepancy in most transsexed people. The initial discrepancy for transsexed people is real but hidden from view until it is revealed once the summit has been reached.

IMPROVING THE LIVES OF TRANSSEXED PEOPLE

Joan Roughgarden[5] has provided a list of demands that if satisfied should substantially improve the lives of transsexed people. She suggests that transsexuality should be "cherished as a normal part of human diversity," just as it is in the animal kingdom; that transsexed people should be cherished and treated with courtesy and dignity; that there should be no social or legal obstacles to stop transsexed people leading the same lives and having the same rights as any other member of the community; and that sponsored health support for transsexed people's special medical needs should be readily available.

To this end, it is worth noting that the formal policy of the Australian Greens Party[6] includes support for

(a) legislation, policies and programmes to protect the right of an individual to live and identify as the gender of their choice and to deliver all the benefits flowing from that recognition;

(b) the provision of accurate, comprehensive, non-stigmatizing and non-pathologising information and education about transgender issues and a complete explanation of the full range of medical options available, including surgical and non-surgical;

(c) community education programmes aimed at reducing the stigmatization associated with being transgender;

(d) transgender medical procedures being available at both public and private hospitals and under Medicare;

(e) access to health care information that encompasses the safe sex issues faced by transgender people;

(f) equal access for transgender people to recreation facilities, coaching, sports education and competition; and

(g) ongoing research aimed at improving medical procedures for transgender people, both surgical and non-surgical.

There is still a long way to go before these admirable goals are attained. In the meantime it is important that all transsexed people fight for their rights as best they can. One way this can be achieved is to promote greater education and understanding by all people of the myriad issues of concern to transsexed people. Rather than sensationalizing transsexed people, the media, with the assistance of concerned individuals, would serve the transsexed community better if it disseminated information about the biological basis of the condition and current research findings; the problems endured by many transsexed people as they strive for happiness; and what society must do to ensure that transsexed people are treated with the respect they deserve.

I hope that by reading the information contained in this book, professionals, laypeople, and importantly, policymakers can become sufficiently knowledgeable to put some of these ideas into practice.

APPENDIX

This appendix contains a list of useful Internet resources with commentary where appropriate.

RESOURCES FOR TRANSSEXED WOMEN AND MEN

The Harry Benjamin International Gender Dysphoria Association, the professional group assisting transsexed people in their transition, has a website at: http://www.hbigda.org/. The latest edition of the standards of care can be downloaded from this site.

The Press for Change organization in the UK fights for the rights of transgendered and transsexed people. Its efforts paid off when the UK Gender Recognition Bill became law in 2004. Its website is: http://www.pfc.org.uk/.

The complete UK Gender Recognition Act 2004 can be read at: http://www.opsi.gov.uk/acts/acts2004/20040007.htm, and information on the Gender Recognition Panel in the UK is contained in: http://www.grp.gov.uk/.

A detailed list of recent bibliographic sources on transsexuality is contained in: http://www.transgenderzone.com/index.htm.

Resources to assist in the transition process are contained in: http://www.transgenderzone.com/index.htm.

A multilingual list of surgeons worldwide is contained in: http://www.europeants.org/surgeons/.

The Gender Centre in Sydney, Australia, is one of the few government-sponsored organizations worldwide that offer day-to-day support for transgendered and transsexed people: http://www.gendercentre.org.au/.

Events of interest in international law for transsexed and transgendered people are contained at the Transgender Law and Policy Institute located at: http://www.transgenderlaw.org/.

RESOURCES FOR TRANSSEXED WOMEN

A comprehensive information resource, including information on surgical procedures and results, is contained in: http://www.annelawrence.com/twr/.

Professor Lynn Conway provides detailed information on all aspects of transsexuality, including her own life story and brief accounts of notable transsexed men and women who have made an impact in their various pursuits. Her comprehensive resource can be found at: http://ai.eecs.umich.edu/people/conway/conway.html.

A well-organized and entertaining site that provides useful information on hormones, surgery, and lifestyle for transsexed women can be accessed from: http://transwoman.tripod.com/.

The Australian Woman Network is a legal and political lobby group. Its website is: http://www.w-o-m-a-n.net.

RESOURCES FOR TRANSSEXED MEN

A comprehensive list of resources for transsexed men is contained in the FTM International website located at: http://www.ftmi.org/.

RESEARCH ON SEXUALITY, TRANSGENDERISM, AND TRANSSEXUALITY

Academic interest in transsexuality and transgenderism is contained in: http://www.trans-academics.org/.

Information on current research is available at: http://www.transcience.org/TransScience_Research_Institute.html.

Division 44 of the American Psychological Association has an interest group in transgender issues. Its webpage is: http://www.apadivision44.org/.

ACADEMIC PROGRAMS IN TRANSSEXUALITY

A list of North American university and college programs in transgender and transsexuality studies is available in: http://www.people.ku.edu/~jyounger/lgbtqprogs.html.

The International Foundation for Gender Education (IFGE) offers detailed information on all aspects of transsexuality. IFGE conducts a highly regarded annual conference in the United States. Information can be obtained from: http://www.ifge.org/index.php.

SUPPORT FOR SIGNIFICANT OTHERS

A support group for the wives, partners, and families of transgendered and transsexed people is contained in: http://www.ssnetwk.org/.

A UK support group for partners, family, and friends of transgendered and transsexed people can be contacted at: http://www.depend.org.uk.

The Mermaids is a support group for children and adolescents with gender identity atypicality. Its website is located at: http://www.mermaids. freeuk.com.

RESOURCES FOR PEOPLE WITH AN INTERSEX CONDITION

The Intersex Society of North America contains a comprehensive guide to intersex conditions, support groups, and research. Its webpage is located at: http://www.isna.org/.

A general information site on intersex conditions from the UK is: http://www.ukia.co.uk/.

INTERESTING INFORMATION FOR EVERYONE

Interesting talks given by transgendered and transsexed people are frequently contained on GenderTalk Radio and are available for download from: http://www.gendertalk.com/.

The PRAAT Speech Recognition program is useful for analyzing one's voice. There are numerous options including fundamental frequency, formants, and amplitude dynamics. General information on the program is available from: http://www.ling.lu.se/persons/Sidney/praate/frames.html.

The PRAAT software can be downloaded from http://www.fon.hum.uva.nl/praat/.

NOTES

PREFACE

1. Zucker, K. J. (2002). Intersexuality and gender identity differentiation. *Journal of Pediatrics and Adolescent Gynecology* 15:3–13.

2. Bockting, W. O. (1999). From construction to context: Gender through the eyes of the transgendered. *SIECUS Report* 28:3–7.

3. Monro, S. (2000). Theorizing transgender diversity: Towards a social model of health. *Sexual and Relationship Therapy* 15:33–45.

4. Wallbank, R. (2004). *Contemporary human rights issues for people with transsexualism*, p. 15. Paper presented at the Gendys Conference, Manchester, UK. Downloaded from http://www.wallbanks.com/main/resources.html on January 31, 2006.

5. The term *gynephilia* was reportedly first used by Kurt Freund, a noted sexologist. The terms *gynephilic* and *androphilic* have been recommended in Diamond, M. (2002). Sex and gender are different: Sexual identity and gender identity are different. *Clinical Child Psychology and Psychiatry* 7:320–334.

6. Miller, W. R. (2004). The phenomenon of quantum change. *Journal of Clinical Psychology/In Session* 1–8.

CHAPTER 1

1. Cited in Benjamin H. (1966). *The transsexual phenomenon.* New York: The Julian Press. Downloaded from http://www.symposion.com/ijt/benjamin/index.htm on January 9, 2006.

2. Bullough, V. L. (1974). Transvestites in the Middle Ages. *American Journal of Sociology* 79:1381–1394.

3. Liveley, G. (2003). Tiresias/Teresa: A man-made-woman in Ovid's Metamorphoses 3.318–38. *Helios* 30:147–162.

4. Blanchard, R. (2005). Early history of the concept of autogynephilia. *Archives of Sexual Behavior* 34:439–466.

5. Norton, J. (1997). "Brain says you're a girl, but I think you're a sissy boy": Cultural origins of transphobia. *Journal of Gay, Lesbian, and Bisexual Identity* 2:139–164, p. 141.

6. Ekins, R. and King, D. (2001). Pioneers of transgendering: The popular sexology of David O. Cauldwell. *International Journal of Transgenderism* 5(1). Downloaded from http://www.symposion.com/ijt/cauldwell/cauldwell_01.htm on January 9, 2006.

7. Pfäfflin, F. (1997). Sex reassignment, Harry Benjamin, and some European roots. *International Journal of Transgenderism* 1(2). Downloaded from http://www.symposion.com/ijt/ijtc0202.htm on January 9, 2006.

8. Haire, N. (1930). *Encyclopaedia of sexual knowledge.* London: Encyclopaedic Press. Summary compiled by S. Johnson.

9. An intersexed condition often involves malformation of the genitals so that it is difficult to determine a child's birth-sex by simple inspection. Some intersexed conditions arise from genetic variations that produce the wrong body chemistry. This can lead to masculinization of female bodies and feminization of male bodies. Klinefelter syndrome, which occurs in about 1 in 750 male births, is characterized by a lack of body and pubic hair, underdeveloped testicles, infertility, and some loss in cognitive function. Some breast development can occur at puberty but generally most people with the syndrome live their lives unaffected. Chen, H. (2005). Klinefelter syndrome. Downloaded from http://www.emedicine.com/ped/topic1252.htm on January 21, 2006.

10. Gilpin, D. C., Raza, S., and Gilpin, D. (1979). Transsexual symptoms in a male child treated by a female therapist. *American Journal of Psychotherapy* 33:453–463.

11. Ettner, R. (1999). *Gender loving care: A guide to counseling gender-variant clients.* New York: Norton & Company.

12. Michel, A., Mormont, C., and Legros, J. J. (2001). A psycho-endocrinological overview of transsexualism. *European Journal of Endocrinology* 145:365–376.

13. Schaefer, L. C. and Wheeler, C. C. (1995). Harry Benjamin's first ten cases (1938–1953): A critical historical note. *Archives of Sexual Behavior* 24:73–93.

14. Gay and Lesbian Historical Society of Northern California (1998). MTF transgender activism in the Tenderloin and beyond, 1966–1975: Commentary and interview with Elliot Blackstone. *Gay & Lesbian Quarterly* 4:349–372.

15. Cohen-Kettenis, P. T. and Gooren, L.J.G. (1999). Transsexualism: A review of etiology, diagnosis and treatment. *Journal of Psychosomatic Research* 46:315–333.

16. Fisk, N. (1973). Gender dysphoria syndrome (The how, what, and why of a disease). In D. Laub and P. Gandy (Eds.), *Proceedings of the Second Interdisciplinary Symposium on Gender Dysphoria Syndrome* (pp. 7–14). Palo Alto, CA: Stanford University Press.

17. Bullough, V. L. (2003). The contributions of John Money: A personal view. *Journal of Sex Research* 40:230–236.

18. Damodaran, S. S. and Kennedy, T. (2000). The Monash Gender Dysphoria Clinic: Opportunities and challenges. *Australasian Psychiatry* 8:355–357.

19. Murjan, S., Shepherd, M., and Ferguson, B. G. (2002). What services are available for the treatment of transsexuals in Great Britain? *Psychiatric Bulletin* 26:210–212.

20. Weitze, C. and Osburg, S. (1996). Transsexualism in Germany: Empirical data on epidemiology and application of the German Transsexuals' Act during its first ten years. *Archives of Sexual Behavior* 25:409–425.

21. Ruan, F.-F. and Bullough, V. L. (1988). The first case of transsexual surgery in mainland China. *Journal of Sex Research* 25:546–547.

22. Stryker, S. (1998). The transgender issue: An introduction. *Gay & Lesbian Quarterly* 4:152.

23. Broad, K. L. (2002). GLB + T?: Gender/sexuality movements and transgender collective identity (de)constructions. *International Journal of Sexuality and Gender Studies* 7:241–264.

24. In Australia and in the UK, a small number of spiteful and regretful men who have undergone feminization surgery have now sued their respective gender clinics for unspecified damages. At least one has used support from religious extremists to both support his case and to instigate a ban on GRS. In the meantime they seek medical help to regain their lost masculinity. See http://www.abc.net.au/austory/content/2003/s934839.htm and http://www.parakaleo.co.uk/MistakenID-Guardian31-07-2004.html accessed on January 21, 2006.

25. Morris, R. C. (1995). All made up: Performance theory and the new anthropology of sex and gender. *Annual Review of Anthropology* 24:567–592.

26. Ibid., p. 579.

27. Ibid., p. 580.

28. Towle, E. B. and Morgan, L. M. (2002). Romancing the transgender native: Rethinking the use of the "Third Gender" concept. *Gay & Lesbian Quarterly* 8:469–497.

29. Brown, K. (2004). "Sistergirls"—Stories from indigenous Australian transgendered people. *Aboriginal and Islander Health Worker Journal* 28:25–26.

30. Bockting, W. O. and Cesaretti, C. (2001). Spirituality, transgender identity, and coming out. *Journal of Sex Education and Therapy* 26:291–300.

31. Sinnott, M. (2000). The semiotics of transgendered sexual identity in the Thai print media: Imagery and discourse of the sexual other. *Culture, Health & Sexuality* 2:425–440.

32. Littlewood, R. (2002). Three into two: The third sex in Northern Albania. *Anthropology & Medicine* 9:37–50.

33. McLelland, M. (2002). The newhalf net: Japan's "intermediate sex" on-line. *International Journal of Sexuality and Gender Studies* 7:163–175.

34. Ramaswami, M. (2003). Essentialism, culture, and beliefs about gender among the Aravanis of Tamil Nadu, India. *Sex Roles* 49:489–496.

35. Raymond, J. G. (1994). *The transsexual empire: The making of the she-male*. New York: Teachers College.

36. For example, Boylan, J. F. (2003). *She's not there. A life in two genders*. New York: Broadway Books; Clark, S. (2004). *Running to normal*. Available from http://www.iUniverse.com; Cummings, K. (1993). *Katherine's diary*. Melbourne: Mandarin; McCloskey, D. N. (1999). *Crossing. A memoir*. Chicago: University of Chicago Press; Morris, J. (1974). *Conundrum*. London: Faber & Faber.

37. Landén, M. and Innala, S. (2000) Attitudes toward transsexualism in a Swedish national survey. *Archives of Sexual Behavior* 29:375–388.

38. Ibid., pp. 376–377.

39. Similar findings to those of the Swedish study were obtained from an Internet survey that used the same questions as well as additional questions on attitudes towards people with an intersex condition. An interesting finding was that although a majority approve the use of public funds to sponsor surgical interventions for people with an intersex condition, they were not so supportive of public funding for GRS. Kemp, E. and Swain, J. (2005). *Attitudes towards transsexualism and intersex conditions: An Internet based survey*. Unpublished Honours thesis, School of Behavioural Sciences, University of Newcastle, Australia.

Using the Swedish survey as a basis, a modified questionnaire was devised to measure tolerance towards transsexuality. Tolerance was greater for those who consider transsexuality to have a biological cause, those who are not regular churchgoers, and those with a same-sex sexual orientation. Rose, L. and Chenhall, J. (2005). *Australian undergraduates' attitudes towards transsexualism: The effect of written information, attributions of causality and personal demographic correlates.* Unpublished Honours thesis, School of Behavioural Sciences, University of Newcastle, Australia.

40. Rogers, L. (1999). *Sexing the brain.* London: Weidenfeld & Nicolson.

41. Raj, R. (2002). Towards a transpositive therapeutic model: Developing clinical sensitivity and cultural competence in the effective support of transsexual and transgendered clients. *International Journal of Transgenderism* 6(2). Downloaded from http://www.symposion.com/ijt/ijtvo06no02_04.htm on January 9, 2006.

42. Van Kesteren, P. J., Gooren, L. J., and Megens, J. A. (1996). An epidemiological and demographic study of transsexuals in the Netherlands. *Archives of Sexual Behavior* 25:589–600.

43. Jarolím, L. (2000). Surgical conversion of genitalia in transsexual patients. *BJU International* 85:851–856.

44. Green, R. (2000). Family co-occurrence of "Gender Dysphoria": Ten sibling or parent–child pairs. *Archives of Sexual Behavior* 29:499–507.

45. See http://ai.eecs.umich.edu/people/conway/TS/TSprevalence.html. Downloaded on January 9, 2006.

CHAPTER 2

1. Gustafson, M. L. and Donahoe, P. K. (1994). Male sex determination: Current concepts of male sexual differentiation. *Annual Review of Medicine* 45:505–524.

2. Ibid., Figure 2.1 on p. 507.

3. Mathews, G. A., Fane, B. A., Pasterski, V. L., Conway, G. S., Brook, C., and Hines, M. (2004). Androgenic influences on neural asymmetry: Handedness and language lateralization in individuals with congenital adrenal hyperplasia. *Psychoneuroendocrinology* 29:810–822.

4. Dewing, P., Shi, T., Horvath, S., and Vilain, E. (2003). Sexually dimorphic gene expression in mouse brain precedes gonadal differentiation. *Molecular Brain Research* 118:82–90.

5. Carruth, L. L., Reisert, I., and Arnold, A. P. (2002). Sex chromosome genes directly affect brain sexual differentiation. *Nature Neuroscience* 5:933–934.

6. Hengstschläger, M., van Trotsenburg, M., Repa, C., Marton, E., Huber, J.C., and Bernaschek, G. (2003). Sex chromosome aberrations and transsexualism. *Fertility and Sterility* 79:639–640.

7. Henningsson, S., Westberg, L., Nilsson, S., et al. (2005). Sex steroid-related genes and male-to-female transsexualism. *Psychoneuroendocrinology* 30:657–664.

8. McEwen, B. S. (1999). Permanence of brain sex differences and structural plasticity of the adult brain. *Proceedings of the National Academy of Sciences, USA* 96:7128–7130.

9. Swaab, D. F., Chung, W.C.J., Kruijver, F.P.M, Hofman, M. A., and Hestiantoro, A. (2003). Sex differences in the hypothalamus in the different stages of human life. *Neurobiology of Aging* 24:S1–S16.

10.   Bishop, K. M. and Wahlsten, D. (1997). Sex differences in the human corpus callosum: Myth or reality? *Neuroscience and Biobehavioral Reviews* 21:581–601; Wahlsten, D. and Bishop, K. M. (1998). Effect sizes and meta-analysis indicate no sex dimorphism in the human or rodent corpus callosum. *Behavioral and Brain Sciences* 21:338–339.

11.   Downloaded from http://www.symposion.com/ijt/ijtc0106.htm on January 21, 2006.

12.   Swaab, D. F., Chung, W.C.J., Kruijver, F.P.M, Hofman, M. A., and Ishunina, T. A. (2001). Structural and functional sex differences in the human hypothalamus. *Hormones and Behavior* 40:93–98.

13.   Dournaud, P., Boudin, H., Schonbrunn, A., Tannenbaum, G. S., and Beaudet, A. (1998). Interrelationships between somatostatin sst2A receptors and somatostatin-containing axons in rat brain: Evidence for regulation of cell surface receptors by endogenous somatostatin. *Journal of Neuroscience* 18:1056–1071.

14.   Pichler, R., Maschek, W., Crespillo, C., Esteva, I., and Soriguer, F. (2002). Is there a gender difference in somatostatin-receptor density in the human brain? *Neuroendocrinology Letters* 23:440–441.

15.   Rogers, L. (1999). *Sexing the brain.* London: Weidenfeld & Nicolson.

16.   Rahman, Q. and Wilson, G.D. (2002). Born gay? The psychobiology of human sexual orientation. *Personality and Individual Differences* 34:1337–1382.

17.   Zhou, J.-N., Hofman, M. A., Gooren, L. L., and Swaab, D. F. (1995). A sex difference in the human brain and its relation to transsexuality. *Nature* 378:68–70.

18.   Kruijver, F.P.M., Zhou, J.-N., Pool, C. W., Hofman, M. A., Gooren, L.J.G., and Swaab, D. F. (2000). Male-to-female transsexuals have female neuron numbers in a limbic nucleus. *Journal of Clinical Endocrinology and Metabolism* 85:2034–2041.

19.   Chung, W.C.J., de Vries, G. J., and Swaab, D. F. (2002). Sexual differentiation of the bed nucleus of the stria terminalis in humans may extend into adulthood. *Journal of Neuroscience* 22:1027–1033.

20.   Lawrence, A. A. (2004). New report: In humans, the central subdivision of the bed nucleus of the stria terminalis does not become sexually dimorphic until adulthood. Downloaded from http://www.annelawrence.com/bstcreport.html on January 9, 2006.

21.   The locations of these hypothalamic nuclei are described in both the text and figures of Kruijver, F.P.M., Balesar, R., Espila, A. M., Unmehopa, U. A., and Swaab, D. F. (2002). Estrogen receptor-α distribution in the human hypothalamus in relation to sex and endocrine status. *Journal of Comparative Neurology* 454:115–139.

22.   Goldstein, J. M., Seidman, L. J., Horton, N. J., Makris, N., Kennedy, D. N., Caviness, V. S., Faraone, S. V., and Tsuang, M. T. (2001). Normal sexual dimorphism of the adult human brain assessed by *in vivo* magnetic resonance imaging. *Cerebral Cortex* 11:490–497.

23.   Adinoff, B., Devous Sr., M. D., Best, S. E., Chandler, P., Alexander, D., Payne, K., Harris, T. S., and Williams, M. J. (2003). Gender differences in limbic responsiveness, by SPECT, following a pharmacologic challenge in healthy subjects. *NeuroImage* 18:697–706.

24.   Durston, S., Hulshoff, H. E., Casey, B. J., Giedd, J. N., Buitelaar, J. K., and van Engeland, H. (2001). Anatomical MRI of the developing brain: What have we learned? *Journal of the American Academy of Child and Adolescent Psychiatry* 40:1012–1020.

25.   Cooke, B. M., Tabibnia, G., and Breedlove, S. M. (1999). A brain sexual dimorphism controlled by adult circulating androgens. *Proceedings of the National Academy of Sciences, USA* 96:7538–7540.

26. Ehrhardt, A. A. and Meyer-Bahlburg, H.F.L. (1979). Prenatal sex hormones and the developing brain: Effects on psychosexual differentiation and cognitive function. *Annual Review of Medicine* 30:417–430.

CHAPTER 3

1. Zucker, K. J. (2002). Intersexuality and gender identity differentiation. *Journal of Pediatrics and Adolescent Gynecology* 15:3–13.

2. Frable, D.E.S. (1997). Gender, racial, ethnic, sexual, and class identities. *Annual Review of Psychology* 48:139–162, p. 144.

3. Kohlberg, L. A. (1966). A cognitive-developmental analysis of children's sex role concepts and attitudes. In E. E. Maccoby (Ed.). *The development of sex differences* (pp. 82-173). Stanford, CA: Stanford University Press.

4. Warin, J. (2000). The attainment of self-consistency through gender in young children. *Sex Roles* 42:209–231.

5. Martin, C. L., Ruble, D. N., and Szkrybalo, J. (2002). Cognitive theories of early gender development. *Psychological Bulletin* 128:903–933.

6. Campbell, A., Shirley, L., and Caygill, L. (2002). Sex-typed preferences in three domains: Do two-year-olds need cognitive variables? *British Journal of Psychology* 93:203–217.

7. Cohen-Kettenis, P. T. and Pfäfflin, F. (2003). *Transgenderism and intersexuality in childhood and adolescence: Making choices.* Thousand Oakes, CA: Sage Publications.

8. Brutsaert, H. (1999). Coeducation and gender identity formation: A comparative analysis of secondary schools in Belgium. *British Journal of Sociology of Education* 20: 343–353.

9. Golombok, S. and Rust, G. (1993). The Pre-School Activities Inventory: A standardized assessment of gender roles in children. *Psychological Assessment* 5:131–136.

10. Albert, A. A. and Porter, J. R. (1988). Children's gender-role stereotypes: A sociological investigation of psychological models. *Sociological Forum* 3:184–210.

11. Martin, C. L., Ruble, D. N., and Szkrybalo, J. (2002). Cognitive theories of early gender development. *Psychological Bulletin* 128:911.

12. Barberá, E. (2003). Gender schemas: Configuration and activation processes. *Canadian Journal of Behavioural Science* 35:176–184.

13. Tenenbaum, H. R. and Leaper, C. (2002). Are parents' gender schemas related to their children's gender-related cognitions? A meta-analysis. *Developmental Psychology* 38:615–630.

14. Sandnabba, N. K., Santtila, P., Wannäs, M., and Krook, K. (2003). Age and gender specific sexual behaviors in children. *Child Abuse & Neglect* 27:579–605.

15. Cohen-Kettenis, P. T., Owen, A., Kaijser, V. G., Bradley, S. J., and Zucker, K. J. (2003). Demographic characteristics, social competence, and behavior problems in children with gender identity disorder: A cross-national, cross-clinic comparative analysis. *Journal of Abnormal Child Psychology* 31:41–53.

16. Bailey, J. M. and Zucker, K. J. (1995). Childhood sex-typed behavior and sexual orientation: A conceptual analysis and quantitative review. *Developmental Psychology* 31:43–55.

17. Roberts, C. W., Goodman, M., Green, R., and Williams, K. (1987). Boyhood gender identity development: A statistical contrast of two family groups. *Developmental Psychology* 23:544–557.

18. Zucker, K. J., Bradley, S. J., Kuksis, M., Pecore, K., Birkenfeld-Adams, A., Doering, R. W., Mitchell, J. N., and Wild, J. (1999). Gender constancy judgments in children with Gender Identity Disorder: Evidence for a developmental lag. *Archives of Sexual Behavior* 28:475–502.

19. Fridell, S. R., Zucker, K. J., Bradley, S. J., and Maing, D. M. (1996). Physical attractiveness of girls with Gender Identity Disorder. *Archives of Sexual Behavior* 25:17–31.

20. McDermid, S. A., Zucker, K. J., Bradley, S. J., and Maing, D. M. (1998). Effects of physical appearance on masculine trait ratings of boys and girls with gender identity disorder. *Archives of Sexual Behavior* 27:253–267.

CHAPTER 4

1. Diamond, M. (2000). Sex and gender: Same or different? *Feminism & Psychology* 10:46–54.

2. Gender identity disorder (GID) is described in the latest version of the *Diagnostic and Statistical Manual*, DSM-IV-TR, published by the American Psychiatric Association. It pathologizes gender identity atypicality, which is more appropriately considered a variation on normal gender identity development. Except when mentioning GID as a diagnostic category, a more appropriate terminology, gender identity atypicality (GIA), will be used in this book.

3. Deaux, K. (1985). Sex and gender. *Annual Review of Psychology* 36:51.

4. Collaer, M. L. and Hines, M. (1995). Human behavioral sex differences: A role for gonadal hormones during early development? *Psychological Bulletin* 118:55–107.

5. Gooren, L.J.G. (1993). *Transsexualism, medicine and law.* Closing speech at the Council of Europe, 23rd Colloquy on European Law: Transsexualism, medicine and law. Downloaded from http://www.pfc.org.uk/gendrpol/lgooren.htm on January 9, 2006.

6. Kimura, D. (1996). Sex, sexual orientation and sex hormones influence human cognitive function. *Current Opinion in Neurobiology* 6:259–263.

7. Maccoby, E. E. and Jacklin, C. N. (1974). *The psychology of sex differences.* Stanford, CA: Stanford University Press.

8. Haraldsen, I. R., Opjordsmoen, S., Egeland, T., and Finset, A. (2003). Sex-sensitive cognitive performance in untreated patients with early onset gender identity disorder. *Psychoneuroendocrinology* 28:906–915.

9. Van Goozen, S.H.M., Cohen-Kettenis, P. T., Gooren, L.J.G., Frijda, N. H., and van der Poll, N. E. (1994). Activating effects of androgens on cognitive performance: Causal evidence in a group of female-to-male transsexuals. *Neuropsychologia* 32:1153–1157.

10. Slabbekoorn, D., van Goozen, S.H.M., Megens, J., Gooren, L.J.G., and Cohen-Kettenis, P. T. (1999). Activating effects of cross-sex hormones on cognitive functioning: A study of short-term and long-term hormone effects in transsexuals. *Psychoneuroendocrinology* 24:423–447.

11. Alexander, G. M. (2003). An evolutionary perspective of sex-typed toy preferences: Pink, blue, and the brain. *Archives of Sexual Behavior* 32:7–14.

12. Thornhill, R. and Gangestad, S. W. (1999). Facial attractiveness. *Trends in Cognitive Sciences* 3:452–460.

13. Fellous, J.-M. (1997). Gender discrimination and prediction on the basis of facial metric information. *Vision Research* 37, 1961–1973.

14. Obleser, J., Eulitz, C., Lahiri, A., and Elbert, T. (2001). Gender differences in functional hemispheric asymmetry during processing of vowels as reflected by the human brain magnetic response. *Neuroscience Letters* 314:131–134.

15. Geschwind, N. and Galaburda, A. M. (1987). *Cerebral lateralization: Biological mechanisms, associations, and pathology.* Cambridge, MA: MIT Press.

16. Philips, S. U. (1980). Sex differences and language. *Annual Review of Anthropology* 9:523–544.

17. Argamon, S., Koppel, M., Fine, J., and Shimoni, A. R. (2003). Gender, genre, and writing style in formal written texts. *Text* 24:321–346; Koppel, M., Argamon, S., and Shimoni, A. R. (2002). Automatically categorizing written texts by author gender. *Literary and Linguistic Computing* 17:401–412.

18. Ho, S.M.Y. and Lee, T.M.C. (2001). Computer usage and its relationship with adolescent lifestyle in Hong Kong. *Journal of Adolescent Health* 29:258–266.

19. Thomson, R. and Murachver, T. (2001). Predicting gender form electronic discourse. *British Journal of Social Psychology* 40:193–208.

20. Palanza, P. (2001). Animal models of anxiety and depression: How are females different? *Neuroscience and Biobehavioral Reviews* 25:219–233.

21. Woodhill, B. M. and Samuels, C. A. (2003). Positive and negative androgyny and their relationship with psychological health and well-being. *Sex Roles* 48:555–565.

22. Costa Jr., P. T., Terracciano, A., and McCrea, R. R. (2001). Gender differences in personality traits across cultures: Robust and surprising findings. *Journal of Personality and Social Psychology* 81:322–331.

23. Visser, I. (2002). Prototypes of gender: Conceptions of feminine and masculine. *Women's Studies International Forum* 25:529–539.

24. Lippa, R. A. (2001). On deconstructing and reconstructing Masculinity-Femininity. *Journal of Research in Personality* 35:168–207.

25. Vingerhoets, A.J.J.M., Cornelius, R.R., van Heck, G.L., and Becht, M.C. (2000). Adult crying: A model and review of the literature. *Review of General Psychology* 4: 354–377.

CHAPTER 5

1. Once transsexed people have completed their transition, or even before then, most consider their sexual orientation relative to their affirmed sex and not their born-sex. For example, homosexual women of transsexual background would have a female partner. However, to reduce confusion when discussing the literature on sexual orientation, the same convention used for nontranssexed people is employed.

2. Elliot, P. and Roen, K. (1998). Transgenderism and the question of embodiment. Promising Queer politics? *Gay & Lesbian Quarterly* 4:231–261, p. 234.

3. Ibid., p. 259.

4. Lutz, D. J., Roback, H. B., and Hart, M. (1984). Feminine gender identity and psychological adjustment of male transsexuals and male homosexuals. *Journal of Sex Research* 20:350–362.

5. Rahman, Q. and Wilson, G. D. (2002). Born gay? The psychobiology of human sexual orientation. *Personality and Individual Differences* 34:1337–1382.

6. Bailey, J. M. (2003). *The man who would be queen: The science of gender-bending and transsexualism.* Washington, DC: Joseph Henry Press. This book received an angry response from transsexed people who detected in it a lack of scientific finesse as well as problems in correctly identifying the lifestyles and needs of transsexed women, in particular.

7. Levitt, H. M., Gerrish, E. A., and Hiestand, K. R. (2003). The misunderstood gender: A model of modern femme identity. *Sex Roles* 48:99–113.

8. Simon, P. A., Reback, C. J., and Bemis, C. C. (2000). HIV prevalence and incidence among male-to-female transsexuals receiving HIV prevention services in Los Angeles County. *Aids* 14:2953–2955.

9. Ogins, J. and Eichenbaum, J. (2002). Engaging transgender substance users in substance use treatment. *International Journal of Transgenderism* 6(2). Downloaded from http://www.symposion.com/ijt/ijtvo06no02_03.htm on January 9, 2006.

10. Hughes, T. L. and Eliason, M. (2002). Substance use and abuse in lesbian, gay, bisexual and transgender populations. *Journal of Primary Prevention* 22:263–298.

11. Dean, L., Meyer, I. H., Robinson, K., Sell, R. L., et al. (2000). Lesbian, gay, bisexual, and transgender health: Findings and concerns. *Journal of the Gay and Lesbian Medical Association* 4:102–151.

12. Murphy, T. E. (2001). Lesbian, gay, bisexual, and transgender medical students and their ethical conflicts. *Journal of the Gay and Lesbian Medical Association* 5:31–35.

13. Schilder, A. J., Laframboise, S., Hogg, R. S., Trussler, T., Goldstone, I., Schechter, M. T., and O'Shaughnessy, M.V. (1998). "They don't see our feelings." The health care experiences of HIV-positive transgendered persons. *Journal of the Gay and Lesbian Medical Association* 2:103–111.

14. Kenagy, G. P and Hsieh, C.-M. (2005). The risk less known: Female-to-male transgender persons' vulnerability to HIV infection. *AIDS Care* 17:195–207.

15. Friedman, R. C., Green, R., and Spitzer, R. L. (1976). Reassessment of homosexuality and transsexuality. *Annual Review of Medicine* 57–62.

16. Blanchard, R., Dickey, R., and Jones, C. L. (1995). Comparison of height and weight in homosexual versus nonhomosexual male gender dysphorics. *Archives of Sexual Behavior* 24:543–554.

17. Van Goozen, S.H.M., Slabbekoorn, D., Gooren, L.J.G., Sanders, G., and Cohen-Kettenis, P. T. (2002). Organizing and activating effects of sex hormones in homosexual transsexuals. *Behavioral Neuroscience* 116:982–988.

18. Bullough, V., Bullough, B., and Smith, R. (1983). A comparative study of male transvestites, male to female transsexuals, and male homosexuals. *Journal of Sex Research* 19:238–257.

19. Bailey, M. J., Dunne, M. P., and Martin, N. G. (2000). Genetic and environmental influences on sexual orientation and its correlates in an Australian twin sample. *Personality and Social Psychology* 78:524–536.

20. McManus, C. (2002). *Right hand, left hand: The origins of asymmetry in brains, bodies, atoms and cultures.* London: Phoenix.

21. Lalumière, M. L., Blanchard, R., and Zucker, K. J. (2000). Sexual orientation and handedness in men and woman: A meta-analysis. *Psychological Bulletin* 126:575–592.

22. Lippa, R. A. (2003). Handedness, sexual orientation, and gender-related personality traits in men and women. *Archives of Sexual Behavior* 32:103–114.

23. Green, R. and Young, R. (2001). Hand preference, sexual preference, and transsexualism. *Archives of Sexual Behavior* 30:565–574; Orlebeke, J. F., Gooren. L.J.G., Verschoor, A. M., and van den Bree, M.J.M. (1992). Elevated sinistrality in transsexuals. *Neuropsychology* 6:351–355.

24. Zucker, K. J., Beaulieu, N., Bradley, S. J., Grimshaw, G. M., and Wilcox, A. (2001). Handedness in boys with Gender Identity Disorder. *Journal of Child Psychology and Psychiatry* 42:767–776.

25. Green, R. and Young, R. (2000). Fingerprint asymmetry in male and female transsexuals. *Personality and Individual Differences* 29:933–942; Slabbekoorn, D., van Goozen, S.H.M., Sanders, G., Gooren, L.J.G, and Cohen-Kettenis, P.T. (2000). The dermatoglyphic

characteristics of transsexuals: Is there evidence for an organizing effect of sex hormones. *Psychoneuroendocrinology* 25:365–375.

26. Manning, J. T. (2002). *Digit ratio: A pointer to fertility, behavior, and health.* New Brunswick, NJ: Rutgers University Press.

27. Buck, J. J., Williams, R. M., Hughes, I. A., and Acerini, C. L. (2003). In-utero androgen exposure and 2nd to 4th digit length ratio—comparisons between healthy controls and females with classical congenital adrenal hyperplasia. *Human Reproduction* 18:976–979.

28. Austin, E. J., Manning, J. T., McInroy, K., and Mathews, E. (2002). A preliminary investigation of the associations between personality, cognitive ability and digit ratio. *Personality and Individual Differences* 33:1115–1124.

29. Schneider, H. J., Pickel, J., and Stalla, G. K. (2006). Typical female 2nd-4th finger length (2D:4D) ratios in male-to-female transsexuals—possible implications for prenatal androgen exposure. *Psychoneuroendocrinology* 31:265–269.

30. Blanchard, R., Zucker, K. J., Cohen-Kettenis, P. T., Gooren, L.J.G., and Bailey, J. M. (1996). Birth order and sibling sex ratio in two samples of Dutch gender-dysphoric homosexual males. *Archives of Sexual Behavior* 25:495–512.

31. Green, R. (2000). Birth order and ratio of brothers to sisters in transsexuals. *Psychological Medicine* 30:789–795.

32. Poasa, K. H., Blanchard, R., and Zucker, K. J. (2004). Birth order in transgendered males from Polynesia: A quantitative study of Samoan *Fa'afāfine*. *Journal of Sex & Marital Therapy* 30:13–23.

33. Green, R. and Keverne, E. B. (2000). The disparate maternal aunt–uncle ratio in male transsexuals: An explanation invoking genomic imprinting. *Journal of Theoretical Biology* 202:55–63.

34. Blanchard, R. (1989). The classification and labeling of nonhomosexual gender dysphorias. *Archives of Sexual Behavior* 18:315–334; Blanchard, R. (2005). Early history of the concept of autogynephilia. *Archives of Sexual Behavior* 34:439–466. Blanchard's discussion of homosexuality is in reference to the person's natal sex. So a homosexual transsexed woman is one who has a sexual preference for men, not women. A nonhomosexual transsexed woman may be heterosexual, bisexual, or asexual. Heterosexual transsexed women prefer women as their sexual partners.

35. Blanchard, R. (1993). Varieties of autogynephilia and their relationship to gender dysphoria. *Archives of Sexual Behavior* 22:241–251, p. 241.

36. Blanchard, R. (1992). Nonmonotonic relation of autogynephilia and heterosexual attraction. *Journal of Abnormal Psychology* 101:271–276.

37. Blanchard, R. (1988). Nonhomosexual gender dysphoria. *Journal of Sex Research* 24:188–193.

38. Blanchard, R. (2000). *Autogynephilia and the taxonomy of gender identity disorders in biological males.* Talk given at International Academy of Sex Research, Paris.

39. Lawrence, A. (2004). Sexuality and transsexuality: A new introduction to autogynephilia. Downloaded from http://www.annelawrence.com/newintroagp.html on January 9, 2006.

40. Daskalos, C. T. (1998). Changes in the sexual orientation of six heterosexual male-to-female transsexuals. *Archives of Sexual Behavior* 27:605–614.

41. Devor, H. (1997). *FTM: Female-to-male transsexuals in society.* Bloomington, IN: Indiana University Press.

42. Lee, T. (2001). Trans(re)lations: Lesbian and female to male transsexual accounts of identity. *Women's Studies International Forum* 24:347–357.

43. McCauley, E. A. and Ehrhardt, A. A. (1980). Sexual behavior in female transsexuals and lesbians. *Journal of Sex Research* 16:202–211.

44. Devor, H. (1993). Sexual orientation identities, attractions, and practices of female-to-male transsexuals. *Journal of Sex Research* 30:303–315.

45. Golombok, S., Perry, B., Burston, A., Murray, C., Mooney-Sumers, J., Stevens, M., and Golding, J. (2003). Children with lesbian parents: A community study. *Developmental Psychology* 39:20–33.

CHAPTER 6

1. A quote from Ekins, R. and King, D. (2001). Transgendering, migrating and love of oneself as a woman: A contribution to a sociology of autogynephilia. *International Journal of Transgenderism* 5(3). Downloaded from http://www.symposion.com/ijt/ijtvo05no03_01.htm on January 9, 2006.

2. Ibid.

3. Mason-Schrock, D. (1996). Transsexuals' narrative construction of the "true self." *Social Psychology Quarterly* 59:176–192.

4. Ringo, C. P. (2002). Media roles in Female-to-Male transsexual and transgender identity formation. *International Journal of Transgenderism* 6(1). Downloaded from http://www.symposion.com/ijt/ijtvo06no03_01.htm on January 9, 2006.

5. Marone, P., Iacoella S., Cecchini M. G., Ravenna A.R., and Ruggieri, V. (1998). An experimental study of body image and perception in gender identity disorders. *International Journal of Transgenderism* 2(3). Downloaded from http://www.symposion.com/ijt/ijtc0501.htm on January 9, 2006.

6. Viglione, D. J. (1999). A review of recent research addressing the utility of the Rorschach. *Psychological Assessment* 11:251–265.

7. Michel, A., Ansseau, M., Legros, J. J., Pitchot, W., Cornet, J. P., and Mormont, C. (2002). Comparisons of two groups of sex-change applicants based on the MMPI. *Psychological Reports* 91:233–240.

8. Kersting, A., Reutemann, M., Gast, U., Ohrmann, P., Suslow, T., Nikolaus, M., and Volker, A. (2003). Dissociative disorders and traumatic childhood experiences in transsexuals. *Journal of Nervous and Mental Disease* 191:182–189.

9. Hartmann, U., Becker, H., and Rueffer-Hesse, C. (1997). Self and gender: Narcissistic pathology and personality factors in gender dysphoric patients. Preliminary results of a prospective study. *International Journal of Transgenderism* 1(1). Downloaded from http://www.symposion.com/ijt/ijtc0103.htm on January 9, 2006.

10. Tsushima, W. T. and Wedding, D. (1979). MMPI results of male candidates for transsexual surgery. *Journal of Personality Assessment* 43:385–387.

11. Althof, S. E., Lothstein, L. M., Jones, P., and Shen, J. (1983). An MMPI Subscale (*Gd*): To identify males with gender identity conflicts. *Journal of Personality Assessment* 47:42–49.

12. Cole, C. M., O'Boyle, M., Emory, L. E., and Meyer, W. J. (1997). Comorbidity of gender dysphoria and other major psychiatric diagnoses. *Archives of Sexual Behavior* 26:13–26.

13. National Institute of Mental Health. Borderline personality disorder. Bethesda (MD): National Institute of Mental Health, National Institutes of Health, U.S. Department of Health and Human Services; 2001, 4 pages. (NIH Publication Number: 01–4928). Downloaded from http://www.nimh.nih.gov/publicat/NIMHbpd.pdf on January 9, 2006.

14. Miach, P. P., Berah, E. F., Butcher, J. N., and Rouse, S. (2000). Utility of the MMPI-2 in assessing gender dysphoric patients. *Journal of Personality Assessment* 75:268–279.

15. Brems, C., Adams, R. L., and Skillman, G. D. (1993). Person drawings by trans-sexual clients, psychiatric clients, and nonclients compared: Indicators of sex-typing and pathology. *Archives of Sexual Behavior* 22:253–264.

16. Wolfradt, U. and Neumann, K. (2001). Depersonalization, self-esteem and body image in male-to-female transsexuals compared to male and female controls. *Archives of Sexual Behavior* 30:301–310.

17. Lippa, R.A. (2001). On deconstructing and reconstructing Masculinity-Femininity. *Journal of Research in Personality* 35:168–207.

18. Costa Jr., P. T., Terracciano, A., and McCrea, R. R. (2001). Gender differences in personality traits across cultures: Robust and surprising findings. *Journal of Personality and Social Psychology* 81:322–331.

19. Papageorgiou, C., Papageorgaki, P., Tolis, G., Rabavilas, A. D., and Christodoulou, G. N. (2003). Psychophysiological correlates in male to female transsexuals studied with a P300 investigation. *Psychological Medicine* 33:555–561.

20. Midence, K. (2005). Attributional style and psychological adjustment in male-to-female transsexuals. *Clinical Psychology Forum* 155:16–19.

21. Docter, R. F. and Prince, V. (1997). Transvestism: A survey of 1032 cross-dressers. *Archives of Sexual Behavior* 26:589–605.

22. Docter, R. F. and Fleming, J. S. (2001). Measures of transgender behavior. *Archives of Sexual Behavior* 30:255–271.

23. Herman-Jeglinska, A., Grabowska, A., and Dulko, S. (2002). Masculinity, feminin-ity, and transsexualism. *Archives of Sexual Behavior* 31:527–534.

24. Brown, G. R., Wise, T. N., Costa Jr., P. T., et al. (1996). Personality characteristics and sexual functioning of 188 cross-dressing men. *Journal of Nervous and Mental Diseases* 184:265–273.

25. Hepp, U. and Milos, G. (2002). Gender identity disorder and eating disorders. *International Journal of Eating Disorders* 32:473–478.

26. Hepp, U., Milos, G., and Braun-Scharm, H. (2004). Gender identity disorder and anorexia nervosa in male monozygotic twins. *International Journal of Eating Disorders* 35:239–243.

27. Fernández-Arana, F., Peri, J. M., Navarro, V., Badía-Casanovas, A., Turón-Gil, V., and Vallejo-Ruiloba, J. (2000). Transsexualism and anorexia nervosa: A case report. *Eating Disorders* 8:63–66.

28. Surgenor, L. J. and Fear, J. L. (1998). Eating disorder in a transgendered patient: A case report. *International Journal of Eating Disorders* 24:449–452.

CHAPTER 7

1. Pregnancy as an example of a normal condition is a useful analogy to transsexuality, which without accompanying medical and psychological complications is itself a normal condition. See Roughgarden, J. (2004). *Evolution's rainbow: Diversity, gender, and sexuality in nature and people.* Berkeley, CA: University of California Press.

2. Dean, L., Meyer, I. H., Robinson, K., Sell, R. L., et al. (2000). Lesbian, gay, bisex-ual, and transgender health: Findings and concerns. *Journal of the Gay and Lesbian Medical Association* 4:102–151.

3. Israel, G. E. and Tarver, D. E. (1997). *Transgender care: Recommended guidelines, prac-tical information & personal accounts.* Philadelphia, PA: Temple University Press.

4. Midence, K. and Hargreaves, I. (1997). Psychosocial adjustment in Male-to-Female transsexuals: An overview of research evidence. *Journal of Psychology* 131:602–614.

5. Michel, A., Mormont, C., and Legros, J. J. (2001). A psycho-endocrinological overview of transsexualism. *European Journal of Endocrinology* 145:365–376.

6. à Compo, J., Nijman, H., Merckelbach, H., and Evers, C. (2003). Psychiatric comorbidity of Gender Identity Disorders: A survey among Dutch psychiatrists. *American Journal of Psychiatry* 160:1332–1336.

7. Benjamin H. (1966). *The transsexual phenomenon.* New York: The Julian Press. Downloaded from http://www.symposion.com/ijt/benjamin/index.htm on January 9, 2006.

8. Blank, R. J. (1981). The partial transsexual. *American Journal of Psychotherapy* 35: 107–112.

9. Wålinder, J. (1967). *Transsexualism: A study of forty-three cases.* Downloaded from http://www.symposion.com/ijt/walinder/index.htm on January 9, 2006.

10. Gooren, L.J.G. (1993). *Transsexualism, medicine and law.* Closing speech at the Council of Europe, 23rd Colloquy on European Law: Transsexualism, medicine and law. Downloaded from http://www.pfc.org.uk/gendrpol/lgooren.htm on January 9, 2006.

11. Chiland, C. (2000). The psychoanalyst and the transsexual patient. *International Journal of Psychoanalysis* 81:21–35.

12. Laub, D. and Fisk, N. (1971). A rehabilitation program for Gender Dysphoria Syndrome by surgical sex change. *Plastic and Reconstructive Surgery* 53:388–403. Cited in Lothstein, L. M. (1979). Psychodynamics and sociodynamics of gender-dysphoric states. *American Journal of Psychotherapy* 33:214–238.

13. Lothstein, L. M. (1979). Psychodynamics and sociodynamics of gender-dysphoric states. *American Journal of Psychotherapy* 33:214–238.

14. Ibid., p. 214.

15. Ibid., p. 232.

16. Levine, E., Shaieva, C., and Mihailovic, M. (1975). Male to female: The role transformation of transsexuals. *Archives of Sexual Behavior* 4:173–185.

17. Lothstein, L. M. (1984). Psychological testing with transsexuals: A 30-year review. *Journal of Personality Assessment* 48:500–507.

18. A recent review published in August 2004 is contained in an article on gender atypicality produced by GIRES in the UK and authored by a group of international experts chaired by Professor Milton Diamond who met in London in 2003. Downloaded from http://www.gires.org.uk on January 19, 2006.

19. In Bradley, S. J. and Zucker, K. J. (2001). Gender identity disorders. In *International encyclopedia of the social & behavioral sciences* (p. 6015). Amsterdam, Elsevier Science, it is stated that "[s]ex reassignment surgery typically is not undertaken until sometime (sic) in early adulthood although those individuals with a history of Transvestic Fetishism may not have surgery until their thirties or forties." This statement suggests an inconsistency in the DSM criteria for transsexualism, as it is frequently assumed that the diagnoses transvestic fetishism and transsexualism are mutually exclusive.

20. Lawrence, A. A. (2003). Factors associated with satisfaction or regret following male-to-female sex reassignment surgery. *Archives of Sexual Behavior* 32:299–316.

21. Doorn, C. D., Poortinga, J., and Verschoor, A. M. (1994). Cross-gender identity in transvestites and male transsexuals. *Archives of Sexual Behavior* 23:185–201.

22. Schott, R. L. (1995). The childhood and family dynamics of transvestites. *Archives of Sexual Behavior* 24:309–327.

23. Blanchard, R. (1994). A structural equation model for age at clinical presentation in nonhomosexual male gender dysphorics. *Archives of Sexual Behavior* 23:311–320.

24. Lawrence, A. A. (2004). Autogynephilia: A paraphilic model of Gender Identity Disorder. In U. Leli and J. Drescher (Eds.), *Transgender subjectivities: A clinician's guide* (pp. 69–87). Binghamton, NY: The Haworth Medical Press.

25. Karasic, D. H. (2000). Progress in health care for transgendered people. *Journal of the Gay and Lesbian Medical Association* 4:157–158.

26. Oriel, K. A. (2000). Medical care of transsexual patients. *Journal of the Gay and Lesbian Medical Association* 4:185–194; Sobralske, M. (2005). Primary care needs of patients who have undergone gender reassignment. *Journal of the American Academy of Nurse Practitioners* 17:133–138.

27. Hausman, K. (2003). Controversy continues to grow over DSM's GID diagnosis. *Psychiatric News* 38:25.

28. McConaghy, N. (1999). Unresolved issues in scientific sexology. *Archives of Sexual Behavior* 28:285–328.

29. Blanchard, R. and Clemmensen, L. H. (1988). A test of the DSM-III-R's implicit assumption that fetishistic arousal and gender dysphoria are mutually exclusive. *Journal of Sex Research* 25:426–432.

30. Långström, N. and Zucker, K. J. (2005). Transvestic Fetishism in the general population: Prevalence and correlates. *Journal of Sex & Marital Therapy* 31:87–95.

31. Vitale, A. (2001). Implications of being gender dysphoric: A developmental review. *Gender and Psychoanalysis* 6:121–141.

32. A full account of the standards of care is located at http://www.hbigda.org/Documents2/socv6.pdf. Downloaded on January 9, 2006.

33. Norton, J. (1997). "Brain says you're a girl, but I think you're a sissy boy": Cultural origins of transphobia. *Journal of Gay, Lesbian, and Bisexual Identity* 2:152.

34. Osborne, M. (2003). *Beyond gatekeeping: Truth and trust in therapy with transsexuals*. IFGE Conference, Philadelphia, PA. Downloaded from http://www.transgenderzone.com/library/st/fulltext/26.htm on January 9, 2006.

35. Carroll, L., Gilroy, P. J., and Ryan, J. (2002). Counseling transgendered, transsexual, and gender-variant clients. *Journal of Counseling and Development* 80:131–139.

36. Bower, H. (2001). The gender identity disorder in the DSM-IV classification: A critical evaluation. *Australian and New Zealand Journal of Psychiatry* 35:1–8.

37. Bodlund, O. and Kullgren, G. (1996). Transsexualism—General outcome and prognostic factors: A five-year follow-up study of nineteen transsexuals in the process of changing sex. *Archives of Sexual Behavior* 25:303–316.

38. Blanchard, R., Steiner, B. W., and Clemmensen, L. H. (1985). Gender dysphoria, gender reorientation, and the clinical management of transsexualism. *Journal of Consulting and Clinical Psychology* 53: 295–304.

39. Cohen-Kettenis, P. T. and Gooren, L.J.G. (1999). Transsexualism: A Review of etiology, diagnosis and treatment. *Journal of Psychosomatic Research* 46:315–333.

40. Heath, R. (2004). A second chance for Alex: sex affirmation in young people. *On Line Opinion*. Downloaded from http://www.onlineopinion.com.au/view.asp?article=2166 on January 9, 2006; Spriggs, M. P. (2004). Ethics and the proposed treatment for a 13-year-old with atypical gender identity. *Medical Journal of Australia,* 181:319–321.

41. Wallbank, R. (2004). *Contemporary human rights issues for people with transsexualism,* p. 5. Paper presented at the Gendys Conference, Manchester, UK.

42. Cohen-Kettenis, P. T. and van Goozen, S.H.M. (1997). Sex reassignment of adolescent transsexuals: A follow-up study. *Journal of the American Academy of Child and Adolescent*

Psychiatry 36:263–271. The quotation is from page 53 of Cohen-Kettenis, P. T. and Pfäfflin, F. (2003). *Transgenderism and intersexuality in childhood and adolescence: Making choices.* Thousand Oaks, CA: Sage Publications. The original reference is *Diagnostic and Statistical Manual of Mental Illnesses: DSM-IV-TR* (4th Edition, Text Revision, 2002). Washington, DC: American Psychiatric Association.

43. Richardson, J. (1999). Response: Finding the disorder in Gender Identity Disorder. *Harvard Review of Psychiatry* 7:43–50.

44. Zucker, K. J. and Spitzer, R. L. (2005). Was the Gender Identity Disorder of Childhood diagnosis introduced into DSM-III as a backdoor maneuver to replace homosexuality? A historical note. *Journal of Sex & Marital Therapy* 31:31–42.

45. Di Ceglie, D. (2000). Gender identity disorder in young people. *Advances in Psychiatric Treatment* 6: 464.

46. Meyenburg, B. (1999). Gender identity disorder in adolescence: Outcomes of psychotherapy. *Adolescence* 34:305–313.

47. Cohen-Kettenis, P. T. and Pfäfflin, F. (2003). *Transgenderism and intersexuality in childhood and adolescence: Making choices.* Thousand Oaks, CA: Sage Publications.

48. Ibid., p. 112.

49. Bradley, S. J. and Zucker, K. J. (1997). Gender identity disorder: A review of the past 10 years. *Journal of the American Academy of Child and Adolescent Psychiatry* 36:872–880.

50. Johnson, L. L., Bradley, S. J., Birkenfeld-Adams, A. S., et al. (2004). A parent-report gender identity questionnaire for children. *Archives of Sexual Behavior* 33:105–116.

51. Di Ceglie, D. (2002). Castaway's corner. *Clinical Child Psychology and Psychiatry* 7:487–491.

52. Di Ceglie, D., Freedman, D., McPherson, S., and Richardson, P. (2002). Children and adolescents referred to a specialist gender identity development service: Clinical features and demographic characteristics, *International Journal of Transgenderism* 6(1). Downloaded from http://www.symposion.com/ijt/ijtvo06no01_01.htm on January 9, 2006.

53. Rekers, G. A. (1979). Sex-role behavior change: Intrasubject studies of boyhood gender disturbance. *Journal of Psychology* 103:255–269.

54. Zucker, K. J. (2005). Gender identity disorder in children and adolescents. *Annual Review of Clinical Psychology* 1:467–492.

55. Cohen-Kettenis, P. T. and van Goozen, S.H.M. (1998). Pubertal delay as an aid in diagnosis and treatment of a transsexual adolescent. *European Child & Adolescent Psychiatry* 7:246–248.

CHAPTER 8

1. See Figure 1 in White, P. C. and Speiser, P. W. (2000). Congenital adrenal hyperplasia due to 21-hydroxylase deficiency. *Endocrine Reviews* 21:247.

2. Cohen-Kettenis, P. T. and Pfäfflin, F. (2003). *Transgenderism and intersexuality in childhood and adolescence: Making choices.* Thousand Oaks, CA: Sage Publications.

3. Vandenbergh, J. G. (2003). Prenatal hormone exposure and sexual variation. *American Scientist* 91:216–225.

4. Wilson, J. D. (2001). Androgens, androgen receptors, and male gender role behavior. *Hormones and Behavior* 40:358–366.

5. Grumbach, M. M. and Auchus, R. J. (1999). Estrogen: Consequences and implications of human mutations in synthesis and action. *Journal of Clinical Endocrinology and Metabolism* 84:4677–4694.

6. Jin, B., Turner, L., Walters, W.A.W., and Handelsman, D. J. (1996). Androgen or estrogen effects on human prostate. *Journal of Clinical Endocrinology and Metabolism* 81:4290–4295.

7. Melmed, S. (2003). Mechanisms for pituitary tumorigenesis: The plastic pituitary. *Journal of Clinical Investigation* 112:1603–1618.

8. Serri, O., Noiseux, D., Robert, F., and Hardy, J. (1996). Lactotroph hyperplasia in an estrogen treated male-to-female transsexual. *Journal of Clinical Endocrinology and Metabolism* 81:3177–3179.

9. Giltay, E. J., Gooren, L.J.G., Emeis, J. J., Kooistra, T., and Stehouwer, C.D.A. (2000). Oral, but not transdermal, administration of estrogens lowers tissue-type plasminogen activation levels in humans without affecting endothelial levels. *Arteriosclerosis, Thrombosis, and Vascular Biology* 20:1396–1403.

10. Toorians, A.W.F.T., Thomassen, M.C.L.G.D., Zweegman, S., Magdeleyns, E.J.P., Tans, G., Gooren, L.J.G., and Rosing, J. (2003). Venous thrombosis and changes of hemostatic variables during cross-sex hormone treatment in transsexual people. *Journal of Clinical Endocrinology and Metabolism* 12:5723–5729.

11. Giltay, E. J., Elbers, J.M.H., Gooren, L.J.G., Emeis, J. J., Kooistra, T., Asscherman, H., and Stehouwer, C.D.A. (1998). Visceral fat accumulation is an important determinant of PAI-1 levels in young, nonobese men and women: Modulation by cross-sex hormone administration. *Arteriosclerosis, Thrombosis and Vascular Biology* 18:1716–1722.

12. Elbers, J.M.H., Asscheman, H., Seidell, J. C., and Gooren, L.J.G. (1999). Effects of sex steroid hormones on regional fat depots as assessed by magnetic resonance imaging in transsexuals. *American Journal of Physiology* 276:E317–E325.

13. Bosinski, H.A.G., Schröder, I., Peter, M., Arndt, R., Wille, R., and Sippell, W.G. (1997). Anthropometrical measurements and androgen levels in males, females, and hormonally untreated female-male transsexuals. *Archives of Sexual Behavior* 26:143–157.

14. Rosenbaum, M. and Leibel, R. L. (1999). Role of gonadal steroids in the sexual dimorphisms in body composition and circulating concentrations of leptin. *Journal of Clinical Endocrinology and Metabolism* 84:1784–1789.

15. Elbers, J.M.H., Asscheman, H., Seidell, J. C., Frölich, M., Meinders, A. E., and Gooren, L.J.G. (1997). Reversal of the sex difference in serum leptin levels upon cross-sex hormone administration in transsexuals. *Journal of Clinical Endocrinology and Metabolism* 82:3267–3270.

16. Van Kesteren, P., Lips, P., Gooren, L.J.G., Asscheman, H., and Megens, J. (1998). Long-term follow-up of bone mineral density and bone metabolism in transsexuals treated with cross-sex hormones. *Clinical Endocrinology* 48:347–354.

17. Reutrakul, S., Ongphiphadhanakul, B., Piaseu, N., Krittiyawong, S., Chanprasertyothin, S., Bunnag P., and Rajatanavin, R. (1998). The effects of oestrogen exposure on bone mass in male to female transsexuals. *Clinical Endocrinology* 49:811–814.

18. Ferriman, D. and Gallwey, J. D. (1971). Clinical assessment of body hair growth in women. *Journal of Clinical Endocrinology* 21:1440–1447.

19. Giltay, E. J. and Gooren, L.J.G. (2000). Effects of sex steroid deprivation/administration on hair growth and skin sebum production in transsexual males and females. *Journal of Clinical Endocrinology & Metabolism* 85:2913–2921.

20. Giltay, E. J., Fonk, J.C.M, von Blomberg, B.M.E., Drexhage, H. A., Schalkwijk, C., and Gooren, L.J.G. (2000). *In Vivo* effects of sex steroids on lymphocyte responsiveness and immunoglobulin levels in humans. *Journal of Clinical Endocrinology & Metabolism* 85:1648–1657.

21. Polderman, K. H., Gooren, L.J.G., Asscheman, H., Bakker, A., and Heine, R. J. (1994). Induction of insulin resistance by androgens and estrogens. *Journal of Clinical Endocrinology and Metabolism* 79:265–271.

22. Miller, V. M. (1999). Gender, estrogen, and NOS. Cautions about generalizations. *Circulation Research* 85:979–981.

23. Valenti, S., Fazzuoli, L., and Giusti, M. (2003). Circulating nitric oxide levels increase after anti-androgen treatment in male-to-female transsexuals. *Journal of Endocrinological Investigation* 26:522–526.

24. Sudhir, K. and Komesaroff, P. A. (1999). Cardiovascular actions of estrogens in men. *Journal of Clinical Endocrinology and Metabolism* 84:3411–3415.

25. Giltay, E. J., Hoogeveen, E. K., Elbers, J.M.H., Gooren, L.J.G., Asscheman, H., and Stehouwer, C.D.A. (1998). Effects of sex steroids on plasma total homocysteine levels: A study in transsexual males and females. *Journal of Clinical Endocrinology and Metabolism* 83:550–553.

26. Giltay, E. J., Verhoef, P., Gooren, L.J.G., Geleijnse, J. M., Schouten, E. G., and Stehouwer, C.D.A. (2003). Oral and transdermal estrogens both lower plasma total homocysteine in male-to-female transsexuals. *Atherosclerosis* 168:139–146.

27. Giltay, E. J., Lambert, J., Gooren, L.J.G., Elbers, J.M.H., Steyn, M., and Stehouwer, C.D.A. (1999). Sex steroids, insulin, and arterial stiffness in women and men. *Hypertension* 34:590–597.

28. Polderman, K. H., Stehouwer, C. D., van Kamp, G. J., Dekker, G. A., Verheugt, F. W., and Gooren, L. J. (2003). Influence of sex hormones on plasma endothelin levels. *Annals of Internal Medicine* 118:429–32.

29. Schwertz, D. W. and Penckhofer, S. (2001). Sex differences and the effects of sex hormones on hemostasis and vascular reactivity. *Heart & Lung* 30:401–426.

30. New, G., Timmins, K. L., Duffy, S. J., Tran, B. T., O'Brien, R. C., Harper, R. W., and Meredith, I. T. (1997). Long-term estrogen therapy improves vascular function in male to female transsexuals. *Journal of the American College of Cardiology* 29:1437–1444.

31. McCrohon, J. A., Walters, W.A.W., Robinson, J.T.C., McCredie, R. J., Turner, L., Adams, M. R., Handelsman, D. J., and Celermajer, D. S. (1997). Arterial reactivity is enhanced in genetic males taking high dose estrogens. *Journal of the American College of Cardiology* 29:1432–1436.

32. Egan, R. A. and Kuyl, J. M. (2002). Ischemic stroke in a man using estrogen. *Journal of Stroke and Cerebrovascular Diseases* 11:117–118.

33. De Sutter, P. (2001). Gender reassignment and assisted reproduction. Present and future reproductive options for transsexual people. *Human Reproduction* 16:612–614.

34. Brothers, D. and Ford, W.C.L. (2000). Gender reassignment and assisted reproduction, an ethical analysis. *Human Reproduction* 15:737–738.

35. De Sutter, P., Kira, K., Verschoor, A., and Hotimsky, A. (2002). The desire to have children and the preservation of fertility in transsexual women: A survey. *International Journal of Transgenderism* 6(3). Downloaded from http://www.symposion.com/ijt/ijtvo06no03_03.htm on January 9, 2006.

36. Bosinski, H.A.G., Peter, M., Bonatz, G., Arndt, R., Heidenreich, M., Sippell, W. G., and Wille, R. (1997). A higher rate of hyperandrogenic disorders in female-to-male transsexuals. *Psychoneuroendocrinology* 22:361–380.

37. Elbers, J.M.H., Asscheman, H., Seidell, J. C., Megens, J.A.J., and Gooren, L.J.G. (1997). Long-term testosterone administration increases visceral fat in female to male transsexuals. *Journal of Clinical Metabolism and Metabolism* 82:2044–2047.

38. Goh, V.H.H. and Ratnam, S. S. (1997). Effects of hormone deficiency, androgen therapy and calcium supplementation on bone mineral density in female transsexuals. *Maturitas* 26:45–52.

39. Goh, V.H.H. (1999). Breast tissues in transsexual women—a nonprostatic source of androgen up-regulated production of prostate-specific antigen. *Journal of Clinical Endocrinology and Metabolism* 84:3313–3315.

CHAPTER 9

1. Gooren, L.J.G. (1999). Hormonal sex reassignment. *International Journal of Transgenderism* 3(3). Downloaded from http://www.symposion.com/ijt/ijt990301.htm on January 9, 2006; for a review of possible medical complications see Asscherman, H., Gooren, L.J.G., and Eklund, P.J.E. (1989). Mortality and morbidity in transsexual patients with cross-gender hormone treatment. *Metabolism* 38:869–873.

2. Kanhai, R.C.J., Hage, J. J., Asscheman, H., and Mulder, J. W. (1999). Augmentation mammoplasty in male-to-female transsexuals. *Plastic and Reconstructive Surgery* 104: 542–549.

3. Meyer, W. J., Walker, P. A., and Suplee, Z. R. (1981). A survey of transsexual hormonal treatment in twenty gender-treatment centers. *Journal of Sex Research* 17:344–349.

4. Barrett, J. (2003). Disorders of gender identity. *The Practitioner* 247(1647):472, 477–482.

5. Keefe, D. F. (2002). Sex hormones and neural mechanisms. *Archives of Sexual Behavior* 31:401–403.

6. Levy, A., Crown, A., and Reid, R. (2003). Endocrine intervention for transsexuals. *Clinical Endocrinology* 59: 409–418. See also Moore, E., Wisniewski, A., and Dobs, A. (2003). Endocrine treatment of transsexual people: A review of treatment regimens, outcomes, and adverse effects. *Journal of Clinical Endocrinology & Metabolism* 88:3467–3473.

7. Slabbekoorn, D., Van Goozen, S., Gooren, L., and Cohen-Kettenis, P. (2001). Effects of cross-sex hormone treatment on emotionality in transsexuals. *International Journal of Transgenderism* 5(3). Downloaded from http://www.symposion.com/ijt/ijtvo05no03_02.htm on January 9, 2006.

8. Van Kesteren, P.J.M., Asscheman, H., Megens, J.A.J., and Gooren, L.J.G. (1997). Mortality and morbidity in transsexual subjects treated with cross-sex hormones. *Clinical Endocrinology* 47:337–342.

9. Futterweit, W. (1998). Endocrine therapy of transsexualism and potential complications of long-term treatment. *Archives of Sexual Behavior* 27:209–226.

10. Tangpricha, V., Afdhal, N. H., and Chipkin, S. R. (2001). Case report: Autoimmune hepatitis in a Male-to-Female transsexual treated with conjugated estrogens. *International Journal of Transgenderism* 5(3). Downloaded from http://www.symposion.com/ijt/ijtvo05no03_03.htm on January 9, 2006.

11. Schlatterer, K., der Yassouridis, A., von Werder, K., Poland, D., Kemper, J., and Stalla, G. K. (1998). A follow-up study for estimating the effectiveness of a cross-gender hormone substitution therapy on transsexual patients. *Archives of Sexual Behavior* 27:475–492.

12. Kanhai, R.C.J., Hage, J. J., Bloemena, E., van Diest, P. J., and Karim, R. B. (1999). Mammary fibroadenoma in a male-to-female transsexual. *Histopathology* 35:183–185.

13. Feldman, J. (2002). New onset of type 2 diabetes mellitus with feminizing hormone therapy: Case series. *International Journal of Transgenderism* 6(2). Downloaded from http://www.symposion.com/ijt/ijtvo06no02_01.htm on January 9, 2006.

14. Van Haast, E. P., Newlind, D.W.W., Gooren. L.J.G., Asscheman, H., and Prenger, D. M. (1998). Metastatic prostatic carcinoma in a male-female transsexual. *British Journal of Urology* 81:776.

15. Pringsheim, T., and Gooren, L. (2004). Migraine prevalence in male to female transsexuals on hormone therapy. *Neurology* 63:593–594.

16. Booth, A., Johnson, D. R., Granger, D. A., Crouter, A. C., and McHale, S. (2003). Testosterone and child and adolescent adjustment: The moderating role of parent-child relationships. *Developmental Psychology* 39:85–98.

17. Van Goozen, S.H.M., Cohen-Kettenis, P. T., Gooren, L.J.G., Frijda, N. H., and van de Poll, N. E. (1995). Gender differences in behavior: Activating effects of cross-sex hormones. *Psychoneuroendocrinology* 20:343–363.

18. Cherrier, M. M., Anawalt, B. D., Herbst, K. L., Amory, J. K., Craft, S., Matsumoto, A. M., and Bremner, W. J. (2002). Cognitive effects of short-term manipulation of serum sex steroids in healthy young men. *Journal of Clinical Endocrinology & Metabolism* 87:3090–3096.

19. Van Goozen, S.H.M., Slabbekoorn, D., Gooren, L.J.G., Sanders, G., and Cohen-Kettenis, P. T. (2002). Organizing and activating effects of sex hormones in homosexual transsexuals. *Behavioral Neuroscience* 116:982–988.

CHAPTER 10

1. Sekvaggi, G., Ceulemans, P., De Cuypere, G., et al. (2005). Gender identity disorder: General overview and surgical treatment for vaginoplasty in male-to-female transsexuals. *Plastic and Reconstructive Surgery* 116:135e-145e.

2. Rubin, H. S. (1998). Phenomenology as method in trans studies. *Gay & Lesbian Quarterly* 4:265.

3. Michel, A. (2001). Le transsexuel: Quel devenir? *Annales Médico-Psychologiques* 159:347–58.

4. Haraldsen, I. R. and Dahl, A. A. (2000). Symptom profiles of gender dysphoric patients of transsexual type compared to patients with personality disorders and healthy adults. *Acta Psychiatrica Scandiavica* 102:276–281.

5. Michel, A., Mormont, C., and Legros, J. J. (2001). A psycho-endocrinological overview of transsexualism. *European Journal of Endocrinology* 145:365–376.

6. Snaith, P. (1987). Gender reassignment today. *British Medical Journal* 295:454. A more recent account of GRS possibilities for transsexed women is contained in: Selvaggi, G., Ceulemans, P., De Cuypere, G., et al. (2005). Gender identity disorder: General overview and surgical treatment for vaginoplasty in male-to-female transsexuals. *Plastic and Reconstructive Surgery* 116:135–145.

7. Rachlin, K. (2002). Transgender individuals' experiences of psychotherapy. *International Journal of Transgenderism* 6(1). Downloaded from http://www.symposion.com/ijt/ijtvo06no01_03.htm on January 9, 2006.

8. Fee, E., Brown, T. M., and Laylor, J. (2003). One size does not fit all in the transgender community. *American Journal of Public Health* 93:899–900.

9. Friedman, R. C., Green, R., and Spitzer, R. L. (1976). Reassessment of homosexuality and transsexuality. *Annual Review of Medicine* 57–62.

10. Perovic, S. V., Stanojevic, D. S., and Djordjevic, M.L.J. (2000). Vaginoplasty in male transsexuals using penile skin and a urethral flap. *BJU International* 86:843–850.

11. Schlatterer, K., der Yassouridis, A., von Werder, K., Poland, D., Kemper, J., and Stalla, G. K. (1998). A follow-up study for estimating the effectiveness of a cross-gender hormone substitution therapy on transsexual patients. *Archives of Sexual Behavior* 27:475–492.

12. Krege, S., Bex, A., Lümmen G., and Rübben, H. (2001). Male-to-female transsexualism: A technique, results and long-term follow-up in 66 patients. *BJU International* 88:396–402.

13. Freundt, I., Toolenaar, T.A.M., Huikeshoven, F.J.M., Jeekel, H., and Drogendijk, A. C. (1993). Long-term psychosexual and psychosocial performance of patients with a sigmoid neovagina. *American Journal of Obstetrics and Gynecology* 169: 1210–1214.

14. Kwun Kim, S., Hoon Park, J., Cheol Lee, K., Min Park, J., Tae Kim, J., and Chan Kim, M. (2003). Long-term results in patients after rectosigmoid vaginoplasty. *Plastic and Reconstructive Surgery* 112:143–151.

15. Maral, T., Aygun, C., and Borman, H. (2002). Management and prevention of ongoing peristaltic contractions of the neovagina following rectosigmoid neocolpopoiesis in male transsexuals. *Plastic and Reconstructive Surgery* 109:1667–1671.

16. Cova, M., Mosconi, E., Liguori, G., Bucci, S., Trombetta, C., Belgrano, E., and Pozzi-Mucelli, R. (2003). Value of magnetic resonance imaging in the evaluation of sex-reassignment surgery in male-to-female transsexuals. *Abdominal Imaging* 28:728–732.

17. Fugate, S. R., Apodaca, C. C., and Hibbert, M. L. (2001). Gender reassignment surgery and the gynecological patient. *Primary Care Update in Obstetrics and Gynecology* 8:22–24.

18. Wilson, N. (2002). The aesthetic vulva: Perineal cosmesis in the male-to-female transsexual. *International Journal of Transgenderism* 6(4). Downloaded from http://www.symposion.com/ijt/ijtvo06no04_01.htm on January 9, 2006.

19. Kuiper, A. J. and Cohen-Kettenis, P. T. (1998). Gender role reversal among postoperative transsexuals. *International Journal of Transgenderism* 2(3). Downloaded from http://www.symposion.com/ijt/ijtc0502.htm on January 9, 2006.

20. Rehman, J., Lazer, S., Benet, A. E., Schaefer, L. C., and Melman, A. (1999). The reported sex and surgery satisfactions of 28 postoperative male-to-female transsexual patients. *Archives of Sexual Behavior* 28:71–89.

21. Rakic, Z., Starcevic, S., Maric, J., and Kelin, K. (1996). The outcome of sex reassignment surgery in Belgrade: 32 patients of both sexes. *Archives of Sexual Behavior* 25: 515–525.

22. Abramowitz, S. I. (1986). Psychosocial outcomes of sex reassignment surgery. *Journal of Consulting and Clinical Psychology* 54:183–189.

23. Lief, H. I. and Hubschman, L. (1993). Orgasm in the postoperative transsexual. *Archives of Sexual Behavior* 22:145–155.

24. Lawrence, A. A. (2005). Sexuality before and after male-to-female sex reassignment surgery. *Archives of Sexual Behavior* 34:147–166.

25. Lawrence, A. (2001). *Sex reassignment surgery without a one year real-life experience: Still no regrets.* XVII Harry Benjamin International Gender Dysphoria Association Symposium, 2001, Galveston, Texas, U.S. Downloaded from http://www.symposion.com/ijt/hbigda/2001/70_lawrence.htm on January 9, 2006.

26. Lawrence, A. A., Latty, E. M., Chivers, M. L., and Bailey, J. M. (2005). Measurement of sexual arousal in postoperative male-to-female transsexuals using vaginal photoplethysmography. *Archives of Sexual Behavior* 34:135–145.

27. Smith, Y.L.S., Cohen, L., and Cohen-Kettenis, P. T. (2002). Postoperative psychological functioning of adolescent transsexuals: A Rorschach study. *Archives of Sexual Behavior* 31:255–261.

28. Fang, R.-H., Chen, T.-J., and Chen, T.-H. (2003). Anatomic study of vaginal width in male-to-female transsexual surgery. *Plastic and Reconstructive Surgery* 112:511–514.

29. Frederick, R. W. and Leach, G. E. (2004). Abdominal sacral colpopexy for repair of neovaginal prolapse in male-to-female transsexuals. *Urology* 64:580–581.

30. Hoebeke, P., Selvaggi, G., Ceulemans, P., et al. (2005). Impact of sex reassignment surgery on lower urinary tract function. *European Urology* 47:398–402.

31. Fitzpatrick, C., Swierzewski, S. J., and McGuire, E. J. (1993). Periurethral collagen for urinary incontinence after gender reassignment surgery. *Urology* 42:458–460.

32. Liguori, G., Trombetta, C., Buttazzi, L., and Belgrano, E. (2001). Acute peritonitis due to introital stenosis and perforation of a bowel neovagina in a transsexual. *Obstetrics & Gynecology* 97:828–829.

33. Brown, J. A. and Wilson, T. M. (1997). Benign prostatic hyperplasia requiring transurethral resection of the prostate in a 60-year-old male-to-female transsexual. *British Journal of Urology* 80:956–957.

34. Lawrence, A. (2001). Vaginal neoplasia in a male-to-female transsexual: Case report, review of the literature, and recommendations for cytological screening. *International Journal of Transgenderism* 5(1). Downloaded from http://www.symposion.com/ijt/ijtvo05no01_01.htm on January 9, 2006.

35. Rachlin, K. (1999). Factors which influence individual's decisions when considering female-to-male genital reconstructive surgery. *International Journal of Transgenderism* 3(3). Downloaded from http://www.symposion.com/ijt/ijt990302.htm on January 9, 2006.

36. Ergeneli, M. H., Duran, E. H., Özcan, G., and Erdogan, M. (1999). Vaginectomy and laparoscopically assisted vaginal hysterectomy as adjunctive surgery for female-to-male transsexual reassignment: preliminary report. *European Journal of Obstetrics & Gynecology and Reproductive Biology* 87:35–37.

37. Fang, R. H., Kao, Y. S., Ma, S., and Lin, J. T. (1999). Phalloplasty in female-to-male transsexuals using free radial osteocutaneous flap: A series of 22 cases. *British Journal of Plastic Surgery* 52:217–222.

38. García de Alba, A., Abel de la Peña-Salcedo, J., López-Monjardin, H., Clifton, J. F., and Palacio-López, E. (2000). Microsurgical penile reconstruction with a sensitive radial forearm free flap. *Microsurgery* 20:181–185.

39. Bettocchi, C., Ralph, D. J., and Pryor, J. P. (2005). Pedicled pubic phalloplasty in females with gender dysphoria. *BJU International* 95:120–124.

40. Rohrmann, D. and Jakse, G. (2003). Urethroplasty in female-to-male transsexuals. *European Urology* 44:611–614.

41. Trombetta, C., Liguori, G., Pacone, M., Bucci, S., Guaschino, S., Papa, G., and Belgrano, E. (2002). Total sex-reassignment surgery in female-to-male transsexuals: A one-stage technique. *BJU International* 90:754–757.

42. Perovic, S. V. and Djordjevic, M. L. (2003). Metoidioplasty: A variant of phalloplasty in female transsexuals. *BJU International* 92:981–985.

CHAPTER 11

1. Oates, J. M. and Dacakis, G. (1983). Speech pathology considerations in the management of transsexualism—A review. *British Journal of Disorders of Communication* 18:139–151.

2. King, J. B., Lindstedt, D. E., Jensen, M., and Law, M. (1999). Transgendered voice: Considerations in case history management. *Logopedics Phoniatrics Vocology* 24:14–18.

3. Oates, J. and Dacakis, G. (1997). Voice change in transsexuals. *Venereology* 10:178–187.

4. Günzberger, D. (1995). Acoustic and perceptual implications of the transsexual voice. *Archives of Sexual Behavior* 24:339–348.

5. Dacakis, G. (2002). The role of voice therapy in male-to-female transsexuals. *Current Opinion in Otolaryngology & Head and Neck Surgery* 10:173–177.

6. Brown, M., Perry, A., Cheesman, A. D., and Pring, T. (2000). Pitch change in male-to-female transsexuals: Has phonosurgery a role to play? *International Journal of Language & Communication Disorders* 35:129–136.

7. Coleman, R. O. (1983). Acoustic correlates of speaker sex identification: Implications for the transsexual voice. *Journal of Sex Research* 19:293–295.

8. White, C. T. (1998). On the pragmatics of an androgynous style of speaking (from a transsexual's perspective). *World Englishes* 17:215–223.

9. Kulick, D. (1999). Transgender and language: A review of the literature and suggestions for the future. *Gay & Lesbian Quarterly* 5:605–622.

10. Byrne, L. A., Dacakis, G., and Douglas, J. M. (2003). Self-perceptions of pragmatic communication abilities in male-to-female transsexuals. *Advances in Speech-Language Pathology* 5:15–25.

11. de Bruin, M. D., Coerts, M. J., and Greven, A. J. (2000). Speech therapy in the management of male-to-female transsexuals. *Folia Phoniatrica et Logopaedica* 52:220–227.

12. Dacakis, G. (2000). Long-term maintenance of fundamental frequency increases in male-to-female transsexuals. *Journal of Voice* 14:549–556.

13. Van Borsel, J., De Cuypere, G., Rubens, R., and Bestaerke, B. (2000). Voice problems in female-to-male transsexuals. *International Journal of Language and Communication Disorders* 35:427–442.

14. Neumann, K., Welzel, C., and Gonnermann, U. (2002). Satisfaction of MtF transsexuals with operative voice therapy—A questionnaire-based preliminary study. *International Journal of Transgenderism* 6(4). Downloaded from http://www.symposion.com/ijt/ijtvo06no04_02.htm on January 9, 2006.

15. Kanagalingam, J., Georgalas, C., Wood, G. R., Suki, A., Guri, S., and Cheesman, A. D. (2005). Cricothyroid approximation and subluxation in 21 male-to-female transsexuals. *Laryngoscope* 115:611–618.

16. Pickuth, D., Brandt, S., Neumann, K., Berghaus, A., Spielmann, R. P., and Heywang-Köbrunner, S. H. (2000). Value of spiral CT with cricothyroid approximation. *British Journal of Radiology* 73:840–842.

17. Matai, V., Chessman, A. D., and Clarke, P. M. (2003). Cricothyroid approximation and thyroid chondroplasty: A patient survey. *Otolaryngology—Head and Neck Surgery* 128:841–847.

18. Yang, C. Y., Palmer, A. D., Murray, K. D., Meltzer, T. R., and Coen, J. I. (2002). Cricothyroid approximation to elevate vocal pitch in male-to-female transsexuals: Results of surgery. *Annals of Otolaryngology, Rhinology and Laryngology* 111:477–485.

19. Wagner, I., Fugain, C., Monneron-Girard, L., Cordier, B., and Chabolle, F. (2003). Pitch-raising surgery in fourteen male-to-female transsexuals. *Laryngoscope* 113:1157–1165.

20. Kanhai, R.C.J., Hage, J. J., and Mulder, J. W. (2000). Long-term outcome of augmentation mammoplasty in male-to-female transsexuals: A questionnaire survey of 107 patients. *British Journal of Plastic Surgery* 53:209–211.

21. Kanhai, R.C.J., Hage, J. J., and Karim, R. B. (2001). Augmentation mammoplasty in male-to-female trans-sexuals: Facts and figures from Amsterdam. *Scandinavian Journal of Plastic and Reconstructive Hand Surgery* 35:203–206.

22. Kanhai, R.C.J., Hage, J. J., Asscheman, H., and Mulder, J. W. (1999). Augmentation mammoplasty in male-to-female transsexuals. *Plastic and Reconstructive Surgery* 104: 542–549.

23. Leslie, K., Buscombe, J., and Davenport, A. (2000). Implant infection in a transsexual with renal failure. *Nephrology Dialysis Transplant* 15:436–437.

24. Fox, L. P., Geyer, A. S., Husain, S., Della-Latta, P., and Grossman, M. E. (2004). *Myobacterium abscessus* cellulites and multifocal abscesses of the breast in a transsexual from illicit intramammary injections of silicone. *Journal of the American Academy of Dermatology* 50:450–454.

25. Duong, T., Schonfeld, A. J., Yungbluth, M., and Slotten, R. (1998). Acute pneumopathy in a nonsurgical transsexual. *Chest* 113:1127–1129.

26. Wylie, K. R. (2000). Suction to the breasts of a transsexual male. *Journal of Sex & Marital Therapy* 26:353–356.

27. Burcombe, R. J., Makris, A., Pittam, M., and Finer, N. (2003). Breast cancer after bilateral subcutaneous mastectomy in a female-to-male trans-sexual. *The Breast* 12: 290–293.

28. Shenenberger, D. W. and Utecht, L. M. (2002). Removal of unwanted facial hair. *American Family Physician* 66:1907–1911.

29. Azziz, R., Carmina, E., and Sawaya, M. E. (2000). Idiopathic hirsutism. *Endocrine Reviews* 21:347–362.

30. Paquet, P., Fumal, I., Piérard-Franchimont, C., and Piérard, G. E. (2002). Long-pulsed ruby laser-assisted hair removal in male-to-female transsexuals. *Journal of Cosmetic Dermatology* 1:8–12.

31. Schroeter, C. A., Groenewegen, J. S., Reineke, T., and Neumann, H.A.M. (2003). Ninety percent permanent hair reduction in transsexual patients. *Annals of Plastic Surgery* 51:243–248.

32. Hage, J. J., Becking, A. G., de Graaf, F. H., and Tuinzing, D. B. (1997). Gender-confirming facial surgery: Considerations on the masculinity and femininity of faces. *Plastic and Reconstructive Surgery* 99:1799–1807.

33. Becking, A. G., Tuinzing, D. B, Hage, J. J., and Gooren, L.J.G. (1996). Facial corrections in male to female transsexuals: A preliminary report on 16 patients. *Journal of Oral and Maxillofacial Surgery* 54:413–418.

CHAPTER 12

1. Bloom, A. (2003). *Normal. Transsexual CEOs, crossdressing cops, and hermaphrodites with attitude.* London: Bloomsbury Publishing.

2. Diamond, M. (1997). Sexual identity and sexual orientation in children with traumatized or ambiguous genitalia. *Journal of Sex Research* 34:199–211; Diamond, M. (1999). Pediatric management of ambiguous and traumatized genitalia. *Journal of Urology* 162:1021–1028; Reiner, W. J. (1999). Assignment of sex in neonates with ambiguous genitalia. *Current Opinion in Pediatrics* 11:363–365.

3. Money, J. and Ehrhardt, A. A. (1972). *Man and woman, boy and girl: Differentiation and dimorphism of gender identity from conception to maturity.* Baltimore, MD: Johns Hopkins University Press.

4. Diamond, M. and Sigmundson, H. K. (1997). Sex reassignment at birth. Long-term review and clinical implications. *Archives of Pediatrics & Adolescent Medicine* 151:298–304.

5. Colapinto, J. (2000). *As nature made him. The boy who was raised as a girl.* New York: HarperCollins.

6. Zucker, K. J. (2002). Intersexuality and gender identity differentiation. *Journal of Pediatrics and Adolescent Gynecology* 15:3–13.

7. Minto, C. L., Liao, K.L.-M., Woodhouse, C.R.J., Ransley, P.G., and Creighton, S.M. (2003). The effect of clitoral surgery on sexual outcome in individuals who have intersex conditions with ambiguous genitalia: A cross-sectional study. *Lancet* 361:1252–1257.

8. Creighton, S. M. (2004). Long-term outcome of feminization surgery: The London experience. *BJU International* 93 (Supplement 3):44–46.

9. Slijper, F.M.E. (2003). Clitoral surgery and sexual outcome in intersex conditions. *Lancet* 361:1236–1237.

10. The Prader scale is illustrated in Figure 3 of White, P. C. and Speiser, P. W. (2000). Congenital adrenal hyperplasia due to 21-hydroxylase deficiency. *Endocrine Reviews* 21:245–291.

11. Wilson, J. D. (2001). Androgens, androgen receptors, and male gender role behavior. *Hormones and Behavior* 40:358–366.

12. Wilson, J. D. (1999). The role of androgens in male gender role behavior. *Endocrine Reviews* 20:726–737.

13. Gustafson, M. L. and Donahoe, P. K. (1994). Male sex determination: Current concepts of male sexual differentiation. *Annual Review of Medicine* 45:505–524.

14. Meyenberg, B. and Sigusch, V. (2001). Kallmann's Syndrome and transsexualism. *Archives of Sexual Behavior* 30:75–81.

15. Minto, C. L., Liao, K.L.-M., Conway, G. S., and Creighton, S. M. (2003). Sexual function in women with complete androgen insensitivity syndrome. *Fertility and Sterility* 80:157–164.

16. Zucker, K. J. (1999). Intersexuality and gender identity differentiation. *Annual Review of Sex Research* 10:1–69.

17. Bailey, M. J., Dunne, M. P., and Martin, N. G. (2000). Genetic and environmental influences on sexual orientation and its correlates in an Australian twin sample. *Personality and Social Psychology* 78:524–536.

18. Kelso, W. M., Nicholls, M.E.R., Warne, G. L., and Zacharin, M. (2000). Cerebral lateralization and cognitive functioning in patients with congenital adrenal hyperplasia. *Neuropsychology* 14:370–378.

19. Merke, D. P., Bornstein, S. R., Avila, N. A., and Chrousos, G. P. (2002). Future directions in the study and management of congenital hyperplasia due to 21-hyroxylase deficiency. *Annals of Internal Medicine* 136:320–334.

20. Servin, A., Nordenström, A., Larsson, A., and Bohlin, G. (2003). Prenatal androgens and gender-typed behavior: A study of girls with mild and severe forms of congenital adrenal hyperplasia. *Developmental Psychology* 39:440–450.

21. White, P. C. and Speiser, P. W. (2000). Congenital adrenal hyperplasia due to 21-hydroxylase deficiency. *Endocrine Reviews* 21:245–291.

22. Ehrhardt, A. A. and Meyer-Bahlburg, H.F.L. (1979). Prenatal sex hormones and the developing brain: Effects on psychosexual differentiation and cognitive function. *Annual Review of Medicine* 30:417–430.

23. Berenbaum, S. A. and Bailey, J. M. (2003). Effects on gender identity of prenatal androgens and genital appearance: Evidence from girls with congenital adrenal hyperplasia. *Journal of Clinical Endocrinology & Metabolism* 88:1102–1106.

24. Mathews, G. A., Fane, B. A., Pasterski, V. L., Conway, G. S., Brook, C., and Hines, M. (2004). Androgenic influences on neural asymmetry: Handedness and language lateralization in individuals with congenital adrenal hyperplasia. *Psychoneuroendocrinology* 29:810–822.

25. Meyer-Bahlburg, H.F.L., Dolezal, C., Baker, S. W., Carlson, A. D., Obeid, J. S., and New, M. I. (2004). Prenatal androgenization affects gender-related behavior but not gender identity in 5–12-year-old girls with congenital adrenal hyperplasia. *Archives of Sexual Behavior* 33:97–104.

26. Swain, A., Narvaez, V., Burgoyne, P., Camerino, G., and Lovell-Badge, R. (1998). *Dax1* antagonizes *Sry* action in mammalian sex determination. *Nature* 391:761–767.

27. Vered, I., Kaiserman, I., Sela, B.-A., and Sack, J. (1997). Cross genotype sex hormone treatment in two cases of hypogonadal osteoporosis. *Journal of Clinical Endocrinology and Metabolism* 82:576–578.

CHAPTER 13

1. Lesser, J. G. (1999). When your son becomes your daughter: A mother's adjustment to a transgender child. *Families in Society* 80:182–189.

2. These vignettes are direct quotes from Green, R. (1998). Transsexuals' children. *International Journal of Transgenderism* 2(3). Downloaded from http://www.symposion.com/ijt/ijtc0601.htm on January 9, 2006.

3. Wallbank, R. (2004). *Re Kevin* in perspective. *Deakin Law Review* 9: 466.

4. Freedman, D., Tasker, F., and Di Ceglie, D. (2002). Children and adolescents with transsexual parents referred to a specialist gender identity development service: A brief report of key developmental features. *Clinical Child Psychology and Psychiatry* 7:423–432.

5. White, T. and Ettner, R. (2004). Disclosure, risks and protective factors for children whose parents are undergoing a gender transition. In U. Leli and J. Drescher (Eds.), *Transgender subjectivities: A clinician's guide* (pp. 129–145). Binghamton, NY: The Haworth Medical Press.

6. Wren, B. (2002). "I can accept my child is transsexual but if I ever see him in a dress I'll hit him": Dilemmas in parenting a transgendered adolescent. *Clinical Child Psychology and Psychiatry* 7:377–397.

7. Levine, S. B. and Davis, L. (2002). What I did for love: Temporary returns to the male gender role. *International Journal of Transgenderism* 6(4). Downloaded from http://www.symposion.com/ijt/ijtvo06no04_04.htm on January 9, 2006.

8. Gagné, P., Tewksbury, R., and McGaughey, D. (1997). Coming out and crossing over. Identity formation and proclamation in a transgender community. *Gender & Society* 11:478–508; Gagné, P. and Tewksbury, R. (1998). Conformity pressures and gender resistance among transgendered individuals. *Social Problems* 45:81–101.

9. Nuttbrock, L., Rosenblum, A., and Blumenstein, R. (2002). Transgender identity affirmation and mental health. *International Journal of Transgenderism* 6(4). Downloaded from http://www.symposion.com/ijt/ijtvo06no04_03.htm on January 9, 2006.

10. Wilson, M. (2002). "I am the Prince of Pain, for I am a Princess in the Brain": Liminal transgender identities, narratives and the elimination of ambiguities. *Sexualities* 5:425–448.

11. Lewins, F. (2002). Explaining stable partnerships among FTMs and MTFs: A significant difference? *Journal of Sociology* 38:76–88.

12. Stryker, S. (1998). The transgender issue: An introduction. *Gay & Lesbian Quarterly* 4:145–158.

13. Kirksey, K. M., Williams, B., and Garza, D. J. (1995). Thoughts on caring for transsexual patients. *Journal of Emergency Nursing* 21:519–20.

14. Lombardi, E. L. and van Servellen, G. (2000). Building culturally sensitive substance use prevention and treatment programs for transgendered populations. *Journal of Substance Abuse Treatment* 19:291–296.

15. Witten, T. M. and Whittle, S. (2004). Transpanthers: The greying of transgender and the law. *Deakin Law Review* 9:503–522.

16. Benjamin H. (1966). *The transsexual phenomenon.* New York: The Julian Press. Downloaded from http://www.symposion.com/ijt/benjamin/index.htm on January 9, 2006.

17. Wojdowski, P. and Tebor, I. B. (1976). Social and emotional tensions during transsexual passing. *Journal of Sex Research* 12:193–205.

18. Roen, K. (2001). "Either/Or" and "Both/Neither": Discursive tensions in transgender politics. *Signs: Journal of Women in Culture and Society* 27:501–522.

19. Ibid., p. 517.

20. Bornstein, K. (1994). *Gender outlaw.* New York: Routledge.

21. Sharon M. (2004). A non-op explains. Downloaded from http://www.xs4all.nl/~txtbreed/gender/nonop.htm on January 6, 2006.

22. Gagné, P., Tewksbury, R., and McGaughey, D. (1997). Coming out and crossing over. Identity formation and proclamation in a transgender community. *Gender & Society* 11: 501.

23. Ibid., p. 502.

24. The phrase "true selves" forms part of the title of this excellent book: Brown, M. L. and Rounsley, C. A. (2003). *True selves: Understanding transsexualism—For families, friends, coworkers, and helping professionals.* San Francisco: Jossey-Bass.

25. Kolakowski, V. S. (1997). Toward a Christian ethical response to transsexual persons. *Theology & Sexuality* 6:10–31.

26. O'Donovan, O. (1983). Transsexualism and Christian marriage. *Journal of Religious Ethics* 11:135–162.

27. Ibid., p. 150.

CHAPTER 14

1. Finlay, H. (2003). *Corbett to Kevin: Legal recognition of transsexualism in England and Australia.* Thirteenth Commonwealth Law Conference, Melbourne, Australia.

2. Ibid., p. 2.

3. Ibid., p. 13.

4. Ibid., p. 24.

5. Sharpe, A. N. (2002). *Transgender jurisprudence: Dysphoric bodies of law.* Sydney: Cavendish Publishing Limited.

6. Monro, S. (2002). Transgender trouble: Legislation beyond binaries? *Res Publica* 8:275–283.

7. Sharpe, A. (2002). English transgender law reform and the *spectre* of Corbett. *Feminist Legal Studies* 10:65–89.

8. Ibid., p. 67.

9. Swartz, L. H. (1997). Updated look at legal responses to transsexualism: Especially three marriage cases in U.K., U.S. and New Zealand. *International Journal of Transgenderism* 1(2). Downloaded from http://www.symposion.com/ijt/ijtc0201.htm on January 9, 2006.

10. Taitz, J. (1987). Judicial determination of the sexual identity of post-operative transsexuals: A new form of sex discrimination. *American Journal of Law & Medicine* 13:60.

11. Family Court of Australia (2001). *Re Kevin* (validity of marriage of transsexual). FamCA 1074. The following paragraph references in the text apply to this legal document.

12. Ibid., Paragraph 169.

13. Ibid., Paragraph 329.

14. Ibid., Paragraph 198.

15. Ibid., Paragraph 208.

16. Wallbank, R. (2004). *Contemporary human rights issues for people with transsexualism.* Paper presented at the Gendys Conference, Manchester, UK, p. 13. Downloaded from http://www.wallbanks.com/main/resources.html on January 31, 2006.

17. The UK Gender Recognition Bill was enacted in 2004. Details can be obtained from http://www.pfc.org.uk/gr-bill/index.htm downloaded on January 30, 2006.

18. Mowbray, A. (1999). Respect for the private lives of transsexuals. *Journal of Forensic Psychiatry* 10:154.

19. Taitz, J. (1987). Judicial determination of the sexual identity of post-operative transsexuals: A new form of sex discrimination. *American Journal of Law & Medicine* 13: 55.

20. Sharpe, A. N. (1997). The transsexual and marriage: Law's contradictory desires. *Australasian Gay and Lesbian Law Journal* 7:1–14.

21. Clough, A. S. (2001). The illusion of protection: Transsexual employment discrimination. *Georgetown Journal of Gender and the Law* 1:849–886.

22. Wintemute, R. (1997). Recognising new kinds of direct sex discrimination: Transsexualism, sexual orientation and dress codes. *Modern Law Review* 60:334–359.

23. Ibid., p. 341.

24. Sandland, R. (2003). Crossing and not crossing: Gender, sexuality and melancholy in the European Court of Human Rights. *Feminist Legal Studies* 11:204.

25. Ibid., p. 195.

26. Kirkland, A. (2003). Victorious transsexuals in the courtroom: A challenge for feminist legal theory. *Law and Social Inquiry* 28:1–37.

27. Ibid., p. 21.

28. Ungar, M. (2000). State violence and lesbian, gay, bisexual and transgender (lgbt) rights. *New Political Science* 22:61–75.

29. Dworkin, S. H. and Yi, H. (2003). LGBT identity, violence, and social justice: The psychological is political. *International Journal for the Advancement of Counselling* 25: 269–279.

30. Ibid., p. 271.

31. Witten, T. M. and Eyler, A. E. (1999). Hate crimes and violence against the transgendered. *Peace Review* 11:461–468.

CHAPTER 15

1. Kemp, E., and Swain, J. (2005). *Attitudes towards transsexualism and intersex conditions: An Internet based survey.* Unpublished Honours thesis, School of Behavioural Sciences, University of Newcastle, Australia.

2. Lev, A. I. (2004). *Transgender emergence: Therapeutic guidelines for working with gender-variant people and their families.* Binghamton, NY: Haworth Clinical Practice Press.

3. van Geert, P. (1994). *Dynamic systems of development: Change between complexity and chaos.* New York: Harvester Wheatsheaf.

4. Heath, R. A. (2004). Complexity and mental health. In Holt, T. (Ed.), *Complexity for clinicians* (pp. 83–94). Oxford, UK: Radcliffe Medical Press.

5. Roughgarden, J. (2004). *Evolution's rainbow: Diversity, gender, and sexuality in nature and people,* (p. 398). Berkeley, CA: University of California Press.

6. Sections 3.56 to 3.62 in *Policies: Lesbian, Gay, Bisexual, Transgender and Intersex People,* downloaded from http://greens.org.au/policies/careforpeople/lgbti on January 31, 2006.

INDEX

About the Author

RACHEL ANN HEATH is Honorary Professor of Psychology at the University of Newcastle, Australia. The author of six books and 18 book chapters, she has earned more than $500,000 in competitive research grants in Australia and the United Kingdom. One of the pioneers in applying chaos theory in both psychology and medicine, she obtained her Ph.D. in psychology from McMaster University in Canada.